Swedish

PHRASE BOOK
& DICTIONARY

120th anniversary
Berlitz

Easy to use features

- Handy thematic colour coding

- Quick Reference Section

- Tipping Guide — inside back cover

- Quick reply panels throughout

How best to use this phrase book

● We suggest that you start with the **Guide to pronunciation** (pp. 6–9), then go on to **Some basic expressions** (pp. 10–15). This gives you not only a minimum vocabulary, but also helps you get used to pronouncing the language. The phonetic transcription throughout the book enables you to pronounce every word correctly.

● Consult the **Contents** pages (3–5) for the section you need. In each chapter you'll find travel facts, hints and useful information. Simple phrases are followed by a list of words applicable to the situation.

● Separate, detailed contents lists are included at the beginning of the extensive **Eating out** and **Shopping guide** sections (Menus, p. 39, Shops and services, p. 97).

● If you want to find out how to say something in Swedish, your fastest look-up is via the **Dictionary** section (pp. 164–189). This will give you the word cross-referenced to its use in a phrase on a specific page.

● If you wish to learn more about constructing sentences, check the **Basic grammar** (pp. 159–163).

● Note the **colour margins** are indexed in Swedish and English to help both listener and speaker. And, in addition, there is also an **index in Swedish** for the use of your listener.

● Throughout the book, this symbol ☞ suggests phrases your listener can use to help you. Hand this phrase book to the Swedish-speaker to encourage pointing to an appropriate answer. The English translation for you is just alongside the Swedish.

Second revised edition–9th printing–May 1998
Printed in Spain

Contents

4

Acknowledgments
We are particularly grateful to Christina Sonesson for her help in the preparation of this book, and to Dr. T.J.A. Bennett who devised the phonetic transcription.

Guide to pronunciation

You'll find the pronunciation of the Swedish letters and sounds explained below, as well as the symbols we use in the transcriptions. The imitated pronunciation should be read as if it were English, with exceptions as indicated below. It is based on Standard British pronunciation, though we have tried to take into account General American pronunciation as well. If you follow the instructions carefully you'll have no difficulty in reading our transcriptions so as to make yourself understood.

Swedish uses intonation (or more correctly "tones"), sometimes to distinguish between words. Without considerable training, a foreigner can't differentiate between the tones, much less use them correctly. Swedes don't expect foreigners to use intonation. Thus we haven't shown the tones in our transcriptions.

In the phonetic transcription of this book you will notice that some letters are placed in parentheses e.g. **mew**ker(t). In daily conversation, these letters are rarely pronounced by Swedes, although it is certainly not incorrect to do so. Syllables printed in **bold type** should be stressed. A bar over a vowel symbol (e.g., sh$\overline{\text{ay}}$f) indicates a long vowel.

Consonants

Letter	Approximate pronunciation	Symbol	Example	
b, c, d, f, h, l, m, n, p, v, w, x	as in English			
ch	at the beginning of words borrowed from French, like **sh** in shut	sh	**chef**	sh$\overline{\text{ay}}$f
g	1) before stressed **i, e, y, ä, ö**, and sometimes after **l** or **r**, like **y** in yet	y	**ge**	y$\overline{\text{ay}}$

	2) before **e** and **i** in many words of French origin, like **sh** in **sh**ut	sh	**geni**	sha̅ynee
	3) elsewhere, generally like **g** in **go**	g	**gaffel**	gahferl
j, dj, gj,	at the beginning of words	y	**ja**	yaa
lj, hj	always like **y** in **y**et		**ljus**	ye̅wss
k	1) before stressed **i, e, y, ä, ö,** generally like **ch** in Scottish lo**ch**, but pronounced in the front of the mouth	kh	**köpa**	khu̅rpah
	2) elsewhere, like **k** in **k**it	k	**klippa**	klippah
kj	like **ch** in Scottish lo**ch**, but pronounced in the front of the mouth	kh	**kjol**	kho̅o̅l
qu	like **k** in **k**it followed by **v** in **v**at	kv	**Lindquist**	lin(d)kvist
r	slightly rolled near the front of the mouth	r	**ryka**	re̅wkah
s	1) in the ending **-sion** like **sh** in **sh**ut	sh	**mission**	misho̅o̅n
	2) elsewhere, like **s** in **s**o	s/ss	**ses**	sa̅yss
	3) the groups **sch, skj, sj, stj** are pronounced like **sh** in **sh**ut	sh	**schema**	sha̅ymah
sk	1) before stressed **e, i, y, ä, ö,** like **sh** in **sh**ut	sh	**skänk**	shehnk
	2) elsewhere, like **sk** in **sk**ip	sk	**skola**	sko̅o̅la
t	1) in the ending **-tion** like **sh** in **sh**ut or like **ch** in **ch**at	sh / tsh	**station** / **nation**	stahsho̅o̅n / nahtsho̅o̅n
	2) elsewhere, like **t** in **t**op	t	**tid**	teed
tj	like **ch** in Scottish lo**ch**, but pronounced in the front of the mouth; sometimes with a **t**-sound at the beginning	kh	**tjäna**	khainah
z	like **s** in **s**o	s	**zenit**	sa̅ynit

N.B. The consonants **d, l, n, s, t,** if preceded by **r,** are generally pronounced with the tip of the tongue turned up well behind the front teeth. The **r** then ceases to be pronounced. We indicate this pronunciation of **d, l, n, s** or **t** by printing a small **r** above the line, e.g. *svart* is pronounced svah^rt.

Vowels

A vowel is generally long in stressed syllables when it's the final letter or followed by only one consonant. If followed by two or more consonants or in unstressed syllables, the vowel is generally short.

a	1) when long, like **a** in car	aa	**dag**	daa(g)
	2) when short, between **a** in cat and **u** in cut	ah	**tack**	tahk
e	1) when long, like **ay** in say, but a *pure* vowel, not a diphthong	a̅y	**sen**	sa̅yn
	2) when followed by **r**, like **a** in man; long or short	æ̅	**erfara**	æ̅rfaarah
	3) when short, like **e** in get	eh	**beck**	behk
	4) when unstressed, like **a** in about	er*	**betala**	bertaalah
ej	like **a** in mate	ay	**nej**	nay
i	1) when long, like **ee** in bee	ee	**vit**	veet
	2) when short, between **ee** in meet and **i** in hit	i	**hinna**	hinnah
	3) in a few words, e.g. in the personal pronoun **mig**, like **a** in mate	ay	**mig**	may
o	1) when long, often like **oo** in soon, but with the lips more tightly rounded, and with a puff of breath at the end	o̅o̅	**sko**	sko̅o̅
	2) the same sound can be short	oo	**solid**	sooleed
	3) when long, sometimes like **aw** in raw, but with the tongue a little higher in the mouth and the lips closely rounded	aw	**son**	sawn
	4) when short, sometimes like **o** in hot	o	**korrekt**	korrehkt
u	1) when long, like Swedish **y**, but with the tongue a little lower in the mouth, and with a puff of breath at the end; you'll find it very hard to distinguish from Swedish **y**, so we'll use the same symbol for both	e̅w̅	**hus**	he̅w̅ss

* The **r** should not be pronounced when reading this transcription.

	2) when short, a little more like the **u** of put; a very difficult sound	ew	**full**	fewl
y	like German **ü** in **über**, or French **u** in **une**; round your lips and try to say **ee** as in **bee**; long or short	ēw ew	**vy** **syster**	vēw sewsterr
å	1) when long, like **aw** in **raw**, but with the tongue a little higher in the mouth and the lips closely rounded	aw	**gå**	gaw
	2) when short, like **o** in **hot**	o	**sång**	song
ä	1) when followed by **r**, like **a** in **man**, long or short	ǣ æ	**ära** **värka**	ǣrah værkah
	2) elsewhere, like **e** in **get**; long or short	ai eh	**läsa** **bäst**	laissah behst
ö	like **ur** in **fur**, but with the lips rounded and without any **r**-sound; long or short; when followed by **r**, it is pronounced with the mouth a little more open	ūr ur	**röd** **köld** **öra**	rūrd khurld ūrrah

Pronunciation of the Swedish alphabet

A	aa	**H**	haw	**O**	ōō	**V**	vāy
B	bāy	**I**	ee	**P**	pāy	**X**	ehkss
C	sāy	**J**	y	**Q**	kēw	**Y**	ēw
D	dāy	**K**	kaw	**R**	ær	**Z**	sǣtah
E	āy	**L**	ehl	**S**	ehss	**Å**	aw
F	ehf	**M**	ehm	**T**	tāy	**Ä**	ǣ
G	gāy	**N**	ehn	**U**	ēw	**Ö**	ūr

The letter **w** occurs only in names, foreign words and their derivatives, as well as in certain abbreviations.

Some basic expressions

Yes.	**Ja.**	yaa
No.	**Nej.**	nay
Please.	**Var snäll och .../ ..., tack.**	vaar snehl ok/ ... tahk
Thank you.	**Tack.**	tahk
Thank you very much.	**Tack så mycket.**	tahk saw **mew**ker(t)
That's all right/ You're welcome.	**Ingen orsak.**	ingern ōōˡsaak

Greetings *Hälsningsfraser*

Generally people say "Goddag" or "Hej" and shake hands when introduced. The terms Mr., Mrs. and Miss (*herr—* hehr, *fru—*frēw, *fröken—*frūrkern) are very rarely used. People are introduced by their full name. *Hej* (hay) is an informal expression you'll hear all the time, similar to "Hallo" ("Hi!"). When speaking to someone use *ni,* the polite form for "you", until you have been introduced. From then on you can use the more informal *du.* Younger people always call each other *du.*

Good morning.	**God morgon.**	goo(d) morron
Good afternoon.	**God middag.**	goo(d) middah(g)
Good evening.	**God afton.**	goo(d) ahfton
Good night.	**God natt.**	goo(d) naht
Goodbye.	**Adjö.**	ahyūr
See you later.	**Vi ses.**	vee sāyss
How do you do? (Pleased to meet you.)	**Goddag.**	goddaa(g)
How are you?	**Hur mår ni/du?**	hēwr mawr nee/dēw
Very well, thanks. And you?	**Bara bra, tack. Och ni/du?**	baarah braa tahk ok nee/dēw

How's life?	**Hur står det till?**	hewr stawr day(t) til
Fine.	**Bra, tack.**	braa tahk
I beg your pardon?	**Förlåt?**	fur'lawt
Excuse me. (May I get past?)	**Förlåt/Ursäkta.**	fur'lawt/ew'sehktah
Sorry!	**Förlåt!**	fur'lawt

Questions *Frågor*

Where?	**Var?**	vaar
How?	**Hur?**	hewr
When?	**När?**	nær
What?	**Vad?**	vaad
Why?	**Varför?**	vahrfurr
Who?	**Vem?**	vehm
Which?	**Vilken?**	vilkern
Where is ...?	**Var är/Var finns/ Var ligger ...?**	vaar ær/vaar finss/ vaar liggerr
Where are ...?	**Var är/Var finns/ Var ligger ...?**	vaar ær/vaar finss/ vaar liggerr
Where can I find ...?	**Var hittar jag ...?**	vaar hittahr yaa(g)
Where can I get ...?	**Var kan jag få tag på ...?**	vaar kahn yaa(g) faw taag paw
How far?	**Hur långt?**	hewr longt
How long?	**Hur länge?**	hewr lehnger
How much?	**Hur mycket?**	hewr mewker(t)
How many?	**Hur många?**	hewr mongah
How much does this cost?	**Hur mycket kostar det här?**	hewr mewker(t) kostahr day(t) hær
When does ... open/ close?	**När öppnar/ stänger ...?**	nær urpnahr/ stehngerr
What do you call this/that in Swedish?	**Vad heter det här/ det där på svenska?**	vaa(d) hayterr day(t) hær/ day(t) dær paw svehnskah
What does this/that mean?	**Vad betyder det här/ det där?**	vaa(d) bertewderr day(t) hær/day(t) dær

Do you speak ...?   *Talar ni ...?*

Do you speak English?	**Talar ni engelska?**	taalahr nee **ehng**erlskah
Does anyone here speak English?	**Finns det någon här som talar engelska?**	finss dāȳ(t) **naw**gon hǣr som **taal**ahr **ehng**erlskah
I don't speak (much) Swedish.	**Jag talar inte (så bra) svenska.**	yaa(g) **taal**ahr inter (saw braa) **svehn**skah
Could you speak more slowly?	**Kan ni tala lite långsammare?**	kahn nee **taal**ah liter **long**sahmahrer
Could you repeat that?	**Kan ni upprepa det där?**	kahn nee **ewp**rāȳpah dāȳ(t) dǣr
Could you spell it?	**Kan ni bokstavera det?**	kahn nee bookstah**vāȳ**rah dāȳ(t)
Could you write it down please?	**Skulle ni kunna skriva det?**	**skewl**er nee **kewn**nah **skreev**ah dāȳ(t)
Can you translate this for me/us?	**Kan ni översätta det här för mig/oss?**	kahn nee **ūr**ver\ʳsehtah dāȳ(t) hǣr fūr may/oss
Could you point to the ... in the book?	**Kan ni peka på ... i boken?**	kahn nee **pāȳ**kah paw ... ee **book**ern
word	**ordet***	**ōō**ʳdert
phrase	**uttrycket**	**ēw**trewkert
sentence	**meningen**	**māȳ**ningern
Just a moment.	**Ett ögonblick.**	eht **ūr**gonblik
I'll see if I can find it in this book.	**Jag skall se om jag kan hitta det i den här boken.**	yaa(g) skah(l) sāȳ om yaa(g) kahn **hitt**ah dāȳ(t) ee dehn hǣr **book**ern
I understand.	**Jag förstår.**	yaa(g) fur**ʳstawr**
I don't understand.	**Jag förstår inte.**	yaa(g) fur**ʳstawr** inter
Do you understand?	**Förstår ni?**	fur**ʳstawr** nee

Can/May ...?   *Kan ...?*

Can I have ...?	**Kan jag få ...?**	kahn yaa(g) faw
Can we have ...?	**Kan vi få ...?**	kahn vee faw
Can you show me ...?	**Kan ni visa mig ...?**	kahn nee **vee**ssah may

---

* For information on the definite article see grammar section page 159

I can't.	Jag kan inte.	yaa(g) kahn inter
Can you tell me ...?	Kan ni säga mig ...?	kahn nee sehyah may
Can you help me?	Kan ni hjälpa mig?	kahn nee yehlpah may
Can I help you?	Kan jag hjälpa er?	kahn yaa(g) yehlpah āyr
Can you direct me to ...?	Kan ni visa mig vägen till ...?	kahn nee veessah may vaigern til

What do you want? *Vad önskar ni?*

I'd like to ...	Jag skulle vilja/ Jag vill ...	yaa(g) skewler vilyah/ yaa(g) vil
We'd like to ...	Vi skulle vilja/ Vi vill ...	vee skewler vilyah
I'd like a ...	Jag skulle vilja ha en/ett ...	yaa(g) skewler vilyah haa ehn/eht
Could you bring/give me ...?	Kan ni ge mig ...?	kahn nee yāy may
Could you show me ...?	Kan ni visa mig ...?	kahn nee veessah may
I'm looking for ...	Jag letar efter ...	yaa(g) lāytahr ehfterr
I'm hungry.	Jag är hungrig.	yaa(g) ǣr hewngri(g)
I'm thirsty.	Jag är törstig.	yaa(g) ǣr turrsti(g)
I'm tired.	Jag är trött.	yaa(g) ǣr trurt
I'm lost.	Jag hittar inte.	yaa(g) hittahr inter
It's important.	Det är viktigt.	day(t) ǣr viktit
It's urgent.	Det är brådskande.	day(t) ǣr broskahnder

It is/There is ... *Det är/Det finns ...*

It is ...	Det är ...	dāy(t) ǣr
Is it ...?	Är det ...?	ǣr dāy(t)
It isn't ...	Det är inte ...	dāy(t) ǣr inter
Here it is.	Här är det.	hǣr ǣr dāy(t)
Here they are.	Här är de.	hǣr ǣr dom
There it is.	Där är det.	dǣr ǣr dāy(t)

There they are.	**Där är de.**	dǣr ǣr dom
There is/There are ...	**Det finns ...**	dāȳ(t) finss
Is there/Are there ...?	**Finns det ...?**	finss dāȳ(t)
There isn't/aren't ...	**Det finns inte ...**	dāȳ(t) finss inter
There isn't/aren't any.	**Det finns ingen/ inga.**	dāȳ(t) finss ingern/ ingah

It's ...   *Den är ...*

big/small	**stor/liten***	stōōr/leetern
quick/slow	**snabb/långsam**	snahb/longsahm
hot/cold	**varm/kall**	vahrm/kahl
full/empty	**full/tom**	fewl/toom
easy/difficult	**lätt, enkel/svår**	leht ehnkerl/svawr
heavy/light	**tung/lätt**	tewng/leht
open/shut	**öppen/stängd**	urpern/stehngd
right/wrong	**rätt/fel**	reht/fāȳl
old/new	**gammal/ny**	gahmahl/nēw
old/young	**gammal/ung**	gahmahl/ewng
next/last	**nästa/sista**	nehstah/sistah
beautiful/ugly	**vacker/ful**	vahkerr/fēwl
free (vacant)/ occupied	**ledig/upptagen**	lāȳdi(g)/ewptaagern
good/bad	**bra/dålig**	braa/dawli(g)
better/worse	**bättre/sämre**	behtrer/sehmrer
early/late	**tidig/sen**	teedi(g)/sāȳn
cheap/expensive	**billig/dyr**	billi(g)/dēwr
near/far	**nära/långt (bort)**	nǣrah/longt (bo^rt)
here/there	**här/där**	hǣr/dǣr

Quantities   *Kvantitet*

a little/a lot	**lite/mycket**	leeter/mewker(t)
few/a few	**få/några**	faw/nawgrah
much/many	**mycket/många**	mewker(t)/mongah
more/less	**mer/mindre**	māȳr/mindrer
more than/less than	**mer än/mindre än**	māȳr ehn/mindrer ehn

* For neuter and plural forms, see grammar section page 160 (adjectives).

| enough/too much | **tillräckligt/för mycket** | tilrehkli(g)t/fürr mewker(t) |
| some/any | **några** | nawgrah |

A few more useful words *Några fler användbara ord*

at	**vid**	veed
on	**på**	paw
in	**i**	ee
to	**till**	til
after	**efter**	ehfterr
before (time)	**innan, före**	innahn, fürrer
before (place)	**framför**	frahmfurr
for	**för**	fürr
from	**från**	frawn
with	**med**	māyd
without	**utan**	ēwtahn
through	**genom**	yāynom
towards	**mot**	mōot
until	**till**	til
during	**under**	ewnderr
next to	**bredvid**	brāy(d)veed
behind	**bakom**	baakom
between	**mellan**	mehlahn
since	**sedan**	sehn
above	**ovanför**	awvahnfürr
below	**nedanför**	nāydahnfürr
under	**under**	ewnderr
inside	**inne**	inner
outside	**ute**	ēwter
up/upstairs	**upp/där uppe**	ewp/dǣr ewper
down/downstairs	**ner/där nere**	nāyr/dǣr nāyrer
and	**och**	ok
or	**eller**	ehlerr
not	**inte**	inter
never	**aldrig**	ahldrig
nothing	**ingenting, inget**	ingernting, ingert
none	**ingen**	ingern
very	**mycket**	mewker(t)
too (also)	**också**	okso
yet	**än**	ehn
soon	**snart**	snaaᶜt
now	**nu**	nēw
then	**då, sedan**	daw, sehn
perhaps	**kanske**	kahnsher
only	**bara**	baarah

Arrival

Passport control   *Passkontroll*

Here's my passport.	**Här är mitt pass.**	hǟr ǟr mit pahss
I'll be staying ...	**Jag tänker stanna ...**	yaa(g) **tehn**kerr **stahn**nah
a few days	**några dagar**	**nawg**rah **daa**(gah)r
a week	**en vecka**	ehn **vehk**kah
a month	**en månad**	ehn **maw**nahd
I don't know yet.	**Jag vet inte än.**	yaa(g) vāyt inter ehn
I'm here on holiday.	**Jag är här på semester.**	yaa(g) ǟr hǟr paw sehm**ehs**terr
I'm here on business.	**Jag är här i affärer.**	yaa(g) ǟr hǟr ee ahf**ǟ**rerr
I'm just passing through.	**Jag är bara på genomresa.**	yaa(g) ǟr **baa**rah paw **yāy**nomrāyssah

If things become difficult:

| I'm sorry, I don't understand. | **Förlåt, jag förstår inte.** | fur‍ᴿ**lawt**, yaa(g) fur‍ᴿ**stawr** inter |
| Does anyone here speak English? | **Finns det någon här som talar engelska?** | finss dāy(t) **naw**gon hǟr som **taa**lahr **ehng**erlskah |

> **TULL**
> CUSTOMS

After collecting your baggage at the airport (*flygplatsen—* **flewg**plahtsern) you have a choice: use the green exit if you have nothing to declare, or leave via the red exit if you have items to declare.

> **varor att förtulla**
> goods to declare

> **inget att förtulla**
> nothing to declare

The chart below shows you what you can bring in duty free (the allowances in parentheses are for non-European residents).*

Cigarettes		Cigars		Tobacco	Spirits		Wine
200 (400)	or	50 (100)	or	250 g. (500 g.)	1 l. (1 l.)	and	1 l. (1 l.)

I have nothing to declare.	Jag har inget att förtulla.	yaa(g) haar ingert aht fur^rtewlah
I have ...	Jag har ...	yaa(g) haar
a carton of cigarettes	en limpa cigarretter	ehn limpah siggahrehterr
a bottle of whisky	en flaska whisky	ehn flahskah wiski
It's for my personal use.	Det är för mitt personliga bruk.	dāy(t) ær fūrr mit pæ^rshōōnliggah brēwk
It's a gift.	Det är en present.	dāy(t) ær ehn prehsehnt

Passet, tack.	Your passport, please.
Har ni något att förtulla?	Do you have anything to declare?
Var snäll och öppna den här bagen.	Please open this bag.
Ni måste betala tull för det här.	You'll have to pay duty on this.
Har ni något mer bagage?	Do you have any more luggage?

---

* All allowances are subject to change.

Baggage—Porter *Bagage – Bärare*

In principle porters are not available at the airports, though if necessary you can book one in advance when you buy your plane ticket. But you'll always find luggage trolleys.

Please take this luggage.	**Var snäll och ta det här bagaget.**	vaar snehl ok taa dāȳ(t) hǣr bahgaashert
That's my suitcase/travelling bag.	**Det där är min väska/bag.**	dāȳ(t) dǣr ǣr min **veh**skah/"bag"
That's mine.	**Det där är mitt.**	dāȳ(t) dǣr ǣr mit
Please take this to the ...	**Var snäll och ta det här till ...**	vaar snehl ok taa dāȳ(t) hǣr til
bus	**bussen**	**bew**ssern
luggage lockers	**förvaringsboxarna**	furr**vaa**ringsboksah^{r}nah
taxi	**taxin**	**tahk**sin
How much is that?	**Vad kostar det?**	vaa(d) **kos**tahr dāȳ(t)
There's one suitcase missing.	**Det fattas en väska.**	dāȳ(t) **fah**tahss ehn **veh**skah
Where are the luggage trolleys (carts)?	**Var finns bagage-kärrorna?**	vaar finss bahgaash-**khæ**ro^{r}nah

Changing money *Växla pengar*

Where's the currency exchange office?	**Var ligger växel-kontoret?**	vaar **lig**gerr **vehk**serl-kont**ōō**rert
Can you change these traveller's cheques (checks)?	**Kan ni lösa in de här resecheckerna?**	kahn nee **lūr**ssah in dom hǣr **rāȳ**sserkhehke^{r}nah
I'd like to change some ...	**Jag skulle vilja växla några ...**	yaa(g) **skew**ler **vil**yah **vehk**slah **naw**grah
dollars	**dollar**	**dol**lahr
pounds	**pund**	pewnd
Can you change this into Swedish crowns?	**Kan ni växla det här till svenska kronor?**	kahn nee **vehk**slah dāȳ(t) hǣr til **svehn**skah **krōō**noor
What's the exchange rate?	**Vilken är växelkursen?**	**vil**kern ǣr **vehk**serlkew^{r}sern

BANK—CURRENCY, see page 129

Where ...? *Var ...?*

Where is the ...?	**Var är ...?**	vaar ǟr
booking office	**biljettkassan**	bilyehtkahssahn
duty-free shop	**tax-free-shopen**	tahks-free-shopern
newsstand	**tidningskiosken**	tee(d)ningskhioskern
restaurant	**restaurangen**	rehstorrahngern
Where can I hire a car?	**Var kan jag hyra en bil?**	vaar kahn yaa(g) hēwrah ehn beel
Where can I get a taxi?	**Var kan jag få tag på en taxi?**	vaar kahn yaa(g) faw taag paw ehn tahksi
How do I get to ...?	**Hur kommer jag till ...?**	hēwr kommerr yaa(g) til
Is there a bus into town?	**Finns det någon buss in till stan?**	finss dāy(t) nawgon bewss in til staan

Hotel reservation *Hotellreservation*

Do you have a hotel guide?	**Har ni någon hotellguide?**	haar nee nawgon hotehl"guide"
Could you reserve a room for me?	**Kan ni beställa ett rum åt mig?**	kahn nee berstehlah eht rewm awt may
in the centre	**i centrum**	ee sehntrewm
near the airport	**nära flygplatsen**	nǟrah flēwgplahtsern
near the railway station	**nära järnvägs-stationen**	nǟrah yǟᶜnvaigs-stahshōōnern
a single room	**ett enkelrum**	eht ehnkerlrewm
a double room	**ett dubbelrum**	eht dewberlrewm
not too expensive	**inte för dyrt**	inter fūrr dēwᶜt
I'll be staying from ... to ...	**Jag tänker stanna från ... till ...**	jaa(g) tehnkerr stahna frawn ... til
Where is the hotel?	**Var ligger hotellet?**	vaar liggerr hotehlert
Can you recommend a guest house?	**Kan ni rekommendera något pensionat?**	kahn nee rehkommerndāy-rah nawgot pahnshōōnaat
Are there any flats (apartments) vacant?	**Finns det några lediga våningar?**	finss dāy(t) nawgrah lāydiggah vawningahr
Do you have a street map?	**Har ni någon karta över stan?**	haar nee nawgon kaaᶜtah ūrverr staan

HOTEL/ACCOMMODATION, see page 22

Car hire (rental)   *Biluthyrning*

To hire a car you must produce a valid driving licence, that you have held for at least one year, and your passport. Some firms set a minimum age of 21, others 25 depending on engine size. Most companies require a deposit, but this is waived if you present an accepted credit card.

I'd like to hire (rent) a car.	**Jag skulle vilja hyra en bil.**	yaa(g) skewler vilyah hewrah ehn beel
small	**liten**	leetern
medium-sized	**mellanstor**	mehlahnstoor
large	**stor**	stoor
automatic	**med automatlåda**	mayd aa(ew)toomaat-lawdah
I'd like it for ...	**Jag vill ha den ...**	yaa(g) vil haa dehn
a day	**en dag**	ehn daa(g)
a week	**en vecka**	ehn vehkah
Are there any week-end arrangements?	**Har ni några speciella weekend-priser?**	haar nee nawgrah spehssiehlah "weekend"-preesserr
Do you have any special rates?	**Har ni några specialpriser?**	haar nee nawgrah spehssiyaalpreesserr
What's the charge ...?	**Vad kostar det ...?**	vaad kostahr day(t)
per day	**per dag**	pær daa(g)
per week	**per vecka**	pær vehkah
Is mileage included?	**Är kilometer-kostnaden inräknad?**	ær khillommayterr-kostnahdern inraiknahd
What's the charge per kilometre?	**Vad är kilometer-kostnaden?**	vaad ær khillommayterr-kostnahdern
I'd like to leave the car in ...	**Jag vill lämna bilen i ...**	yaa(g) vil lehmnah beelern ee
I'd like full insurance.	**Jag vill ha helförsäkring.**	yaa(g) vil haa haylfurᶠsaikring
How much is the deposit?	**Hur stor är depo-neringsavgiften?**	hewr stoor ær dehponnayringsaavyiftern
I have a credit card.	**Jag har kreditkort.**	yaa(g) haar krehdeetkooᶠt
Here's my driving licence.	**Här är mitt körkort.**	hær ær mit khurrkooᶠt

CAR, see page 75

Taxi   *Taxi*

Taxis are clearly marked and available in every town. All taxis are metered, but it's advisable to ask the approximate fare if travelling a long distance. After midnight and if you order the taxi in advance there is an extra charge. The tip is not included in the fare.

Where can I get a taxi?	**Var kan jag få tag på en taxi?**	vaar kahn yaa(g) faw taag paw ehn **tahk**si
Where is the taxi stand?	**Var är taxi-stationen?**	vaar ǟr **tahk**si-stahshōōnern
Could you get me a taxi?	**Kan ni skaffa mig en taxi?**	kahn nee **skah**fah may ehn **tahk**si
What's the fare to ...?	**Vad kostar det till ...?**	vaad **kos**tahr dāȳ(t) til
How far is it to ...?	**Hur långt är det till ...?**	hēwr longt ǟr dāȳ(t) til
Take me to ...	**Kör mig till ...**	khūrr may til
this address	**den här adressen**	dehn hǟr ah**dreh**ssern
the airport	**flygplatsen**	**flēw**gplahtsern
the town centre	**(stads)centrum**	**(stahds)sehn**trewm
the ... Hotel	**hotell ...**	ho**tehl**
the railway station	**järnvägsstationen**	yǟr'nvaigsstashōōnern
Turn ... at the next corner.	**Sväng till ... vid nästa gathörn.**	svehng til ... veed **neh**stah gaathūr'n
left/right	**vänster/höger**	**vehn**sterr/**hū**rgerr
Go straight ahead.	**Kör rakt fram.**	khūrr raakt frahm
Please stop here.	**Var snäll och stanna här.**	vaar snehl ok **stah**nah hǟr
I'm in a hurry.	**Jag har bråttom.**	yaa(g) haar **brot**tom
Could you drive more slowly?	**Kan ni köra lite långsammare?**	kahn nee **khū**rah **lee**ter **long**sahmahrer
Could you help me carry my luggage?	**Kan ni hjälpa mig att bära bagaget?**	kahn nee **yehl**pah may aht **bǟ**rah bah**gaa**shert
Could you wait for me?	**Kan ni vänta på mig?**	kahn nee **vehn**tah paw may
I'll be back in 10 minutes.	**Jag är tillbaka om 10 minuter.**	yaa(g) ǟr til**baa**kah om 10 mi**nēw**terr

TIPPING, see inside back-cover

Hotel — Other accommodation

Early reservation and confirmation are essential in most major tourist centres during the high season. Most towns and arrival points have a tourist information office (*turistbyrå*— tēwristbēwraw) and that's the place to go to if you're stuck without a room. You can get an up-to-date price list for all Swedish hotels, called "Hotels in Sweden", from the Swedish tourist office in your country.

Although there is no official rating system, there are different classes of accommodation.

Hotell (hotehl)	In the bigger towns you will find a number of first-class and some de-luxe hotels. Facilities —and prices—vary across a wide range, but standards are always high. Breakfast is almost always included.
Familjehotell (fahmilyerhotehl)	In summer a number of hotels, particularly in large cities, offer special rates for families with children in rooms with three to six beds.
Turisthotell/ Pensionat (tēwristhotehl)/ (pahnshōōnaat)	Simple but clean and comfortable, many tourist hotels and guest houses are found in summer resorts and winter sports centres. As a rule, breakfast and dinner are included. Rates are usually based on a three-day stay.
Sommarhotell (sommahrhotehl)	In Stockholm, Gothenburg and Lund, modern blocks of student flats are opened to tourists in the summer. These are rooms particularly suitable for groups.
Motell (mootehl)	Accommodation for motorists, usually with restaurant and car-service facilities.
Privatrum (privvaatrewm)	Local and regional tourist associations can recommend rooms in private homes.
Stugor (stēwgoor)	Summer chalets, quite expensive, are let by the week. Booking in advance is advisable.
Vandrarhem (vahndrahrhehm)	The Swedish Touring Club (STF) operates these comfortable, cheap hostels all over Sweden.

Checking in—Reception / receptionen

My name is ...	**Mitt namn är ...**	mit nahmn ǟr
I have a reservation.	**Jag har beställt rum.**	yaa(g) haar ber**stehlt** rewm
We've reserved 2 rooms.	**Vi har beställt 2 rum.**	vee haar ber**stehlt** 2 rewm
Here's the confirmation.	**Här är bekräftelsen.**	hǟr ǟr ber**krehf**terlsern
Do you have any vacancies?	**Har ni några lediga rum?**	haar nee **naw**grah **lāy**diggah rewm
I'd like a ...	**Jag skulle vilja ha ett ...**	yaa(g) **skew**ler **vil**yah haa eht
single room	**enkelrum**	**ehn**kerlrewm
double room	**dubbelrum**	**dew**berlrewm
We'd like a room ...	**Vi skulle vilja ha ett rum ...**	vee **skew**ler **vil**yah haa eht rewm
with twin beds	**med två sängar**	māyd tvaw **sehng**ahr
with a double bed	**med dubbelsäng**	māyd **dew**berlsehng
with a bath	**med bad**	māyd baad
with a shower	**med dusch**	māyd dewsh
with a balcony	**med balkong**	māyd bahl**kong**
with a view	**med utsikt**	māyd **ewt**sikt
at the front	**på framsidan**	paw **frahm**seedahn
at the back	**på baksidan**	paw **baak**seedahn
It must be quiet.	**Det måste vara tyst.**	dāy(t) **mos**ter vaarah tewst
What floor is it on?	**Vilken våning ligger det på?**	**vil**kern **vaw**ning **lig**gerr dāy(t) paw
Is there ...?	**Finns det ...?**	finss dāy(t)
air conditioning	**luftkonditionering**	**lewft**kondishonn**āy**ring
a conference room	**konferensrum**	konfeh**rahns**rewm
heating	**värme**	**vær**mer
hot water	**varmvatten**	**vahrm**vahtern
a laundry service	**tvättservice**	tveht"service"
room service	**rumsbetjäning**	rewmsber**khai**ning
a radio/television in the room	**radio/TV på rummet**	**raa**dyo/**tāy**veh paw **rewm**ert
running water	**rinnande vatten**	**rin**nahnder **vah**tern
a sauna	**bastu**	**bah**stew
a swimming pool	**swimmingpool**	"swimming pool"
a private toilet	**toalett på rummet**	tooah**leht** paw **rewm**ert

CHECKING OUT, see page 31

| Could you put an extra bed/a cot in the room? | **Kan ni ställa in en extra säng/barnsäng i rummet?** | kahn nee **steh**lah in ehn **ehk**strah sehng/**baa**ʳnsehng ee **rew**mert |

How much? *Hur mycket?*

How much does it cost ...?	**Vad kostar det ...?**	vaad **kos**tahr dāȳ(t)
per night	**per natt**	pæʳr naht
per week	**per vecka**	pæʳr **veh**kah
for bed and breakfast	**för rum med frukost**	fūʳr rewm māȳd **frew**kost
excluding meals	**utan måltider**	**ēw**tahn **mawl**teederr
for full board (A.P.)	**för helpension**	fūʳr **hāȳl**pahnshōōn
for half board (M.A.P.)	**för halvpension**	fūʳr **hahlv**pahnshōōn
Does the price include ...?	**Ingår ... i priset?**	**ing**gawr ... ee **pree**sert
breakfast	**frukost**	**frew**kost
service	**betjäningsavgift**	ber**khai**ningsaavyift
value-added tax (VAT)*	**moms**	moms
Is there any reduction for children?	**Ger ni någon rabatt för barn?**	yāȳr nee **naw**gon rah**baht** fūʳr baaʳn
Do you charge for the baby?	**Kostar det något för babyn?**	**kos**tahr dāȳ(t) **naw**got fūʳr **bai**bin
That's too expensive.	**Det är för dyrt.**	dāȳ(t) ær fūʳr **dēw**ʳt
Don't you have anything cheaper?	**Har ni inte något billigare?**	haar nee **in**ter **naw**got **bil**liggahrer

How long? *Hur länge?*

We'll be staying ...	**Vi tänker stanna ...**	vee **tehn**kerr **stah**nah
overnight only	**bara över natten**	**baa**rah **ūr**verr **nah**tern
a few days	**några dagar**	**naw**grah **daa**(gah)r
a week (at least)	**en vecka (minst)**	ehn **veh**kah (minst)
I don't know yet.	**Jag vet inte än.**	yaa(g) vāȳt **in**ter ehn

---

* Americans note: a type of sales tax in Sweden

NUMBERS, see page 147

Decision *Beslut*

May I see the room?	**Kan jag få se på rummet?**	kahn yaa(g) faw sāȳ paw **rew**mert
That's fine. I'll take it.	**Det är bra. Jag tar det.**	dāȳ(t) ǣr braa. yaa(g) taar dāȳ(t)
No. I don't like it.	**Nej. Jag tycker inte om det.**	nay. yaa(g) **tew**kerr inter om dāȳ(t)
It's too ...	**Det är för ...**	dāȳ(t) ǣr fūrr
cold/hot	**kallt/varmt**	kahlt/vahrmt
dark/small	**mörkt/litet**	murrkt/**lee**tert
I asked for a room with a bath.	**Jag bad om ett rum med bad.**	yaa(g) baa(d) om eht rewm māȳd baad
Do you have anything ...?	**Har ni något ...?**	haar nee **naw**got
better	**bättre**	**beh**trer
bigger	**större**	**stu**rrer
cheaper	**billigare**	**bil**liggahrer
quieter	**tystare**	**tew**stahrer
Do you have a room with a (better) view?	**Har ni något rum med (bättre) utsikt?**	haar nee **naw**got rewm māȳd (**beh**trer) **ēw**tsikt

Registration *Incheckning*

Upon arrival at a hotel or guesthouse you'll be asked to fill in a registration form (*inskrivningsblankett*—**in**skreev-ningsblahnkeht).

Efternamn/Förnamn	Name/First name
Hemort/Gata/Nummer	Home town/Street/Number
Hemland	Country of origin
Medborgare i .../Yrke	Citizen of .../Occupation
Födelsedatum/Födelseort	Date/Place of birth
Inrest ...	Arrived on ...
Passnummer	Passport number
Ort/Datum	Place/Date
Underskrift	Signature

| What does this mean? | **Vad betyder det här?** | vaad bertewderr dāy(t) hǟr |

Kan jag få se passet, tack?	May I see your passport, please?
Skulle ni vilja fylla i den här blanketten?	Would you mind filling in this form?
Kan ni skriva under här?	Please sign here.
Hur länge tänker ni stanna?	How long will you be staying?

What's my room number?	**Vilket rumsnummer har jag?**	vilkert rewmsnewmerr haar yaa(g)
Will you have our luggage sent up?	**Kan ni skicka upp bagaget?**	kahn nee shikkah ewp bahgaashert
Where can I park my car?	**Var kan jag parkera bilen?**	vaar kahn yaa(g) pahrkāyrah beelehn
Does the hotel have a garage?	**Har hotellet något garage?**	haar hotehleht nawgot gahraash
I'd like to leave this in the hotel safe.	**Jag skulle vilja lämna det här i kassaskåpet.**	yaa(g) skewler vilyah lehmnah dāy(t) hǟr ee kahssahskawpert

Hotel staff *Hotellpersonal*

hall porter	**portiern**	poʳtyāyʳn
maid	**städerskan**	staiderʳskahn
manager	**direktören**	dirrerktǖrrern
page (bellboy)	**pickolon**	pikkolon
porter	**bäraren**	bǟrahrern
receptionist	**receptionisten**	rehsehphshoonistern
switchboard operator	**telefonisten**	tehlerfonnistern
waiter	**kyparen/ servitören**	khēwpahrern/ sehrvitǖrrern
waitress	**servitrisen**	sehrvitreessern

To attract the attention of staff members say "Excuse me"— *Ursäkta* or *Förlåt*.

TELLING THE TIME, see page 153

General requirements   *Allmänna förfrågningar*

The key to room ... please.	**Nyckeln till rum ..., tack.**	**new**ker(l)n til rewm ... tahk
Could you wake me at ..., please?	**Kan ni väcka mig klockan ... tack?**	kahn nee **veh**kah may **klok**kahn ... tahk
May we have breakfast in our room, please?	**Skulle vi kunna få frukost på rummet?**	**skew**ler vee **kew**nah faw **frew**kost paw **rew**mert
Is there a bath on this floor?	**Finns det bad på den här våningen?**	finss dāȳ(t) baad paw dehn hǣr **vaw**ningern
What's the voltage here?	**Vilken spänning är det?**	**vil**kern **speh**ning ǣr dāȳ(t)
Where's the shaver socket (outlet)?	**Var är uttaget för rakapparaten?**	vaar ǣr **ēwt**taagert fūr **raak**ahpahraatern
Can you find me a ...?	**Kan ni skaffa mig en ...?**	kahn nee **skah**fah may ehn
babysitter	**barnvakt**	**baa**ʳnvahkt
secretary	**sekreterare**	sehkrer**tāȳ**rahrer
typewriter	**skrivmaskin**	**skreev**mahsheen
May I have a/an/ some ...?	**Skulle jag kunna få ...?**	**skew**ler yaa(g) **kew**nah faw
ashtray	**en askkopp**	ehn **ahs**kop
bath towel	**ett badlakan**	eht **baad**laakahn
(extra) blanket	**en (extra) filt**	ehn (**ehk**strah) filt
envelopes	**några kuvert**	**naw**grah kew**vǣr**
(more) hangers	**(fler) hängare**	(flāȳr) **hehng**ahrer
hot-water bottle	**en varmvattenflaska**	ehn **vahrm**vahternflahskah
ice cubes	**lite is**	**lee**ter ees
needle and thread	**nål och tråd**	nawl ok trawd
(extra) pillow	**en (extra) kudde**	ehn (**ehk**strah) **kew**der
reading lamp	**en läslampa**	ehn **lais**lahmpah
soap	**en tvål**	ehn tvawl
writing paper	**några brevpapper**	**naw**grah **brāȳv**pahperr
Where's the ...?	**Var är ...?**	vaar ǣr
bathroom	**badrummet**	**baad**rewmert
dining room	**matsalen**	**maat**saalern
emergency exit	**nödutgången**	**nūrd**ēwtgawngern
hairdresser's	**frisersalongen**	friss**āȳ**ʳsahlongern
lift (elevator)	**hissen**	**hiss**ern
telephone	**telefonen**	tehler**faw**nern
Where are the toilets?	**Var är toaletten?**	vaar ǣr tooah**leh**tern

BREAKFAST, see page 38

Telephone—Post (mail) *Telefon – Post*

Can you get me Malmö 123 45 67?	**Kan ni ringa upp 123 45 67 i Malmö åt mig?**	kahn nee ringah ewp 123 45 67 ee mahlmur awt may
Do you have any stamps?	**Har ni några frimärken?**	haar nee nawgrah freemærkern
Would you post this for me, please?	**Kan ni posta det här åt mig, tack?**	kahn nee postah dāȳ(t) hǟr awt may tahk
Are there any letters for me?	**Finns det några brev till mig?**	finss dāȳ(t) nawgrah brāȳv til may
Are there any messages for me?	**Finns det något meddelande till mig?**	finss dāȳ(t) nawgot māȳdāȳlahnder til may
How much is my telephone bill?	**Hur stor är min telefonräkning?**	hēwr stōōr ǟr min tehlerfawnraikning

Difficulties *Svårigheter*

The … doesn't work.	**… fungerar inte.**	… fewnggāȳrahr inter
air conditioning	**luftkonditio- neringen**	lewftkondisho- nnāȳringern
bidet	**bidén**	beedāȳn
heating	**värmen**	værmern
light	**ljuset**	yēwssert
radio	**radion**	raadyon
television	**TV:n**	tāȳvehn
The tap (faucet) is dripping.	**Kranen droppar.**	kraanern droppahr
There's no hot water.	**Det finns inget varmvatten.**	dāȳ(t) finss ingert vahrmvahtern
The washbasin is blocked.	**Det är stopp i handfatet.**	dāȳ(t) ǟr stop ee hahn(d)faatert
The window is jammed.	**Fönstret har fastnat.**	furnstrert haar fahsnaht
The curtains are stuck.	**Gardinerna har hakat upp sig.**	gah^rdeener^rnah haar haakaht ewp say
The bulb is burned out.	**Glödlampan är trasig.**	glēwdlahmpahn ǟr traassig
My bed hasn't been made up.	**Min säng har inte blivit bäddad.**	min sehng haar inter bleevit behdahd

POST OFFICE AND TELEPHONE, see page 132

The ... is/are broken.	... är trasig.	... ǣr traassig
blind	rullgardinen	rewlgah^rdeenern
lamp	lampan	lahmpahn
plug	stickkontakten	stikkontahktern
switch	strömbrytaren	strurmbrēwtahrern
venetian blinds	persiennen	peh^rsiehnern
Can you get it repaired?	Kan ni laga den?	kahn nee laagah dehn

Laundry—Dry cleaner's   Tvätt – Kemtvätt

I'd like these clothes ...	Jag skulle vilja ha de här kläderna ...	yaa(g) skewler vilyah haa dom hǣr klaider^rnah
dry-cleaned	kemtvättade	khāymtvehtahder
ironed	strukna	strēwknah
pressed	pressade	prehssahder
washed	tvättade	tvehtahder
I need them ...	Jag behöver dem ...	yaa(g) berhūrverr dom
today	idag	eedaa(g)
tonight	i kväll	ee kvehl
tomorrow	i morgon	ee morron
before Friday	före fredag	fūrrer frāydaa(g)
Can you ... this?	Kan ni ... det här?	kahn nee ... dāy(t) hǣr
mend	laga	laagah
stitch	sy ihop	sēw ihoop
Can you sew on this button?	Kan ni sy i den här knappen?	kahn nee sēw ee dehn hǣr knahpern
Can this be invisibly mended?	Kan det här lagas så att det inte syns?	kahn dāy(t) hǣr laagahss saw aht dāy(t) inter sewnss
Can you get this stain out?	Kan ni få bort den här fläcken?	kahn nee faw bo^rt dehn hǣr flehkern
Is my laundry ready?	Är min tvätt klar?	ǣr min tveht klaar
This isn't mine.	Det här är inte mitt.	dāy(t) hǣr ǣr inter mit
There's something missing.	Det fattas något.	dāy(t) fahtahss nawgot
There's a hole in this.	Det har gått hål på det här.	dāy(t) haar got hawl paw dāy(t) hǣr

Hairdresser—Barber *Damfrisör – Herrfrisör*

Is there a ... in the hotel?	**Finns det någon ... på hotellet?**	finss dāȳ(t) nawgon ... paw hotehlert
hairdresser	**frisersalong**	frissāȳ^rsahlong
beauty salon	**skönhetssalong**	shūrnhāȳtssahlong
Can I make an appointment for Thursday?	**Kan jag få en tid på torsdag?**	kahn yaa(g) faw ehn teed paw too^rsdaa(g)
Could you ... my hair, please?	**Skulle ni kunna ... mitt hår?**	skewler nee kewnah ... mit hawr
blow-dry	**föna**	fūrnah
cut	**klippa**	klippah
dye	**färga**	færyah
tint	**tona**	tōōnah
with a fringe (bangs)	**med lugg**	māȳd lewg
I'd like a/some ...	**Jag skulle vilja ha ...**	yaa(g) skewler vilyah haa
colour rinse	**en färgsköljning**	ehn færyshurlyning
face pack	**en ansiktsmask**	ehn ahnsiktsmahsk
manicure	**manikyr**	mahnikkēwr
perm(anent wave)	**en permanent**	ehn pehrmahnehnt
setting lotion	**en läggningsvätska**	ehn lehgningsvehtskah
shampoo and set	**tvättning och läggning**	tvehtning ok lehgning
I'd like a shampoo for ... hair.	**Jag vill ha ett schampo för ... hår.**	yaa(g) vil haa eht shahmpoo fūrr ... hawr
normal/dry/ greasy (oily)	**normalt/torrt/ fett**	normaalt/to^rt/ feht
Do you have a colour chart?	**Har ni en färgkarta?**	haar nee ehn færykaa^rtah
I don't want any hairspray.	**Jag vill inte ha någon spray.**	yaa(g) vil inter haa nawgon "spray"
I'd like a haircut, please.	**Klippning, tack.**	klipning tahk
Don't cut it too short.	**Klipp inte för kort.**	klip inter fūrr ko^rt
A little more off the ...	**Ta lite mer ...**	taa liter māȳr
back/top	**där bak/på hjässan**	dǣr baak/paw yehssahn
neck/sides	**i nacken/på sidorna**	ee nahkern/paw seedo^rnah

DAYS OF THE WEEK, see page 150

I'd like a shave.	**Rakning, tack.**	raakning tahk
Would you trim my ..., please?	**Kan ni putsa ...,** **tack.**	kahn nee pewtsah ... tahk
beard	**skägget**	shehgert
moustache	**mustaschen**	mewstaashern
sideboards (sideburns)	**polisongerna**	polissonger'nah

Checking out *Avresa*

May I have my bill, please?	**Kan jag få** **räkningen, tack?**	kahn yaa(g) faw raikningern tahk
I'm leaving early in the morning.	**Jag åker tidigt i** **morgon bitti.**	yaa(g) awkerr teedi(g)t ee morron bitti
Please have my bill ready.	**Kan ni ha räkningen** **klar?**	kahn nee haa raikningern klaar
We'll be checking out around noon.	**Vi checkar ut vid** **tolvtiden.**	vee khehkahr ēwt veed tolvteedern
I must leave at once.	**Jag måste åka** **genast.**	yaa(g) moster awkah yāÿnahst
Is everything included?	**Är allt inkluderat?**	ǣr ahlt inklewdāÿraht
Can I pay by credit card?	**Kan jag betala med** **kreditkort?**	kahn yaa(g) bertaalah māÿd krehdeetkoo't
I think there's a mistake in the bill.	**Jag tror att det** **är ett fel på** **räkningen.**	yaa(g) trōōr aht dāÿ(t) ǣr eht fāÿl paw raikningern
Can you get us a taxi?	**Kan ni skaffa oss** **en taxi?**	kahn nee skahfah oss ehn tahksi
Would you send someone to bring down our luggage?	**Kan ni be någon** **ta ner bagaget?**	kahn nee bāÿ nawgon taa nāÿr bahgaashert
Here's the forward-ing address.	**Här är efter-** **sändningsadressen.**	hǣr ǣr ehfterr-sehn(d)ningsahdrehssern
You have my home address.	**Ni har min** **bostadsadress.**	nee haar min bōōstaadsahdrehss
It's been a very enjoyable stay.	**Det har varit en** **mycket trevlig** **vistelse.**	dāÿ(t) haar vaarit ehn mewker(t) trāÿvli(g) visterlser

TIPPING, see inside back-cover

Camping   *Camping*

Camping is extremely popular and very well organized in Sweden. There are more than 700 sites, classified by one, two or three stars according to facilities offered. A camping carnet is needed except for holders of the "Camping International" card. If you camp on private property, ask the owner for permission.

Is there a camp site near here?	**Finns det någon campingplats i närheten?**	finss dāȳ(t) nawgon kahmpingplahtss ee nǣrhāȳtern
Can we camp here?	**Kan vi campa här?**	kahn vee kahmpah hǣr
Do you have room for a ...?	**Har ni plats för ...?**	haar nee plahtss fūrr
tent	**ett tält**	eht tehlt
caravan (trailer)	**en husvagn**	ehn hēwsvahngn
What's the charge ...?	**Vad kostar det ...?**	vaa(d) kostahr dāȳ(t)
per day	**per dag**	pǣr daa(g)
per person	**per person**	pǣr peh‿shōōn
for a car	**för en bil**	fūrr ehn beel
for a tent	**för ett tält**	fūrr eht tehlt
for a caravan (trailer)	**för en husvagn**	fūrr ehn hēwsvahngn
Is there/Are there (a) ...?	**Finns det ...?**	finss dāȳ(t)
cooking facilities	**kokmöjligheter**	kookmuyrlighāȳterr
drinking water	**dricksvatten**	driksvahtern
electricity	**elektricitet**	ehlehktrissitāȳt
playground	**någon lekplats**	nawgon lāȳkplahts
restaurant	**någon restaurang**	nawgon rehstorrahng
shopping facilities	**någon affär**	nawgon ahfǣr
sauna	**bastu**	bahstew
swimming pool	**någon swimmingpool**	nawgon "swimmingpool"
Where are the showers/toilets?	**Var är duscharna/ toaletterna?**	vaar ǣr dewshah‿nah/ tooahlehter‿nah
Where can I get butane gas?	**Var kan jag få tag på butangas?**	vaar kahn yaa(g) faw taag paw bewtaangaass
Is there a youth hostel near here?	**Finns det något vandrarhem i närheten?**	finss dāȳ(t) nawgot vahndrahrhehm ee nǣrhāȳtern

CAMPING EQUIPMENT, see page 106

Eating out

Eating places in Sweden range from the ultra chic to the very quick. The following rundown will help you decide what to look for to suit your appetite and mood. Though if you want to have a drink, you'll have to wait till noon—the law is strict about licensing hours.

Cocktail bar ("cocktail bar")	Only in hotels in important towns. Sometimes snacks are served along with the drinks.
Dansrestaurang (**dahns**rehstorrahng)	For dancing and dining. Usually in big towns and hotels.
Fiskrestaurang (**fisk**rehstorrahng)	Fish and seafood specialities.
Gatukök (**gaa**tewkhūrk)	Typically Scandinavian "kitchen on the street" for a quick snack. Sausages or hamburgers with mashed potatoes or chips (French fries), meatballs or spring rolls, ice cream and soft drinks.
Grillbar (**gril**baar)	Self-service hamburgers, steaks, chips, etc., usually with beer or soft drinks only.
Gästgivargård (**yeh**shivvahrgaw^rd)	Old coaching inns in the countryside of southern Sweden (mainly Skåne) with rustic decor and often high culinary standards; many local specialities including *smörgåsbord* (see p. 41) which is usually served on Sundays and around Christmas.
Kafé (kah**fāy**)	Local coffee house that serves snacks (open sandwiches, buns, etc.). If called *Ölkafé* then beer and basic meals are served.
Konditori (kondit**torree**)	A coffee shop serving tea, coffee, soft drinks, pastries and ice cream. You may also find open sandwiches and other snacks.
Korvstånd (**korv**stond)	Swedish hot-dog stand.
Kvarterskrog (kvah^r**tāy**^rskrōōg)	Small inexpensive neighbourhood restaurant. The food is generally good. Wine or beer may be served but no spirits.

Restaurang (rehstorr**rahng**)	Restaurants have no official rating system. You can take your meals in a variety of settings: classically elegant, modern or simply utilitarian. For something a little special, try dinner in a renovated medieval cellar, or on an old boat.
	Most restaurants will serve international food, although you can get excellent Swedish specialities too.
Salladsbar (**sah**lahdssbaar)	Mostly self-service restaurants serving a variety of salads and vegetarian food.
Stekhus (st**ay**kh**ew**ss)	Steakhouse.
Värdshus (vae**ʳ**(d)sh**ew**ss)	Styled after old coaching inns, found on the outskirts of towns or in the country, some with high culinary standards. Many motels also call their restaurants *värdshus*.

Eating habits   *Matvanor*

The Swedes have altered their eating habits to suit the modern way of life. Breakfast is usually a quick cup of tea or coffee with a sandwich, though cereals and yoghurt are also popular. Lunch used to be the most important meal of the day, but as lunch hours became shorter, people started to settle for a one-course meal. Dinner is served quite early—between 5 and 6 p.m. Hefty snacks bridge the gap between meals. The *smörgås* or open sandwich, is immensely popular, and fast food is on the up and up accompanied by the indispensable cup of coffee—black or with cream.

Meal times   *När äter man?*

Breakfast (*frukost*—**frew**kost) is usually served from 7 to 10 a.m. and is generally included in the hotel arrangement.

Lunch (*lunch*—lewnsh) is normally served from 11.30 a.m. and dinner (*middag*—**mi**ddah(g)) from around 6 p.m.

Meal times are very flexible and many restaurants will serve a meal at any hour of the afternoon or evening.

Swedish cuisine *Det svenska köket*

Natural is the best way to describe the Swedish approach to food. A Swede can be lyrical at the thought of *färskpotatis,* new potatoes boiled with dill (one of the most commonly used herbs) and served simply with a pat of butter (always salted). Each season has its traditional specialities, and there is a number of genuine national dishes worth trying. Some may seem a bit strange to you, but if you have the chance to taste them you will probably be pleasantly surprised.

Dairy products have by tradition played an important part in the Swedish diet. Milk is the drink taken with everyday meals.

Nowadays Swedish cuisine is more cosmopolitan than it used to be, and the influence of French, Italian, Japanese and Chinese cuisine among others is apparent.

Vad önskar ni?	What would you like?
Jag rekommenderar det här.	I recommend this.
Vad önskas att dricka?	What would you like to drink?
Vi har inte ...	We don't have ...
Önskar ni ...?	Would you like ...?

Hungry? *Hungrig?*

I'm hungry/I'm thirsty.	**Jag är hungrig/ Jag är törstig.**	yaa(g) ǟr **hewng**ri(g)/ yaa(g) ǟr tur^rsti(g)
Can you recommend a good restaurant?	**Kan ni föreslå en bra restaurang?**	kahn nee **fur**rerslaw ehn braa rehstorrahng
Are there any inexpensive restaurants around here?	**Finns det någon billig restaurang i närheten?**	finss dāy(t) **naw**gon **bil**lig rehstorrahng ee **nǟr**hāytern

If you want to be sure of getting a table in a well-known restaurant, it's better to book in advance.

I'd like to reserve a table for 4.	**Jag skulle vilja beställa ett bord för 4.**	yaa(g) skewler vilyah berstehlah eht bōo͞rd fūrr 4
We'll come at 8.	**Vi kommer klockan 8.**	vee kommerr klokkahn 8
Could we have a ...?	**Skulle vi kunna få ett ...?**	skewler vee kewnah faw eht
table in the corner	**hörnbord**	hūr͠rnbōo͞rd
table by the window	**fönsterbord**	furnsterrbōo͞rd
table outside	**bord ute**	bōo͞rd ēw͞ter
table in a non-smoking area	**bord för icke rökare**	bōo͞rd fūrr ikker rūrkahrer

Asking and ordering   *Fråga och beställa*

Waiter/Waitress!	**Ursäkta.**	ēw͞r͠sehktah
I'd like something to eat/drink.	**Jag skulle vilja ha något att äta/dricka.**	yaa(g) skewler vilyah haa nawgot aht aitah/drikkah
May I have the menu, please?	**Kan jag få matsedeln, tack?**	kahn yaa(g) faw maatsāyderln tahk
Do you have a ...?	**Har ni någon ...?**	haar nee nawgon
set menu	**meny**	mehnēw͞
local speciality	**lokal specialitet**	lookaal spehssiahlitāy(t)
What do you recommend?	**Vad rekommenderar ni?**	vaad rehkommerndāyrahr nee
Could we have a/an ..., please?	**Kan vi få ... tack?**	kahn vee faw ... tahk
ashtray	**en askkopp**	ehn ahskop
cup	**en kopp**	ehn kop
fork	**en gaffel**	ehn gahfehl
glass	**ett glas**	eht glaass
knife	**en kniv**	ehn kneev
napkin (serviette)	**en servett**	ehn sehrveht
plate	**en tallrik**	ehn tahlrik
spoon	**en sked**	ehn shāyd
May I have some ...?	**Kan jag få lite ...?**	kahn yaa(g) faw leeter
bread	**bröd**	brūrd
butter	**smör**	smūrr

lemon	**citron**	sitrōōn
oil	**olja**	olyah
pepper	**peppar**	pehpahr
salt	**salt**	sahlt
seasoning	**kryddor**	krewdoor
sugar	**socker**	sokkerr
vinegar	**vinäger**	vinnaigerr

Some useful expressions for those with special requirements:

I'm on a special diet.	**Jag håller diet.**	yaa(g) hollerr deeāÿt
I don't drink alcohol.	**Jag dricker inte alkohol.**	yaa(g) drikkerr inter ahlkohawl
I mustn't eat food containing ...	**Jag får inte äta mat som innehåller ...**	yaa(g) fawr inter aitah maat som innerhollerr
flour/fat	**mjöl/fett**	myūrl/feht
salt/sugar	**salt/socker**	sahlt/sokkerr
Do you have ... for diabetics?	**Har ni ... för diabetiker?**	haar nee ... fūrr deeahbāÿtikkerr
cakes	**kakor**	kaakoor
fruit juice	**juice**	yōōss
a special menu	**en specialmeny**	ehn spehssiyaalmehnēw
Do you have any vegetarian dishes?	**Har ni några vegetariska rätter?**	haar nee nawgrah vehgertaariskah rehterr
Could I have ... instead of dessert?	**Kan jag få ... i stället för efterrätt?**	kahn yaa(g) faw ... ee stehleht fūrr ehfterreht
Can I have an artificial sweetener?	**Kan jag få sötningsmedel?**	kahn yaa(g) faw sūrtningsmāÿderl

And ...

I'd like some more.	**Jag skulle vilja ha lite mer.**	yaa(g) skewler vilyah haa leeter māÿr
Can I have more ... please?	**Kan jag få lite mer ..., tack?**	kahn yaa(g) faw leeter māÿr ... tahk
Just a small portion.	**Bara en liten portion.**	baarah ehn leetern po^rtshōōn
Nothing more, thanks.	**Tack, inte mer.**	tahk inter māÿr
Where are the toilets?	**Var är toaletten?**	vaar ǣr tooahlehtern

Breakfast   *Frukost*

Almost every hotel has a breakfast buffet consisting of a variety of breads (try *knäckebröd*—**kneh**kerbrūrd, crispbread), butter, cheese, ham, eggs, marmalade, juice, milk, tea and coffee. Try cornflakes with fermented milk (*filmjölk*—**feel**myurlk), a Swedish favourite.

I'd like breakfast, please.	**Jag skulle vilja ha frukost, tack.**	yaa(g) **skewler vil**yah haa **frew**kost tahk
I'll have a/an/ some ...	**Jag skall be att få ...**	yaa(g) skah(l) bāy aht faw
bacon and eggs	**bacon och ägg**	"bacon" ok ehg
boiled egg	**ett kokt ägg**	eht kookt ehg
soft/hard	**löskokt/hårdkokt**	**lūrs**kookt/**haw**ʳdkookt
cereal	**flingor**	**fling**or
cheese	**ost**	oost
eggs	**ägg**	ehg
fried egg	**ett stekt ägg**	eht **stāy**kt ehg
scrambled eggs	**äggröra**	**ehg**rūrrah
fruit juice	**juice**	yōōss
grapefruit	**grapefrukt-**	"grape"frewkt
orange	**apelsin-**	**ah**perlseen
ham and eggs	**skinka och ägg**	**shink**ah ok ehg
jam	**lite sylt**	**lee**ter sewlt
marmalade	**lite apelsin- marmelad**	**lee**ter **ah**perlseen- **mahr**merlaad
roll	**ett småfranska**	eht **smaw**frahnskah
toast	**lite rostat bröd**	**lee**ter **ro**staht brūrd
yoghurt	**en yoghurt**	ehn **yawg**(h)ewʳt
May I have some ...?	**Kan jag få ...?**	kahn yaa(g) faw
bread	**lite bröd**	**lee**ter brūrd
butter	**lite smör**	**lee**ter smūrr
(hot) chocolate	**(varm) choklad**	(vahrm) shoklaa(d)
coffee	**kaffe**	**kah**fer
decaffeinated	**koffeinfritt**	**koffe**heenfrit
black	**utan grädde**	**ēw**tahn **greh**der
with cream	**med grädde**	māyd **greh**der
honey	**lite honung**	**lee**ter **haw**newng
(cold/hot) milk	**(kall/varm) mjölk**	(kahl/vahrm) myurlk
pepper	**lite peppar**	**lee**ter **peh**pahr
salt	**lite salt**	**lee**ter sahlt
tea	**te**	tāy
with milk/lemon	**med mjölk/citron**	māyd myurlk/si**trōōn**
(hot) water	**(varmt) vatten**	(vahrmt) **vah**tern

What's on the menu? *Vad står det på matsedeln?*

Restaurants now often display a menu *(matsedel)* outside. Besides ordering à la carte, you can usually order a fixed-price menu *(meny)*. Some restaurants offer a dish of the day *(dagens rätt)* including bread, butter, drink (non-alcoholic) and coffee at quite a modest price.

Under the headings below you'll find alphabetical lists of dishes that might be offered on a Swedish menu, with their English equivalent. You can simply show the book to the waiter. If you want some cheese, for instance, let *him* point to what's available on the appropriate list. Use pages 36 and 37 for ordering in general.

Reading the menu   *Att läsa matsedeln*

Meny	Set menu
Dagens rätt	Dish of the day
Barnmatsedel	Children's menu
Kökschefen rekommenderar ...	The chef proposes ...
Husets specialiteter	Specialities of the house
Veckans Grill	This week's grilled specialities
Valfria tillbehör	Choice of side-dishes
På beställning	Made on request
Mot extra kostnad	Extra charge
Två personer	For two
Serveringsavgift inräknad	Service charge included

bakverk	baakvehrk	pastries
drycker	drewkkerr	drinks
efterrätter	ehfterrehterr	desserts
fisk	fisk	fish
frukt	frewkt	fruit
från grillen	frawn grillern	grilled (broiled)
fågel	fawgerl	poultry
förrätter	fürrehterr	first course
glass	glahss	ice cream
grönsaker	grürnsaakerr	vegetables
huvudrätter	hewvewdrehterr	main course
kött	khurt	meat
ost	oost	cheese
pastarätter	pahstahrehterr	pasta
risrätter	reesrehterr	rice
sallader	sahlahderr	salads
skaldjur	skaalyewr	seafood
soppor	soppoor	soups
smårätter	smawrehterr	snacks
smörgåsar	smurrgawssahr	open sandwiches
smörgåsbord	smurrgawsbooʳd	smörgåsbord
varmrätter	vahrmrehterr	main course
vilt	vilt	game
vinlista	veenlistah	wine list
äggrätter	ehgrehterr	egg dishes

Smörgåsbord

The Swedish *smörgåsbord* (**smurr**gawsbōō^rd), of ancient origin, is well known abroad. It was originally intended as a large-scale hors d'œuvre but has become a kind of buffet meal. It is not usual to have both a *smörgåsbord* and a main course. These beautifully decorated tables, groaning under the weight of a multitude of hot and cold platters, used to be a common sight in homes and restaurants, especially around Christmas. Nowadays the *smörgåsbord* is usually only served in restaurants, especially *gästgivargårdar* and *värdshus* in the country.

You start at one end of the table, with a variety of herring, salmon, seafood, salads and other appetizers, serving yourself as many times as you like. Work your way through the cold meat, meatballs, small sausages and omelets. Then move on to the cheeses. If you still have room, you might manage a light dessert. The price is the same for big or small eaters alike. During the Christmas season the *smörgåsbord* becomes *julbord,* Yuletide table, even more lavish and served in almost all big restaurants every day of the week.

Aquavit and beer go especially well with this spread. It is rare to drink wine with *smörgåsbord*. Normally this is a lunchtime experience and it can take hours.

Are you serving smörgåsbord today?	**Serverar ni smörgås-bord idag?**	sehrvā**y**rahr nee **smurr-**gawsbōō^rd ee**daa**(g)
gravad strömming i senapssås (**graa**vahd **strur**ming ee **sāy**nahpssawss)	marinated Baltic herring in mustard sauce, eaten with boiled potatoes sprinkled with dill (as are all herring dishes)	
inkokt ål (**inkookt** awl)	jellied eel	
inlagd sill (**inlahgd** sil)	herring marinated in vinegar, sugar and spices	
Janssons frestelse (**yaan**sonss **frehst**erlser)	"Jansson's temptation"—layers of sliced potatoes, marinated sprats and onions, baked in cream	

kalvsylta (kahlvsewltah)	jellied veal loaf (usually around Christmas)
kryddsill (krewdsil)	herring marinated in vinegar, sugar, allspice, mustard seeds and cloves
köttbullar (khurtbewlahr)	meatballs of minced beef and/or pork, flavoured with onion, salt, pepper and allspice
leverpastej (lāyverrpahstay)	liver paté, usually of pork or veal liver
löjrom med lök och gräddfil (luryrom māyd lūrk ok grehdfeel)	bleak roe; served with raw, chopped onion and sour cream, and eaten on toast
matjessill med gräddfil och gräslök (mahtyerssil māyd grehdfil ok graislūrk)	marinated herring with sour cream and chopped chives; often served with small boiled potatoes
revbensspjäll (rāyvbāynsspyehl)	roasted spareribs (usually around Christmas)
rökt korv (rūrkt korv)	smoked sausage; variously flavoured according to region
rökt lax (rūrkt lahks)	smoked salmon; usually served with toast and wedges of lemon
rökt renstek (rūrkt rāynstāyk)	smoked roast reindeer; sometimes served with horseradish cream
rökt ål (rūrkt awl)	smoked eel; often served with scrambled eggs
senapssill (sāynahpssil)	salted herring in mustard sauce
sillsallad (silsahlahd)	herring salad with pickled beetroot and gherkins, apples, potatoes, onions and whipped cream (usually served around Christmas)
solöga (soōlūrga)	marinated sprats, chopped onions, capers and beetroot, with an egg yolk in the center
stekt prinskorv (stāykt prinskorv)	small fried sausages
ägg med kaviar (ehg māyd kahvyahr)	hard-boiled eggs with red salted cod's roe or black salted lumpfish roe

Starters (Appetizers)   *Förrätter*

It's by no means the rule to take a starter. Swedes are usually content with the main course, except on special occasions. Many dishes from the *smörgåsbord* are also served as starters.

I'd like a starter (an appetizer).	Jag skulle vilja ha en förrätt.	yaa(g) skewler vilyah haa ehn fūrreht
grodlår	gröodlawr	frog's legs
gåslever	gawsläyverr	goose liver
hummer	hewmerr	lobster
kaviar	kahvyahr	caviar
röd	rūrd	red (cod's roe, salted)
svart	svahᶠt	black (lumpfish roe)
krabba	krahbah	crab
lax	lahks	salmon
gravad	graavahd	marinated
rökt	rūrkt	smoked
löjrom	luryrom	bleak roe
musslor	mewsloor	mussels
ostron	oostron	oysters
paté	pahtāy	paté
fisk-	fisk-	fish
grönsaks-	grūnsaaks-	vegetable
skaldjurs-	skaalyēwᶠs-	seafood
vilt-	vilt-	game
räkcocktail	raik"cocktail"	prawn (shrimp) salad
sikrom	seekrom	whitefish roe
sniglar	sneeglahr	snails

färska räkor (fæᶠskah raikoor)	unshelled prawns (shrimp), boiled while still on the trawler; generally served with toast and butter
sandwiches ("sandwiches")	3 small open sandwiches, generally with salmon or shrimps, meat and cheese
sillbricka/silltallrik (silbrikkah/siltahlrik)	a choice of almost every kind of herring available
smör, ost och sill (smūrr, oost ok sil)	butter, cheese and herring; small plate of herring with bread, butter and cheese often seen on menus in its abbreviated form: S.O.S.
toast Skagen ("toast" skaagern)	toast with chopped shrimps in mayonnaise, topped with bleak roe

Soups   *Soppor*

I'd like some soup.	**Jag skulle vilja ha en soppa.**	yaa(g) **skewl**er **vil**yah haa ehn **sopp**ah
What do you recommend?	**Vad föreslår ni?**	vaad **fürr**erslawr nee

buljong	bewl**yong**	consommé
champinjonsoppa	shamhpin**yōōn**soppah	mushroom soup
fisksoppa	**fisk**soppah	fish soup
grönsakssoppa	**grür**nsaakssoppah	vegetable soup
hummersoppa	**hew**merrsoppah	lobster soup
kålsoppa	**kawl**soppah	cabbage soup
löksoppa	**lür**ksoppah	onion soup
nässelsoppa	**neh**sserlsoppah	nettle soup
oxvanssoppa	**ooks**svahnssoppah	oxtail soup
räksoppa	**raik**soppah	shrimp soup
sparrissoppa	**spahr**issoppah	asparagus soup
spenatsoppa	speh**naat**soppah	spinach soup

svartsoppa (**svah**ʳ**t**soppah)	black soup made from goose blood and giblets; a southern Swedish speciality served in November, as a starter in a goose meal
ärtsoppa (**æ**ʳ**t**soppah)	yellow pea soup with lightly salted pork; traditionally served on Thursdays in winter as a main course, along with hot sweet Swedish *punsch,* and pancakes as dessert
blåbärssoppa (**blaw**bæ͞ʳssoppah)	sweet bilberry soup; served as a dessert or as a vitamin-packed pick-me-up

Salads   *Sallader*

What salads do you have?	**Vad har ni för sallader?**	vaad haar nee fürr **sahl**ahderr

grönsallad (**grür**nsahlahd)	lettuce, cucumber, tomatoes, parsley, dill, with oil and vinegar dressing; accompanies the main course
tonfisksallad (**tōōn**fisksahlahd)	tuna fish salad—Swedish version of salad Niçoise
skaldjurssallad (**skaal**ye͞wʳssahlahd)	assorted seafood salad (mostly mussels and shrimps)
västkustsallad (**vehst**kewstsahlahd)	assorted seafood salad with mushrooms, tomatoes, lettuce, cucumber, asparagus and dill

Egg dishes *Äggrätter*

crêpe	krehp	crepe
skaldjurs-	**skaal**yēw'rs-	seafood
förlorat ägg	fur'lōōraht ehg	poached egg
omelett	omer**leht**	omelet
med ost	māyd oost	with cheese
med skinka	mayd **shink**ah	with ham
med svamp	mayd svahmp	with mushrooms
pannkaka	**pahn**kaakah	pancake
stekt ägg	stāykt ehg	fried egg
äggröra	ehg**rūr**rah	scrambled eggs

Fish and seafood *Fisk och skaldjur*

Sweden has a long coastline and many lakes, so it's not surprising that fish plays an important part in the country's diet. On the west coast the specialities are shellfish, fresh mackerel and cod. In the south and east, look for fresh herring, Baltic herring and whitefish. And in northern Sweden enjoy river trout and salmon as well as a distinctive red fish, char *(röding)*.

As for herring—the Swedish favourite—ask for *silltallrik* (**sil**tahlrik) and you'll get a sample of almost every variety available.

The crayfish season starts at midnight on the second Wednesday in August. It's taken quite seriously in Sweden, when the nights are long and the parties, floating on aquavit, flow into the early hours.

ansjovis	ahn**shōō**viss	marinated sprats
abborre	**ah**borrer	perch
bergtunga	**bǣry**tewngah	type of dab
bläckfisk	**blehk**fisk	octopus
böckling	**burk**ling	smoked Baltic herring
flundra	**flewn**drah	flounder
forell	for**rehl**	trout
gråsej	**graw**say	coley
gädda	**yeh**dah	pike
gös	yūrss	pike-perch
havskräfta	**hahvs**krehftah	Dublin Bay prawn (saltwater crayfish)

hälleflundra	hehlerflewndrah	halibut
hummer	hewmerr	lobster
kolja	kolyah	haddock
kräfta	krehftah	(freshwater) crayfish
krabba	krahbah	crab
kummel	kewmerl	hake
lake	laaker	burbot
lax	lahks	salmon
laxöring	lahksürring	salmon trout
långa	longah	ling
makrill	mahkril	mackerel
marulk	maarewlk	monkfish, anglerfish
multe	mewlter	mullet
piggvar	pigvaar	turbot
räkor	raikoor	prawns (shrimp)
röding	rürding	char
rödspätta	rür(d)spehtah	plaice
rödtunga	rür(d)tewngah	lemon sole
sardell	sah^rdehl	anchovy
sardin	sah^rdeen	sardine
sik	seek	whitefish
sill	sil	herring
sjötunga	shürtewngah	sole
skarpsill	skahrpsil	sprats
slätvar	slaitvaar	brill
stenbit	stäynbeet	lump-fish
strömming	strurming	Baltic herring
stör	sturr	sturgeon
tonfisk	toonfisk	tuna (tunny)
torsk	to^rsk	cod
vitling	vitling	whiting
ål	awl	eel

baked	**ugnstekt**	ewngnstäykt
deep fried	**friterad**	fritäyrahd
fried	**stekt**	stäykt
grilled	**halstrad, grillad**	hahlstrahd, grillahd
marinated	**marinerad, gravad**	mahrinnäyrahd, graavahd
poached	**pocherad**	poshäyrahd
sautéed	**brynt**	brewnt
simmered	**kokt**	kookt
slightly salted	**rimmad**	rimmahd
smoked	**rökt**	rürkt
steamed	**ångkokt**	ongkookt

You'll probably come across some of the following fish and seafood dishes when eating out:

gravlax
(graavlahks)
salmon marinated with salt, sugar (pepper) and dill; served with a sweet-sour mustard-vinegar-oil sauce with plenty of dill

gubbröra
(gewbrūrrah)
marinated sprats, onions and hard-boiled eggs, fried in butter; served hot

inkokt lax
(inkookt lahks)
simmered fresh salmon; served cold with mayonnaise or a hollandaise sauce

krabba
(krahbah)
crab, available during the crab season (autumn); served with a mustard-dill sauce

kräftor
(krehftoor)
freshwater crayfish simmered with dill, served cold; the season for this Swedish speciality starts on the second Wednesday in August

kräftströmming
(krehftstrurming)
Baltic herring baked with crushed tomatoes and lots of dill; served warm or cold with boiled potatoes

lutfisk
(lēwtfisk)
dried ling, soaked in lye; simmered and served with a béchamel sauce, mustard or black pepper (traditional Christmas dish)

lättrökt lax
(lehtrūrkt lahks)
lightly smoked salmon, often served with creamed spinach, poached egg and lemon

rimmad lax med stuvad potatis
(rimmad lahks māyd stēwvahd pootaatiss)
lightly salted salmon with creamed potatoes and dill

sotare
(sōōtahrer)
Baltic herring soaked in water and salt, grilled until black; served hot, often with dill butter

strömmingsflundror
(strurmingsflewndror)
Baltic herrings, opened out and sandwiched in pairs with a parsley or dill filling, fried; served with mashed potatoes

stuvad abborre
(stēwvahd ahborrer)
perch, poached with onion, parsley and lemon; served with boiled potatoes

surströmming
(sēwᵣstrurming)
Baltic herring, specially processed, marinated and fermented (an autumnal northern Swedish speciality); served with small almond-shaped potatoes, chopped onions and un-leavened barley bread; not for those with delicate noses

Meat *Kött*

What kind of meat is this?	Vad för slags kött är det här?	vaad fūrr slahgss khurt ǣr dāy(t) hǣr
beef/lamb	oxkött/lamm	**ooks**khurt/lahm
pork/veal	fläskkött/kalv	**flehsk**khurt/kahlv
I'd like some ...	Jag skulle vilja ha ...	yaa(g) **skewl**er **vil**yah haa
biff	bif	beef steak
fläskfilé	**flehsk**fillāȳ	fillet of pork
fläskkarré	**flehsk**kahrāȳ	loin of pork
fläskkotlett	**flehsk**kotleht	pork chop
kalvbräss	**kahlv**brehss	sweetbread
kalvfilé	**kahlv**fillāȳ	fillet of veal
kalvkotlett	**kahlv**kotleht	veal chop
kalvlever	**kahlv**lāȳverr	calf's liver
kalvstek	**kahlv**stāȳk	roast veal
kalvsylta	**kahlv**sewlta	jellied veal loaf
kassler	**kahs**lerr	lightly salted, smoked loin of pork
korv	korv	sausage
falukorv	**faa**lewkorv	lightly spiced sausage, fried in slices
fläskkorv	**flehsk**korv	spicy boiled pork sausage
isterband	**is**terrbahnd	fried sausage of pork, beef and barley grain
köttbullar	**khurt**bewlahr	meat balls
köttfärslimpa	**khurt**fæᶜslimpah	meat loaf
lammbog	**lahm**bōōg	shoulder of lamb
lammkotlett	**lahm**kotleht	lamb chop
lammsadel	**lahm**saaderl	saddle of lamb
lammstek	**lahm**stāȳk	roast lamb
njure	**nyēw**rer	kidney
oxbringa	**ooks**bringah	brisket of beef
oxfilé	**ooks**fillāȳ	fillet of beef
oxrulader	**ooks**rewlaaderr	braised rolls of beef
pannbiff	**pahn**bif	hamburger
ragu	rah**gēw**	ragout
revbensspjäll	**rāȳv**bāȳnsspyehl	spareribs
rostbiff	**rost**bif	roast beef
råbiff	**raw**bif	steak tartare
skinka	**shin**kah	ham
kokt skinka	kookt **shin**kah	boiled ham
rökt skinka	rūrkt **shin**kah	smoked ham
tunga	**tewn**gah	tongue
wienerschnitzel	**vee**nerrshnitserl	breaded veal escalope

roast	**ugnstekt**	ewngnstaȳkt
boiled	**kokt**	kookt
braised	**bräserad**	brehssaȳrahd
fried	**stekt**	staȳkt
grilled (broiled)	**grillad**	grillahd
whole roasted	**helstekt**	haȳlstaȳkt
sautéed	**brynt**	brewnt
smoked	**rökt**	rūrkt
underdone (rare)	**blodig**	blōōdig
medium	**medium**	maȳdeeyewm
well-done	**genomstekt**	yaȳnomstaȳkt

biff à la Lindström
(bif à la lin(d)strurm)

minced beef mixed with pickled beetroot, capers and onions, shaped into patties and fried

blodpudding med lingonsylt
(blōō(d)pewding maȳd lingonsewlt)

black pudding (blood sausage), fried and served with cranberries; eaten as a main course

bruna bönor med fläsk
(brewnah būrnoor maȳd flehsk)

stewed brown beans flavoured with vinegar and golden syrup; served with thick slices of lightly salted pork

dillkött
(dilkhurt)

chunks of veal in a lemon and dill sauce

fläskpannkaka
(flehskpahnkaakah)

thick oven-baked pancake with bacon, served with cranberries

kåldolmar
(kawldolmahr)

cabbage rolls, stuffed with minced meat and rice; served with cream gravy

lövbiff
(lūrvbif)

fried thinly sliced beef; served with fried onions

pepparrotskött
(pehpahrrōōtskhurt)

boiled beef with horseradish sauce

pytt i panna
(pewt ee pahnah)

Swedish hash; chunks of fried meat, sausages, onions and potatoes; served with a fried egg and pickled beetroot

sjömansbiff
(shūrmahnsbif)

casserole with fried beef, onions and potatoes, braised in beer

slottsstek
(slotsstaȳk)

pot roast with marinated sprats and golden syrup

Game and poultry   *Vilt och fågel*

During the hunting season you'll find game on restaurant menus. Some varieties—woodland grouse, black grouse, ptarmigan and hazelhen—may be new to you. Try them!

Often game is marinated, for example with juniper berries, before being cooked, then served with an exceptionally rich sauce. Vegetables, cranberries and fruit jellies are also served with game. If you happen to be in southern Sweden on November 11; join in the celebration of *Mårten gås* and eat *svartsoppa,* black soup, and goose.

I'd like some game.	**Jag skulle vilja ha en vilträtt.**	yaa(g) skewler vilyah haa ehn viltreht
anka	ahnkah	duck
björnstek	byūr̶nstāy̶k	roast bear
fasan	fahsaan	pheasant
gås	gawss	goose
hare	haarer	hare
hjort	yoo^rt	deer
järpe	yærper	hazelhen
kalkon	kahlkōōn	turkey
kyckling	khewkling	chicken
morkulla	mōōrkewlah	woodcock
orre	orrer	black grouse
rapphöna	rahphūr̶nah	partridge
ren	rāy̶n	reindeer
renbog	rāy̶nbōōg	shoulder of reindeer
renfilé	rāy̶nfillāy̶	fillet of reindeer
renskav	rāy̶nskaav	dried leg of reindeer, thinly sliced
renstek	rāy̶nstāy̶k	roast reindeer
rökt renstek	rūr̶kt rāy̶nstāy̶k	smoked roast reindeer
torkat renkött	torkaht rāy̶nkhurt	dried fillet of reindeer
ripa	reepah	ptarmigan
rådjur	rawyēw̶r	venison
rådjursfilé	rawyēw̶^rsfillāy̶	fillet of venison
rådjurssadel	rawyēw̶^rssaaderl	saddle of venison
rådjursstek	rawyēw̶^rsstāy̶k	roast venison
tjäder	khaiderr	woodland grouse
vildand	vildahnd	wild duck
älg	ehly	elk
älgfilé	ehlyfillāy̶	fillet of elk
älgstek	ehlystāy̶k	roast elk

Vegetables   *Grönsaker*

Could I have some vegetables?	**Skulle jag kunna få lite grönsaker?**	skewler yaa(g) kewnah faw leeter grūrnsaakerr

blomkål	bloomkawl	cauliflower
broccoli	brokkoli	broccoli
brysselkål	brewsserlkawl	Brussels sprouts
bönor	būrnoor	beans
endiv	ehndeev	chicory (endive)
fänkål	fænkawl	fennel
grönkål	grūrnkawl	kale
grönsallad	grūrnsahlahd	lettuce
gurka	gewrkah	cucumber
haricots verts	ahrikkovær	French (green) beans
kronärtskocka	krōōnærtskokkah	artichoke
kålrot	kawlrōōt	swede (rutabaga)
lök	lūrk	onions
majs	mahyss	sweet corn (corn)
morötter	mōōrurterr	carrots
paprika	paaprikkah	sweet pepper
grön/röd/gul	grūrn/rūrd/gēwl	green/red/yellow
purjolök	pewryoolūrk	leeks
rädisor	rehdissoor	radishes
rödbetor	rūr(d)bāytoor	beetroots
rödkål	rūr(d)kawl	red cabbage
saltgurka	sahltgewrkah	salted gherkin
sparris	spahriss	asparagus
spenat	spehnaat	spinach
svamp	svahmp	mushrooms
champinjoner	shahmpinyōōnerr	button mushrooms
kantareller	kahntahrehlerr	chanterelle mushrooms
tomater	toomaaterr	tomatoes
vitkål	veetkawl	white cabbage
äggplanta	ehgplahntah	aubergine (eggplant)
ärtor	ærtoor	peas
ättiksgurka	ehtiksgewrkah	pickled gherkin (pickle)

rotmos (rōōtmōōss)	mashed swedes, potatoes and carrots; served with boiled, lightly salted pig's knuckle

au gratin	**gratinerade**	grahtināyrahder
boiled	**kokta**	kooktah
in a sauce	**stuvade**	stēwvahder
stuffed	**fyllda**	fewldah

Potatoes, rice and noodles *Potatis, ris och pasta*

bakad potatis	baakad pootaatiss	baked potatoes
färskpotatis	fæ^rskpootaatiss	new potatoes
kokt potatis	kookt pootaatiss	boiled potatoes
pommes frites	pom frit	chips (French fries)
potatis	pootaatiss	potato
-gratäng	-grahtehng	gratin
-kroketter	-krokehterr	croquettes
-mos	-mōōss	mashed
-puffar	-pewfahr	fritters
-sallad	-sahlahd	salad
ris	reess	rice
råstekt potatis	rawstäykt pootaatiss	fried potatoes
stekt potatis	stäykt pootaatiss	sautéed potatoes
stuvade makaroner	stēwvahderr mahkahrōōnerr	creamed macaroni

hasselbackspotatis (hahsserlbahkspootaatiss)	potatoes coated with melted butter, breadcrumbs and sometimes grated cheese, baked
kroppkakor (kropkaakoor)	potato dumplings with a filling of minced bacon and onions; served with melted butter
raggmunk med fläsk (rahgmewnk mäyd flaisk)	potato pancake with lightly salted pork; served with cranberries

Sauces *Såser*

gräddfil	grehdfil	sour cream
kryddsmör	krewdsmūrr	herb butter
löksås	lūrksawss	onion sauce
persiljesmör	peh^rsilyersmūrr	parsley butter
skarpsås	skahrpsawss	sweet-sour mustard-cream sauce
sky	shēw	gravy
vitlökssmör	veetlūrkssmūrr	garlic butter

hovmästarsås (hawvmehstah^rsawss)	sweet-sour mustard-vinegar-oil sauce with dill; served with fish and seafood
pepparotssås (pehpahrōōtssawss)	béchamel sauce flavoured with horseradish
örtagårdssås (ur^rtahgaw^rdssawss)	mayonnaise mixed with sour cream, dill, parsley, chives, (garlic) and tarragon

... as for the herbs, *örter,* and spices, *kryddor:*

basilika	bah**ssee**likkah	basil
dill	dil	dill
dragon	drah**gōōn**	tarragon
enbär	**āȳn**bǟr	juniper berries
gräslök	**grais**lṻrk	chives
ingefära	**inger**fǟrah	ginger
kanel	kah**nāȳl**	cinnamon
kardemumma	kah**ʳdermew**mah	cardamom
krasse	**krahs**ser	cress
kryddpeppar	**krewd**pehpahr	allspice
kummin	**kew**min	caraway seeds
lagerblad	**laager**blaad	bay leaf
mejram	**may**rahm	marjoram
muskot	**mew**skot	nutmeg
(krydd) nejlika	(krewd) **nay**likkah	clove
persilja	peh**ʳsil**yah	parsley
peppar	**peh**pahr	pepper
rosmarin	**raws**mahreen	rosemary
saffran	**sahf**rahn	saffron
salvia	**sahl**veeah	sage
salt	sahlt	salt
vitlök	**veet**lṻrk	garlic

Cheese *Ost*

Why not do like the Swedes and start the day with a slice or two on bread?

Grevé (grāȳvāȳ)	semi-hard cheese; a mixture between Gouda and Emmental
herrgårdsost (hehrgaw^rdsoost)	very popular cheese; semi-hard with large holes. Nutty flavour; eaten young and mature
kryddost (krewdoost)	firm, strong, semi-dry cheese with caraway seeds
mesost (māȳssoost)	amber coloured, sweet whey cheese; definitely an acquired taste
Svecia (svāȳssiah)	popular semi-hard cheese; can be spiced depending on the region
Västerbotten (vehsterrbottern)	hard, pungent cheese from the north of Sweden
ädelost (aiderloost)	blue cheese; sharp taste

Fruit *Frukt*

Do you have (fresh) fruit?	**Har ni (färsk) frukt?**	haar nee (fæ^{r}sk) frewkt
I'd like a fruit salad.	**Jag skulle vilja ha fruktsallad.**	yaa(g) **skew**ler **vil**yah haa **frewkt**sahlahd

ananas	**ah**nahnahss	pineapple
apelsin	ahperl**seen**	orange
aprikos	ahpri**kko̅o̅ss**	apricot
banan	bah**naan**	banana
bigarråer	biggah**raw**err	sweet cherries
björnbär	**byu̅r̅^{r}n**bæ̅r	blackberries
blåbär	**blaw**bæ̅r	bilberries (blueberries)
citron	sit**ro̅o̅n**	lemon
dadlar	**dahd**lahr	dates
fikon	**fee**kon	figs
grapefrukt	"**grape**"frewkt	grapefruit
hallon	**hah**lon	raspberries
hasselnöt	**hah**sserlnu̅r̅t	hazelnut
hjortron	**yoo^{r}**tron	Arctic cloudberries
jordgubbar	**yo̅o̅^{r}d**gewbahr	strawberries
katrinplommon	kah**treen**ploomon	prunes
krusbär	**kre̅w̅s**bæ̅r	gooseberries
kvitten	**kvi**ttern	quince
körsbär	**khur^{r}s**bæ̅r	cherries
lingon	**ling**on	cranberries
mandel	**mahn**derl	almond
melon	meh**lo̅o̅n**	melon
persika	**pæ^{r}**sikkah	peach
plommon	**ploo**mon	plums
päron	**pæ̅**ron	pear
rabarber	rah**bahr**berr	rhubarb
russin	**rew**ssin	raisins
rönnbär	**rurn**bæ̅r	rowanberries
smultron	**smewl**tron	wild strawberries
tranbär	**traan**bæ̅r	type of cranberries
valnöt	**vaal**nu̅r̅t	walnut
vattenmelon	**vah**ternmehlo̅o̅n	watermelon
vinbär	**veen**bæ̅r	currants
röda	**ru̅r̅**dah	red
svarta	**svah^{r}**tah	black
vita	**vee**tah	white
vindruvor	**veen**dre̅w̅voor	grapes
blå	blaw	black
gröna	**gru̅r̅**nah	green
äpple	**eh**pler	apple

Dessert   *Efterrätter*

I'd like a dessert, please.	**Jag skulle vilja ha en efterrätt.**	yaa(g) skewler vilyah haa ehn ehfterreht
Something light, please.	**Någonting lätt, tack.**	nawgonting leht tahk
with/without ...	**med/utan ...**	mayd/ewtahn ...
cream	**grädde**	grehder
whipped cream	**vispgrädde**	vispgrehder

chokladmousse	shoklaa(d)mooss	chocolate mousse
citronfromage	sitroonfroomaash	lemon mousse
fläderblomssorbet	flæderrbloomssorbay	elderflower sorbet
friterad camembert med hjortronsylt	fritayrahd kahmahnbær mayd yoo^rtronsewlt	deep fried camembert with cloudberry jam
glass	glahss	ice cream
jordgubbs-	yoo^rdgewbs-	strawberry
vanilj-	vahnily-	vanilla
hjortron med glass	yoo^rtron mayd glahss	Arctic cloudberries with ice cream
jordgubbar med grädde	yoo^rdgewbahr mayd grehder	strawberries with cream
katrinplommonsufflé	kahtreenploomonsewflay	prune soufflé
lingonsorbet	lingonsorbay	cranberry sorbet
melon och hallon	mehloon ok hahlon	melon and raspberries
ris à la Malta	reess ah lah mahltah	rice cream dessert with fruit juice
smultron med grädde	smewltron mayd grehder	wild strawberries with cream
syltomelett	sewltomerleht	sweet omelet with jam
våfflor med sylt	vofloor mayd sewlt	waffles with jam
äppelkaka med vaniljsås	ehperlkaakah mayd vanilysawss	apple cake with vanilla custard

marängsviss (mahrehngsviss)	meringues with whipped cream and chocolate sauce
nyponsoppa (newponsoppah)	rose-hip soup; served with almond flakes and whipped cream
plättar (plehtahr)	small pancakes; eaten with sugar or jam, sometimes whipped cream
småländsk ostkaka (smawlehnsk oostkaakah)	curd cake from southern Sweden; served with jam
toscaäpplen (toskahehplern)	stewed apples covered with toffee sauce and almond flakes

Drinks *Alkoholhaltiga drycker*

High taxes make most alcohol expensive in Sweden. But if money is no object, you can get just about any drink you like. Note that alcohol is not served anywhere before noon.

Beer *Öl*

Beer is a very popular drink in Sweden. The stronger brew is called *starköl* (**stahrkūrl**) and the weaker beer *lättöl* (**lehtūrl**).

I'd like a beer, please.	**Jag skulle vilja ha en öl, tack.**	yaa(g) **skew**ler vil**yah haa ehn ūrl tahk
Do you have draught beer?	**Har ni fatöl?**	haar nee **faat**ūrl

Aquavit *Brännvin*

The national drink is served ice-cold in small glasses, to go with the *smörgåsbord* or appetizers. Aquavit, popularly known as *snaps* (snahps), contains about 40 per cent pure alcohol; it's often served with a beer chaser. Aquavit can be flavoured with various spices and herbs. In restaurants it is sold in measures of 2, 4, 6 or 8 centilitres (1 cl. = ⅓ oz.).

Bäska Droppar (**behskah droppahr**)	bitter-tasting aquavit, flavoured with wormwood
Herrgårds (Aquavit) (**hehrgaw**ʳds **ahkvahveet**)	flavoured with caraway seeds and whisky, matured in sherry barrels
O.P. (Anderson Aquavit) (oo pāy)	flavoured with aniseed, caraway seeds and fennel
Renat (Brännvin) (**rāy**naht)	colourless, unflavoured
Skåne (Akvavit) (**skaw**ner)	same as O.P. but with a weaker flavour
Svart-Vinbärs-Brännvin (svah**ʳt veen**bā=ʳs-brehnveen)	flavoured with blackcurrants

Glögg

Around Christmas the Swedes drink a sweet, hot punch called *glögg* (glurg). It is made of red wine, sugar, cloves, cinnamon, Seville orange peel and flavourless aquavit, and served with almonds and raisins.

Punsch

This popular after-dinner drink is a very sweet, power-packed liqueur made of arrack, sugar and pure alcohol. *Punsch* (pewnsh) is also served warm with the traditional Thursday pea soup.

Wine   *Vin*

Sweden imports wine from France, Italy, Spain, Australia, California and elsewhere. You'll find excellent Bordeaux and Burgundy vintages in hotels and good restaurants, together with less expensive wines which can be ordered by the carafe or the glass.

May I have the wine list, please?	**Kan jag få vinlistan, tack?**	kahn yaa(g) faw **veen**listahn tahk
I'd like a ... of red wine.	**Jag skulle vilja ha ... rött vin.**	yaa(g) **skewler** vilyah haa ... rurt veen
carafe	**en karaff**	ehn kah**rahf**
glass	**ett glas**	eht glaass
half bottle	**en halv flaska**	ehn hahlv **flah**skah
A bottle of champagne, please.	**En flaska champagne, tack.**	ehn **flah**skah shahm**pahny** tahk
Please bring me another ...	**Kan jag få en ... till, tack?**	kahn yaa(g) faw ehn ... til tahk
Where does this wine come from?	**Varifrån kommer det här vinet?**	**vaa**rifrawn **kom**mer dāȳ(t) hær **vee**nert

red/white/rosé	**rött/vitt/rosé**	rurt/vit/rossāy
dry	**torrt**	to^rt
light	**lätt**	leht
full-bodied	**fylligt**	fewlit
sparkling	**mousserande**	moossāyrahnder
very dry	**mycket torrt**	mewker(t) to^rt
sweet	**sött**	surt
chilled	**kylt**	khewlt
at room temperature	**rumstempererat**	rewmstehmperrāyraht

Other alcoholic drinks   *Andra alkoholhaltiga drycker*

In bars and restaurants you can get almost all the drinks you're used to at home. The customary international names are used and the drinks are mixed the same way.

I'd like a/an ..., please.	**Jag skulle vilja ha ..., tack.**	yaa(g) skewler vilyah haa ... tahk
aperitif	**en aperitif**	ehn ahperritif
brandy	**en cognac**	ehn konyahk
gin and tonic	**en gin och tonic**	ehn yin ok tonnik
liqueur	**ett glas likör**	eht glaass likūrr
port	**ett glas portvin**	eht glaass paw^rtveen
rum	**rom**	rom
sherry	**ett glas sherry**	eht glaass shehri
vermouth	**ett glas vermouth**	eht glaass vehrmewt
vodka	**en vodka**	ehn vodkah
whisky	**en whisky**	ehn viski
neat (straight)	**ren**	rāyn
on the rocks	**med is**	māyd ees
with water	**med vatten**	māyd vahtern
with soda water	**med sodavatten**	māyd sōōdahvahtern

SKÅL!
(skawl)
CHEERS!

Nonalcoholic drinks *Alkoholfria drycker*

Of course you don't have to order wine or spirits in a bar. If you prefer, ask for a *juice* or *läsk* (soft drink):

I don't drink alcohol.	**Jag dricker inte alkohol.**	yaa(g) drikkerr inter ahlkohawl
I'd like a/an ...	**Jag skulle vilja ha ...**	yaa(g) skewler vilyah haa
apple juice	**äppeljuice**	ehperlyōōss
grapefruit juice	**grapefruktjuice**	"grape"frewktyōōss
iced tea	**iste**	eestāȳ
lemonade	**en läsk**	ehn lehsk
(glass of) milk	**(ett glas) mjölk**	(eht glaass) myurlk
milkshake	**en milkshake**	ehn "milkshake"
mineral water	**mineralvatten**	minerraalvahtern
fizzy (carbonated)	**med kolsyra**	māȳd kawlsēȳwrah
still	**utan kolsyra**	ēȳwtahn kawlsēȳwrah
orange juice	**apelsinjuice**	ahperlseenyōōss
pineapple juice	**ananasjuice**	ahnahnahsyōōss
tomato juice	**tomatjuice**	toomaatyōōss
tonic water	**tonic**	tonnik

Hot drinks *Varma drycker*

The best place to go for your afternoon tea or coffee is a cake shop. Pay for your cake or pastry at the counter and then take it through to the seating area. There's usually a table with tea and coffee on it—self-service—and you can have as many cups as you like! In more elegant or old-fashioned cafés a waitress will serve you.

I'd like a/an ...	**Jag skulle vilja ha ...**	yaa(g) skewler vilyah haa
(hot) chocolate	**(varm) choklad**	(vahrm) shoklaa(d)
coffee	**kaffe**	kahfer
a pot of	**en kanna**	ehn kahnah
decaffeinated	**koffeinfritt**	koffeheenfrit
espresso	**en espresso**	ehn ehsprehsso
with cream	**med grädde**	māȳd grehder
tea	**te**	tāȳ
a cup of	**en kopp**	ehn kop
with lemon	**med citron**	māȳd sitrōōn
with milk	**med mjölk**	māȳd myurlk

Complaints *Klagomål*

There's a ... missing.	**Det fattas ...**	dāȳ(t) **fahtahss**
plate	**en tallrik**	ehn **tahl**rik
glass	**ett glas**	eht glaass
I don't have a knife/fork/spoon.	**Jag har inte någon kniv/gaffel/sked.**	yaa(g) haar inter **naw**gon kneev/**gahf**erl/shāȳd
That's not what I ordered.	**Det där har jag inte beställt.**	dāȳ(t) dær haar yaa(g) inter ber**stehlt**
I asked for ...	**Jag bad om ...**	yaa(g) baa(d) om
There must be a mistake.	**Det måste vara ett misstag.**	dāȳ(t) **mos**ter **vaa**rah eht **mis**taag
May I change this?	**Kan jag få byta ut det här?**	kahn yaa(g) faw **bēw**tah **ēw**t dāȳ(t) hær
I asked for a small portion (for the child).	**Jag bad om en liten portion (till barnet).**	yaa(g) baa(d) om ehn **lee**tern po**ʳtshōōn** (til **baaʳ**nert)
The meat is ...	**Köttet är ...**	**khur**tert **ær**
overdone	**för mycket stekt**	fūrr **mew**ker(t) stāȳkt
underdone	**inte tillräckligt genomstekt**	inter **til**rehkli(g)t **yāȳ**nomstāȳkt
too rare	**för blodigt**	fūrr **blōō**di(g)t
too tough	**för segt**	fūrr **sāȳ**gt
This is too ...	**Det här är för ...**	dāȳ(t) hær **ær** fūrr
bitter	**beskt**	behskt
salty	**salt**	sahlt
sweet	**sött**	surt
I don't like this.	**Jag tycker inte om det här.**	yaa(g) **tew**kerr inter om dāȳ(t) hær
The food is cold.	**Maten är kall.**	**maa**tern ær kahl
This isn't fresh.	**Det här är inte färskt.**	dāȳ(t) hær ær inter **fæ**ʳskt
What's taking so long?	**Varför tar det så lång tid?**	vahr**furr** taar dāȳ(t) saw long teed
Have you forgotten our drinks?	**Har ni glömt våra drinkar?**	haar nee glurmt **vaw**rah **drink**ahr
The wine doesn't taste right.	**Vinet smakar inte bra.**	**vee**nert **smaa**kahr inter braa

| This isn't clean. | **Det här är inte rent.** | dā̄y(t) hǣr ǟr inter rāȳnt |
| I'd like to speak to the head waiter. | **Kan jag få tala med hovmästaren?** | kahn yaa(g) faw taalah mā̄yd hawvmehstahˈn |

The bill (check) *Notan*

The service charge is automatically included in restaurant bills. Anything extra for the waiter is optional. Credit cards may be used in an increasing number of restaurants.

I'd like to pay.	**Får jag betala?**	fawr yaa(g) bertaalah
We'd like to pay separately.	**Vi skulle vilja betala var och en för sig.**	vee skewler vilyah bertaalah vaar ok ehn fūr say
I think there's a mistake in this bill.	**Jag tror att det är ett fel på notan.**	yaa(g) trōōr aht dā̄y(t) ǟr eht fāȳl paw nōōtahn
What's this amount for?	**Vad står den här summan för?**	vaad stawr den hǣr sewmahn fūr
Is everything included?	**Är allting inräknat?**	ǟr ahlting inraiknaht
Do you accept traveller's cheques?	**Tar ni emot resecheker?**	taar nee ehmōōt rāȳsserkhehkerr
Can I pay with this credit card?	**Kan jag betala med det här kreditkortet?**	kahn yaa(g) bertaalah mā̄yd dā̄y(t) hǣr krehdeetkooˈtert
Keep the change.	**Behåll växeln.**	berhol vehkserln
That was a delicious meal.	**Det var en utsökt måltid.**	dā̄y(t) vaar ehn ēwtsūrkt mawlteed
We enjoyed it, thank you.	**Det var mycket gott.**	dā̄y(t) vaar mewker(t) got

---

SERVERINGSAVGIFT INRÄKNAD
SERVICE INCLUDED

TIPPING, see inside back-cover

Snacks *Mellanmål*

If you want a quick snack, every self-respecting village has its own *gatukök,* street kitchen, where you can get everything from a hot dog to spring rolls, ice cream and soft drinks. If you want to sit down, look for a *café* or *cafeteria,* where you will get pastries, open sandwiches or maybe a salad.

I'll have one of those.	**Jag skulle vilja ha en av de där.**	yaa(g) **skewl**er vil**yah** haa ehn aav dom dǟr
Can I have two of these, please.	**Kan jag få två av de här, tack?**	kahn yaa(g) faw tvaw aav dom hǟr tahk
to the left/right above/below	**till vänster/höger ovanför/nedanför**	til **vehn**sterr/**hǖ**gerr **aw**vahnfür/**nā̄y**dahnfür
It's to take away.	**Jag tar det med mig.**	yaa(g) taar dā̄y(t) mā̄yd may
I'd like a frankfurter with mashed potatoes.	**Jag skulle vilja ha en varm korv med (potatis)mos.**	yaa(g) **skewl**er vil**yah** haa ehn vahrm korv mā̄yd (poo**taa**tis)**mōō**ss
Can I have an open sandwich with eggs and marinated sprats?	**Kan jag få en smörgås med ägg och ansjovis?**	kahn yaa(g) faw ehn **smurr**gawss mā̄yd ehg ok ahn**shōō**viss
cheese	**ost**	oost
ham	**skinka**	**shin**kah
liver paté	**leverpastej**	**lā̄y**verrpahstay
shrimps	**räkor**	**rai**koor
I'd like a/an/some …	**Jag skulle vilja ha …**	yaa(g) **skewl**er vil**yah** haa
fried sausage	**en grillad korv**	ehn **gril**lahd korv
in a roll	**med bröd**	mā̄yd brǖd
with chips	**med pommes frites**	mā̄yd pom frit
ice cream	**en glass**	ehn glahss
chocolate	**choklad-**	shook**laa**(d)-
pear	**päron-**	**pǟ**ron-
strawberry	**jordgubbs-**	**yōō'd**gewbss-
vanilla	**vanilj-**	**vah**nily-
meat balls	**köttbullar**	**khurt**bewlahr
spring roll	**vårrulle**	**vawr**rewler
landgång (**lahn(d)**gong)		a long open sandwich with at least 3 different toppings

Pastries and cakes   *Bakverk och kakor*

Sweden is famous for its pastries and cakes so either buy them in a pastry shop or try some with coffee in a café.

I'd like a ...	**Jag skulle vilja ha en ...**	yaa(g) skewler vilyah haa ehn
bun	**bulle**	bewler
cake	**kaka**	kaakah
piece of gâteau	**tårtbit**	taw**ʳ**tbeet

kanelbulle	kah**nāȳl**bewler	cinnamon bun
mjuk pepparkaka	my**ēw**k **peh**pahrkaakah	gingerbread cake
sockerkaka	**so**kkerrkaakah	sponge cake
wienerbröd	**vee**nerbr**ūr**d	Danish pastry

chokladbiskvi
(sho**klaa(d)**biskvee)
— chocolate-covered macaroon with a filling of chocolate-flavoured butter-cream

drömtårta
(drurmtaw**ʳ**tah)
— chocolate Swiss roll with a vanilla-butter filling

gräddtårta
(**grehd**taw**ʳ**tah)
— cream sponge with jam filling

mazarin
(mahssa**reen**)
— Sweden's most beloved pastry; almond tart topped with icing

napoleonbakelse
(nah**pōōlāȳon**-baaker**l**ser)
— iced flaky pastry filled with whipped cream and apple sauce

prinsesstårta
(prin**sehss**taw**ʳ**tah)
— sponge cake with vanilla custard, whipped cream and strawberry jam, covered with green marzipan

rulltårta
(**rewl**taw**ʳ**tah)
— Swiss roll filled with jam or chocolate cream

saffransbulle
(**sahf**rahnsbewler)
— saffron bun; traditionally a Christmas bun

semla, fastlagsbulle
(**sehm**lah, **fahst**-laagsbewler)
— bun filled with almond paste and whipped cream, served either as a pastry or in a bowl with hot milk and cinnamon; available from Christmas to Easter

spettekaka
(**speh**terkaakah)
— tall, cone-shaped dry cake, made of egg and sugar paste on a spit; speciality from southern Sweden

64

Picnic *Picknick*

Just a little information to make shopping for a picnic easier. Almost all butter and margarine in Sweden is salted; unsalted butter does exist but is difficult to find. Or buy easy-spread butter/margarine mixtures (not for frying).

For fillings there's a variety of pre-packed smoked or boiled meat and sausages. You can also buy food at the fresh-meat counter—the sales person will slice it for you. Try *medvurst* (**mayd**vewrst), a very popular smoked or boiled sausage (one variety is flavoured with cognac), or juniper-smoked ham, *enrisrökt skinka* (**ayn**reesrürkt **shin**kah). You can also buy a whole sausage and slice it yourself. There are different kinds of liver paté worth trying and an interesting selection of cheeses.

And if you like fermented milk, *filmjölk* (**feel**myurlk), try a variety called *filbunke* (**feel**bewnker)—you eat it like yoghurt.

I'd like a/an/ some ...	**Jag skulle vilja ha ...**	yaa(g) **skewl**er **vil**yah haa
biscuits (Br.)	**kex**	kehks
beer	**öl**	ürl
bread	**bröd**	brürd
butter	**smör**	smürr
cheese	**ost**	oost
chips (Am.)	**chips**	khips
chocolate bar	**en chokladkaka**	ehn shok**laa(d)**kaakah
(instant) coffee	**(snabb)kaffe**	(snahb)**kah**fer
cookies	**kex**	kehks
crisps	**chips**	khipss
eggs	**ägg**	ehg
gherkins (pickles)	**ättiksgurka**	**eht**iksgewrkah
ginger biscuits	**pepparkakor**	**peh**pahrkaakor
ham	**skinka**	**shin**kah
liver paté	**leverpastej**	**lay**verrpahstay
milk	**mjölk**	myurlk
mustard	**senap**	**say**nahp
sausage	**korv**	korv
sugar	**socker**	**sok**kerr
tea	**te**	tay
yoghurt	**en yoghurt**	ehn **yawg**(h)ew'rt

Travelling around

Plane *Flyg*

Is there a flight to Luleå?	**Finns det något flyg till Luleå?**	finss dāy(t) nawgot flewg til lewlāyaw
Is it a direct flight?	**Är det ett direktflyg?**	ǣr dāy(t) eht direhktflewg
When's the next flight to Malmö?	**När går nästa flyg till Malmö?**	nǣr gawr nehstah flewg til mahlmūr
Is there a connection to ...?	**Finns det någon anslutning till ...?**	finss dāy(t) nawgon ahnslewtning til
I'd like a ticket to ...	**Jag skulle vilja ha en biljett till ...**	yaa(g) skewler vilyah haa ehn bilyeht til
single (one-way)	**enkel**	ehnkerl
return (round trip)	**tur och retur**	tewr ok rertewr
aisle seat	**plats vid gången**	plahtss veed gongern
window seat	**plats vid fönstret**	plahtss veed furnstrert
What time do we take off?	**Hur dags går planet?**	hewr dahgss gawr plaanert
What time should I check in?	**Hur dags måste jag checka in?**	hewr dahgss moster yaa(g) khehkah in
Is there a bus to the airport?	**Går det någon buss till flygplatsen?**	gawr dāy(t) nawgon bewss til flewgplahtsern
What time do we arrive?	**Hur dags är vi framme?**	hewr dahgss ǣr vee frahmer
I'd like to ... my reservation.	**Jag skulle vilja ... min reservation.**	jaa(g) skewler vilyah ... min rehsehrvahshōōn
cancel	**annullera**	ahnewlāyrah
change	**ändra**	ehndrah
confirm	**bekräfta**	berkrehftah
I'd like to cancel my ticket.	**Jag skulle vilja avbeställa min biljett.**	yaa(g) skewler vilyah aavberstehlah min bilyeht

ANKOMST ARRIVAL	**AVGÅNG** DEPARTURE

Train *Tåg*

Trains in Sweden are operated by Swedish State Railways (SJ). They are extremely comfortable—in fact, second class in Sweden is often as luxurious as first class in many other countries. On long-distance trains there is always a restaurant car or a buffet. Some trains have special compartments, marked "Bk", for mothers with infants.

Seat reservations are not normally necessary for short distances but are often compulsory on long-distance trains, and during the Christmas and Easter periods it's recommended to book your seat well ahead.

Eurocity (EC) (ehewroositti)	International express train with first and second class
Intercity (IC) ("Intercity")	Long-distance inter-city train with first and second class; reservation compulsory; has telephone, a shop for small items such as perfume, chocolate, books, etc., and a dining car
City Express ("city-express")	Business train on special runs; reservation compulsory; surcharge payable; telephone
Lokaltåg (lookaaltawg)	Local train
Motorvagnståg (mootorvahngnstawg)	Small diesel train used on short runs
Pendeltåg (pehnderltawg)	Local train serving the city suburbs

Coach (long-distance bus) *Expressbuss*

A cheap, comfortable way to travel is by express coach, mainly run by the Swedish State Railways (SJ). These buses operate between major towns in the southern and central parts of Sweden and between the capital and coastal towns further north. In the northern region, the rail network is extended by a postal bus service.

Note: Most of the phrases on the following pages can be used for both train and bus travel.

To the railway station *Till stationen*

Where's the railway station?	**Var ligger järnvägs-stationen?**	vaar liggerr yǣ^rnvaigs-stahshōōnern
Where's the coach station.	**Var ligger buss-stationen?**	vaar liggerr **bews**-stahshōōnern
Taxi!	**Taxi!**	**tah**ksi
Take me to the ..., please.	**Till ..., tack.**	til ... tahk

INGÅNG	ENTRANCE
UTGÅNG	EXIT
TILL TÅGEN	TO THE TRAINS
INFORMATION	INFORMATION

Where's the ...? *Var är ...?*

Where is/are (the) ...?	**Var är ...?**	vaar ǣr
booking office	**biljettexpeditionen**	bil**yeht**ehkspehdishōōnern
cafeteria	**cafeterian**	kahfert**āy**reeahn
currency exchange office	**växelkontoret**	**veh**kserlkont**ōō**rert
left-luggage office (baggage check)	**effektförvaringen**	eh**fehkt**furrvaaringern
lost property (lost and found) office	**hittegods-expeditionen**	**hitter**goods-ehkspehdishōōnern
luggage lockers	**förvaringsboxarna**	furr**vaa**ringsboksah^rnah
newsstand	**tidningskiosken**	**tee**(d)ningskhioskern
platform 2	**perrong 2**	pehrong 2
reservations office	**biljettexpeditionen**	bil**yeht**ehkspehdi-shōōnern
restaurant	**restaurangen**	rehstor**rahng**ern
snack bar	**snackbaren**	**snahk**baarern
ticket office	**biljettluckan**	bil**yeht**lewkahn
track 5	**spår 5**	spawr 5
waiting room	**väntsalen**	**vehnt**saalern
Where are the toilets?	**Var är toaletten?**	vaar ǣr tooah**leht**ern

TAXI, see page 21

Inquiries *Förfrågningar*

In Sweden **i** means information office.

When is the ... train to Uppsala?	**När går ... tåget till Uppsala?**	nær gawr ... **taw**gert til ewp**saa**lah
first/last	**första/sista**	fur[r]stah/**sis**tah
When is the next train to ...?	**När går nästa tåg till ...?**	nær gawr **neh**stah tawg til
What time does the train to Göteborg leave?	**Hur dags går tåget till Göteborg?**	hēwr dahgss gawr **taw**gert til yurter**bory**
What's the fare to Örebro?	**Vad kostar en biljett till Örebro?**	vaad **kos**tahr ehn bil**yeht** til ūrer**brōō**
Is it a through train?	**Är det ett direkt-gående tåg?**	ær dāȳ(t) eht di**rehkt**-gawehnder tawg
Is there a connection to ...?	**Finns det någon anslutning till ...?**	finss dāȳ(t) **naw**gon **ahns**lēwtning til
Do I have to change trains?	**Måste jag byta tåg?**	**mos**ter yaa(g) **bew**tah tawg
Is there enough time to change?	**Hinner man byta tåg?**	**hin**nerr mahn **bēw**tah tawg
Is the train running on time?	**Går tåget i tid?**	gawr **taw**gert ee teed
What time does the train arrive in Helsingborg?	**Hur dags är tåget framme i Helsing-borg?**	hēwr dahgss ær **taw**gert **frah**mer ee **hehl**sing**bory**
Is there a dining car/sleeping car on the train?	**Finns det någon restaurangvagn/sovvagn i tåget?**	finss dāȳ(t) **naw**gon reh**stor**rahng**vahn**gn/**saw**vahngn ee **taw**gert
Does the train stop in Norrköping?	**Stannar tåget i Norrköping?**	**stah**nahr **taw**gert ee norkh**ūr**ping
Which platform does the train to Malmö leave from?	**Från vilken perrong går tåget till Malmö?**	frawn **vil**kern peh**rong** gawr **taw**gert til **mahl**mūr
Which track does the train from Göteborg arrive at?	**På vilket spår kommer tåget från Göteborg in?**	paw **vil**kert spawr **kom**merr **taw**gert frawn yurter**bory** in
I'd like a time-table, please.	**Skulle jag kunna få en tidtabell, tack?**	**skew**ler yaa(g) **kew**nah faw ehn **tee(d)**tahbehl tahk

Det är ett direktgående tåg.	It's a through train.
Ni måste byta i ...	You have to change at ...
Byt i ... och ta lokaltåget.	Change at ... and get a local train.
Perrong 2 är ...	Platform 2 is ...
där borta/uppför trappan till vänster/till höger	over there/upstairs on the left/right
Det går ett tåg till Gävle kl ...	There's a train to Gävle at ...
Tåget avgår från spår 8.	Your train will leave from track 8.
Det är ... minuter försenat.	It's running ... minutes late.
Första klass längst fram/ i mitten/längst bak.	First class at the front/in the middle/at the rear.

Tickets—Reservation   *Biljetter – Beställning*

I'd like a ticket to Lund.	**Jag skulle vilja ha en biljett till Lund.**	yaa(g) **skew**ler **vil**yah haa ehn bily**eht** til lewnd
single (one-way)	**enkel**	**ehn**kerl
return (round trip)	**tur och retur**	tewr ok reh**tewr**
first class	**första klass**	fur^rstah klahss
second class	**andra klass**	**ahn**drah klahss
half price	**halv biljett**	hahlv bily**eht**
full fare	**fullt pris**	fewlt preess
I'd like to reserve a ...	**Jag skulle vilja reservera en ...**	yaa(g) **skew**ler **vil**yah rehsehr**vay**rah ehn
couchette	**liggplats**	**lig**plahtss
window seat	**fönsterplats**	**furn**sterrplahtss
I'd like to reserve a berth in the sleeping car.	**Jag skulle vilja reservera en sovplats.**	yaa(g) **skew**ler **vil**yah rehsehr**vay**rah ehn **sawv**plahts
upper berth	**överbädd**	**ur**verrbehd
middle berth	**mellanbädd**	**meh**lahnbehd
lower berth	**underbädd**	**ewn**derrbehd

All aboard   *Tag plats*

Is this the right platform for the train to Luleå?	**Är det här rätt perrong för tåget till Luleå?**	ǣr dāȳ(t) hǣr reht pehrong fürr tawgert til lēwlāȳaw
Is this the train to Östersund?	**Är det här tåget till Östersund?**	ǣr dāȳ(t) hǣr tawgert til urster‹sewnd
Excuse me. Could I get by?	**Ursäkta, kan jag få komma förbi?**	ēw‹sehktah kahn yaa(g) faw kommah furrbee
Is this seat taken?	**Är den här platsen upptagen?**	ǣr dehn hǣr plahtsern ewptaagern

| **RÖKARE** | **ICKE RÖKARE** |
| SMOKER | NONSMOKER |

I think that's my seat.	**Jag tror att det där är min plats.**	yaa(g) trōōr aht dāȳ(t) dǣr ǣr min plahtss
Would you let me know before we get to Växjö?	**Skulle ni kunna säga till innan vi kommer till Växjö?**	skewler nee kewnah sehyah til innahn vee kommer til vehksshūr
What station is this?	**Vilken station är det här?**	vilkern stahshōōn ǣr dāȳ(t) hǣr
How long does the train stop here?	**Hur länge står tåget här?**	hēwr lehnger stawr tawgert hǣr
When do we get to Kiruna?	**När kommer vi till Kiruna?**	nǣr kommer vee til kirrewnah

Sleeping   *I sovvagnen*

Are there any free compartments in the sleeping car?	**Finns det någon ledig kupé i sovvagnen?**	finns dāȳ(t) nawgon lāȳdi(g) kewpāȳ ee sawvahngnern
Where's the sleeping car?	**Var är sovvagnen?**	vaar ǣr sawvahngnern
Where's my berth?	**Var är min sovplats?**	vaar ǣr min sawvplahtss
I'd like a lower berth.	**Jag skulle vilja ha en underbädd.**	yaa(g) skewler vilyah haa ehn ewnderrbehd

Would you make up our berths?	**Skulle ni kunna göra i ordning våra bäddar?**	skewler nee kewnah yūrrah ee aw^rdning vawrah behdahr
Would you wake me at 7 o'clock?	**Kan ni väcka mig kl. 7?**	kahn nee vehkah may klokkahn 7

Eating *I restaurangvagnen*

On every long-distance train there's a restaurant car and/or a buffet car for drinks and snacks. In some trains there are cars with table space for each passenger so that you can take your coffee back to your own seat.

Where's the dining car/buffet car?	**Var är restaurang-vagnen/cafévagnen?**	vaar ær rehstorrangvahng-nern/kahfāyvahngnern

Baggage and porters *Bagage och bärare*

Where can I find a porter?	**Var kan jag få tag på en bärare?**	vaar kahn yaa(g) faw taag paw ehn bǣrahrer
Can you help me with my luggage?	**Kan ni hjälpa mig med bagaget?**	kahn nee yehlpah may māyd bahgaashert
Where are the ...?	**Var är ...?**	vaar ǣr
luggage trolleys (carts)	**bagagekärrorna**	bahgaashkhæroo^rnah
luggage lockers	**förvaringsboxarna**	furrvaaringsboksah^rnah
Where's the left-luggage office (baggage check)?	**Var är effektförvaringen?**	vaar ǣr ehfehktfurrvaaringern
I'd like to leave my luggage, please.	**Jag skulle vilja lämna in mitt bagage.**	yaa(g) skewler vilyah lehmnah in mit bahgaash
I'd like to register (check) my luggage.	**Jag skulle vilja pollettera mitt bagage.**	yaa(g) skewler vilyah pollehtāyrah mit bahgaash

---

· **RESGODS**
REGISTERING (CHECKING) BAGGAGE

PORTERS, see also page 18

Bus—Tram (streetcar) *Buss – Spårvagn*

Get your ticket from the driver when you board the bus. In major cities it's worthwhile buying a booklet of tickets at a reduced price if you plan to travel extensively. The fare on buses and taxis doubles after midnight.

I'd like a booklet of tickets.	**Jag skulle vilja ha ett biljetthäfte.**	yaa(g) **skewl**er **vil**yah haa eht bil**yeht**hehfter
Which tram (streetcar) goes to the town centre?	**Vilken spårvagn går till centrum?**	**vil**kern **spawr**vahngn gawr til **sehn**trewm
Does this bus stop at ...?	**Stannar den här bussen vid ...?**	**stah**nahr dehn hæær **bew**ssern veed
Where can I get a bus to the opera?	**Varifrån går bussen till operan?**	**vaa**rifrawn gawr **bew**ssern til **ōō**perrahn
Which bus do I take to Skansen?	**Vilken buss skall jag ta till Skansen?**	**vil**kern bewss skah(l) yaa(g) taa til **skahn**sern
Where's the bus stop?	**Var är busshåll-platsen?**	vaar ǣr **bewss**hol-plahtsern
When is the next bus to ...?	**När går nästa buss till ...?**	nǣr gawr **nehs**tah bewss til
How much is the fare to ...?	**Hur mycket kostar det till ...?**	hēwr **mew**ker(t) **kos**tahr dāȳ(t) til
Do I have to change buses?	**Måste jag byta buss?**	**mos**ter yaa(g) **bēw**tah bewss
How many stops are there to ...?	**Hur många håll-platser är det till ...?**	hēwr **mong**ah **hol**-plahtserr ǣr dāȳ(t) til
Will you tell me when to get off?	**Kan ni säga till när jag skall stiga av?**	kahn nee **seh**yah til nǣr yaa(g) skah(l) **stee**gah aav
I want to get off at ...	**Jag vill stiga av vid ...**	yaa(g) vil **stee**gah aav veed

```
BUSSHÅLLPLATS
BUS STOP
```

Underground (subway) *Tunnelbana*

Stockholm's underground system, the *Tunnelbana,* extends from the centre of the city to the suburbs. Maps of the entire system are displayed inside every station and aboard every train. Stations are marked with a blue "T". Services begin at 5 a.m. and continue until midnight; reduced service continues late into the night on certain lines. You can transfer from bus to underground on the same ticket, which is valid for one hour.

Where's the nearest underground station?	**Var ligger närmaste tunnelbanestation?**	vaar liggerr nærmahster tewnerlbaanerstahshōōn
Does this train go to Central Station?	**Går det här tåget till Centralen?**	gawr dāy(t) hær tawgert til sehntraalern
Where do I change for ...?	**Var byter jag till ...?**	vaar bēwterr yaa(g) til
Is the next station ...?	**Är nästa station ...?**	ær nehstah stahshōōn
Which line should I take to ...?	**Vilken linje skall jag ta till ...?**	vilkern linyer skah(l) yaa(g) taa til

Boat service *Båt*

Regular boat and ferry services, carrying trains and cars as well as passengers, link Sweden to the neighbouring countries. Ferries and steamers also join the Swedish mainland to many of the thousands of islands dotted round the coast. Steamer trips on Sweden's lakes and waterways offer beautiful sightseeing opportunities; one of the best is the Göta Canal tour which takes you from one side of the country to the other.

If you would like to rent a boat you should know the regulations applying to Swedish territorial waters, and where guest harbours are located. Get in touch with the Swedish Touring Club (STF). Or hire a canoe for more leisurely excursions on lakes and canals.

I'd like to take a boat trip.	**Jag skulle vilja göra en båttur.**	yaa(g) skewler vilyah yūrrah ehn bawttēwr

When does the boat for ... leave?	**När går båten till ...?**	nair gawr **baw**tern til
Where's the embarkation point?	**Var lägger båten till?**	vaar **lehg**err **baw**tern til
How long does the crossing take?	**Hur lång tid tar överfarten?**	hewr lawng teed taar ūrverrfaa'tern
boat	en båt	ehn bawt
cabin	en hytt	ehn hewt
single/double	enkel/dubbel	ehnkerl/dewberl
canoe	en kanot	ehn kahnōōt
cruise	en kryssning	ehn krewsning
deck	ett däck	eht dehk
ferry	en färja	ehn færyah
gangway	en landgång	ehn lahn(d)gong
hydrofoil	en svävare	ehn svaivahrer
jetty	en brygga	ehn brewgah
life belt	ett livbälte	eht leevbehlter
life boat	en livbåt	ehn leevbawt
pier	en pir	ehn peer
rowing boat	en roddbåt	ehn roodbawt
sailing boat	en segelbåt	ehn sāygerlbawt
ship	ett fartyg	eht faa'tēwg
steamer	en ångbåt	ehn ongbawt

Bicycle hire *Cykeluthyrning*

It is very easy to hire bicycles in Sweden and the local tourist office can give you all the information you will need.

| I'd like to hire a bicycle. | **Jag skulle vilja hyra en cykel.** | yaa(g) **skew**ler vilyah hēwrah ehn sewkerl |

Other means of transport *Andra transportmedel*

cable car	en linbana	ehn leenbaanah
helicopter	en helikopter	ehn hehlikopterr
moped	en moped	ehn moopāyd
motorbike	en motorcykel	ehn mōōto'sewkerl
scooter	en skoter	ehn skōōterr

Or perhaps you prefer:

| to hitchhike | att lifta | aht liftah |
| to walk | att gå | aht gaw |

Car *Bil*

Cars drive on the right in Sweden. All vehicles (including motorcycles) must have dipped headlights switched on at all times, even in broad daylight. A red reflector warning triangle must be carried for use in case of a breakdown, and seat belts *(bilbälte)* are obligatory. Crash helmets are compulsory for both drivers and passengers on motorcycles and scooters.

Where's the nearest filling station?	**Var ligger närmaste bensinstation?**	vaar liggerr **nær**mahster behnseenstahshōōn
Fill it up, please.	**Full tank, tack.**	fewl tahnk tahk
Give me ... litres of petrol (gasoline).	**Kan jag få ... liter bensin?**	kahn yaa(g) faw ... leeterr behnseen
super (premium)	**högoktanig**	**hū̄g**oktaanig
regular	**lågoktanig**	**law**goktaanig
unleaded	**blyfri**	**blē̄w**free
diesel	**diesel**	**dees**serl
Please check the ...	**Var snäll och kontrollera ...**	vaar snehl ok kontrol**lā̄y**rah
battery	**batteriet**	bahter**ri**ert
brake fluid	**bromsvätskan**	**broms**vehtskahn
oil	**oljan**	**ol**yahn
water	**vattnet**	**vaht**nert
Would you check the tyre pressure?	**Skulle ni kunna kontrollera trycket i däcken?**	**skew**ler nee **kew**nah kontrol**lā̄y**rah **trew**kert ee **dehk**ern
1.6 front, 1.8 rear.	**1,6 fram, 1,8 bak.**	1 **kom**mah 6 frahm 1 **kom**mah 8 baak
Could you check the spare tyre, too?	**Kan ni kontrollera reservdäcket också?**	kahn nee kontrol**lā̄y**rah reh**sær**vdehkert **ok**so
Can you mend this puncture (fix this flat)?	**Kan ni laga den här punkteringen?**	kahn nee **laa**gah dehn hǣr pewngt**ā̄y**ringern
Would you change the ..., please?	**Skulle ni kunna byta ... tack?**	**skew**ler nee **kew**nah **bē̄w**tah ... tahk
bulb	**glödlampan**	**glū̄d**lahmpahn
fan belt	**fläktremmen**	**flehkt**rehmern
spark(ing) plugs	**tändstiften**	**tehn(d)**stiftern
tyre	**däcket**	**dehk**ert
wipers	**vindrutetorkarna**	vind**rē̄w**tertorkah^rnah

CAR HIRE, see page 20

| Would you clean the windscreen (windshield)? | **Skulle ni kunna torka av vindrutan?** | skewler nee kewnah torkah aav vindrew̄tahn |

TANKA SJÄLV   SELF SERVICE

Asking the way — Street directions   *Fråga om vägen – Visa vägen*

In which direction is ...?	**I vilken riktning ligger ...?**	ee vilkern riktning liggerr
Can you tell me the way to ...?	**Kan ni tala om hur man kommer till ...?**	kahn nee taalah om hew̄r mahn kommerr til
Can you tell me where ... is?	**Kan ni säga mig var ... ligger?**	kahn nee sehyah may vaar ... liggerr
How do I get to ...?	**Hur kommer jag till ...?**	hew̄r kommerr yaa(g) til
Am I on the right road for ...?	**Är det här vägen till ...?**	ær dāy(t) hær vaigern til
How far is the next village?	**Hur långt är det till nästa samhälle?**	hew̄r longt ær dāy(t) til nehstah sahmhehler
How far is it to ... from here?	**Hur långt är det till ... härifrån?**	hew̄r longt ær dāy(t) til ... hærifrawn
Is there a motorway (expressway)?	**Är det motorväg?**	ær dāy(t) mōōtorvaig
Is there a road with little traffic?	**Finns det någon väg med lite trafik?**	finss dāy(t) nawgon vaig māyd leeter trahfeek
Can I drive to the centre of town?	**Kan jag köra in i centrum?**	kahn yaa(g) khūrrah in ee sehntrewm
How long does it take by car/on foot?	**Hur lång tid tar det med bil/till fots?**	hew̄r long teed taar dāy(t) māyd beel/til fōōtss
How can I find this place/address?	**Hur kommer jag till den här platsen/adressen?**	hew̄r kommerr yaa(g) til dehn hær plahtsern/ahdrehssern
Where's this?	**Var ligger det?**	vaar liggerr dāy(t)
Can you show me on the map where I am?	**Kan ni visa mig på kartan var jag är?**	kahn nee veessah may paw kaaʳtahn vaar yaa(g) ær

Ni har kört fel.	You're on the wrong road.
Kör rakt fram.	Go straight ahead.
Det är där nere till vänster/höger.	It's down there on the left/right.
mitt emot/bakom ... bredvid/efter ...	opposite/behind ... next to/after ...
norr/söder/öster/väster	north/south/east/west
Kör till första/andra korsningen.	Go to the first/second crossroads (intersection).
Sväng till vänster vid trafikljusen.	Turn left at the traffic lights.
Sväng till höger vid nästa gathörn.	Turn right at the next corner.
Ta ... vägen.	Take the ... road.
Det är en enkelriktad gata.	It's a one-way street.
Ni måste köra tillbaka till ...	You have to go back to ...
Följ skyltarna mot Malmö.	Follow signs for Malmö.

Parking *Parkering*

In town centres, most street parking is metered. The police are normally lenient with tourists, but don't push your luck. Parking fines are high in Sweden.

Where can I park?	**Var kan jag parkera?**	vaar kahn yaa(g) pahrkāyrah
Is there a car park nearby?	**Finns det en parkering i närheten?**	finss dāy(t) ehn pahrkāyring ee nǟrhāytern
May I park here?	**Får jag parkera här?**	fawr yaa(g) pahrkāyrah hǟr
How long can I park here?	**Hur länge får jag stå här?**	hēwr lehnger fawr yaa(g) staw hǟr
What's the charge per hour?	**Vad är avgiften per timme?**	vaad ǟr aavyiftern pǟr timmerr
Do you have some change for the parking meter?	**Ni har inte lite växel till parkeringsautomaten?**	nee haar inter leeter vehkserl til pahrkāyringsahtommaatern

Breakdown—Road assistance *Motorstopp – Hjälp på vägen*

Where's the nearest garage?	**Var ligger närmaste verkstad?**	vaar liggerr nærmahster værkstaa(d)
My car has broken down.	**Min bil har gått sönder.**	min beel haar got surnderr
I've had a break-down at ...	**Jag har fått motorstopp vid ...**	yaa(g) haar fot mōōtoʳstop veed
Can you send a mechanic?	**Kan ni skicka en mekaniker?**	kahn nee shikkah ehn mehkaanikkerr
My car won't start.	**Bilen startar inte.**	beelern stahʳtahr inter
The battery is dead.	**Batteriet är slut.**	bahterriert ær slewt
I've run out of petrol (gasoline).	**Bensinen är slut.**	behnseenern ær slewt
I have a flat tyre.	**Jag har fått punktering.**	yaa(g) haar fot pewngtāyring
The engine is over-heating.	**Motorn har gått varm.**	mōōtoʳn haar got vahrm
There is something wrong with the ...	**Det är något fel på ...**	dāy(t) ær nawgot fāyl paw
brakes	**bromsarna**	bromsahʳnah
carburettor	**förgasaren**	furrgaassahrern
exhaust pipe	**avgasröret**	aavgaasrūrert
radiator	**kylaren**	kēwlahrern
wheel	**hjulet**	yēwlert
Can you send a breakdown van (tow truck)?	**Kan ni skicka en bärgningsbil?**	kahn nee shikkah ehn bæryningsbeel
How long will you be?	**När kan ni komma?**	nær kahn nee kommah

Accident—Police *Olycka – Polis*

Please call the police.	**Var snäll och ring polisen.**	vaar snehl ok ring pooleessern
There's been an accident.	**Det har hänt en olycka.**	dāy(t) haar hehnt ehn ōōlewkah
It's about 2 km. from ...	**Det är cirka 2 kilometer från ...**	dāy(t) ær sirkah 2 khillommāyterr frawn
Where's there a telephone?	**Var finns det en telefon?**	vaar finns dāy(t) ehn tehlehfawn

Call a doctor/an ambulance quickly.	**Ring fort efter en läkare/ambulans.**	ring foo^{r}t **ehf**terr ehn **lai**kahrer/ahmbew**lahn**ss
There are people injured.	**Några är skadade.**	**naw**grah ǟr **skaa**dahder
Here's my driving licence.	**Här är mitt körkort.**	hǟr ǟr mit **khürr**koo^{r}t
What's your name and address?	**Kan jag få namn och adress?**	kahn yaa(g) faw nahmn ok ah**dre**hss
What's your insurance company?	**Vilket är ert försäkringsbolag?**	**vil**kert ǟr āy^{r}t fur^r**saik**ringsboolaag

Road signs *Vägmärken*

BEGRÄNSAD FRAMKOMLIGHET	Road narrows
CYKELBANA	Cycle path
EJ MOTORFORDON	No motor vehicles
ENSKILD VÄG	Private road
FARLIG KURVA	Dangerous bend (curve)
HUVUDLED	Main road
INFART	Entrance
JÄRNVÄGSKORSNING	Level (railroad) crossing
KÖR SAKTA	Slow down
KORSANDE ARBETSFORDON	Works vehicles merging
KORSANDE TIMMERVÄG	Lumber-track merging
LIVSFARLIG LEDNING	High-tension cable
LÄMNA FÖRETRÄDE	Give way (yield)
MOTORVÄG	Motorway (expressway)
MÖTESPLATS	Passing place
OMKÖRNING FÖRBJUDEN	No overtaking (no passing)
PARKERING	Parking
PRIVAT VÄG	Private road
RASTPLATS	Roadside picnic site
RIDVÄG	Bridle path
SKOLA	School
STENSKOTT	Loose gravel
STOP	Stop
TJÄLSKOTT	Potholes
TRAFIKOMLÄGGNING	Diversion (detour)
TRAFIKPLATS	Roundabout
TULL	Customs
UTFART	Exit
VÄGARBETE	Roadworks (men working)
VÄNDZON	Turning place
ÅTERVÄNDSVÄG/GATA	No through road

Sightseeing

Where's the tourist office?	Var ligger turistbyrån?	vaar liggerr tewristbewrawn
What are the main points of interest?	Vad finns det för sevärdheter?	vaad finss day(t) fürr sayvä‍ʳdhäyterr
We're here for ...	Vi är här ...	vee ä‍r hä‍r
only a few hours	bara några timmar	baarah nawgrah timmahr
a day	en dag	ehn daa(g)
a week	en vecka	ehn vehkah
Can you recommend a/an ...?	Kan ni föreslå någon ...?	kahn nee fürrerslaw nawgon
sightseeing tour	sightseeingtur	"sightseeing"tewr
excursion	rundtur	rewn(d)tewr
Where do we leave from?	Varifrån startar vi?	vaarifrawn stah‍ʳtahr vee
Will the bus pick us up at the hotel?	Kommer bussen och hämtar oss vid hotellet?	kommerr bewssern ok hehmtahr oss veed hotehlert
How much does the tour cost?	Hur mycket kostar turen?	hewr mewker(t) kostahr tewrern
What time does the tour start?	Hur dags startar turen?	hewr dahgss stah‍ʳtahr tewrern
Is lunch included?	Ingår lunch?	ingawr lewnsh
What time do we get back?	Hur dags är vi tillbaka?	hewr dahgss ä‍r vee tilbaakah
Do we have free time in ...?	Har vi någon ledig tid i ...?	haar vee nawgon laydig teed ee
Is there an English-speaking guide?	Finns det någon engelsktalande guide?	finss day(t) nawgon ehngerlsktaalahnder "guide"
I'd like to hire a private guide for ...	Jag skulle vilja ha en privat guide ...	yaa(g) skewler vilyah haa ehn privaat "guide"
half a day	en halv dag	ehn hahlv daa(g)
a day	en dag	ehn daa(g)

Where is/Where are the ...?	**Var ligger ...?**	vaar liggerr
artists' quarter	**konstnärskvar-teren**	konstnæ^rs-kvah^rtāyrern
art museum	**konstmuseet**	konstmewssāyert
botanical gardens	**botaniska trädgården**	bootaaniskah trai(d)gaw^rdern
bridge	**bron**	brōōn
building	**byggnaden**	bewgnahdern
business district	**affärskvarteren**	ahfæ^rskvah^rtāyrern
castle	**slottet**	slottert
cathedral	**domkyrkan**	doomkhewrkahn
cave	**grottan**	grottahn
cemetery	**kyrkogården**	khewrkoogaw^rdern
chapel	**kapellet**	kahpehlert
church	**kyrkan**	khewrkahn
citadel	**fästningen**	fehstningern
city centre	**(stads)centrum**	(stahds)sehntrewm
city hall	**stadshuset**	stahdshewssert
concert hall	**konserthuset**	konsærhewssert
court house	**tingshuset**	tingshewssert
downtown area	**(stads)centrum**	(stahds)sehntrewm
exhibition	**utställningen**	ewtstehlningern
factory	**fabriken**	fahbreekern
fair	**mässan**	mehssahn
flea market	**loppmarknaden**	lopmahrknahdern
fortress	**borgen**	boryern
fountain	**fontänen**	fontainern
gardens	**trädgårdarna**	trai(d)gaw^rdah^rnah
harbour	**hamnen**	hahmnern
lake	**sjön**	shurn
library	**biblioteket**	bibliotāykert
memorial	**minnesmärket**	minnehsmærkert
monastery	**klostret**	klostrert
monument	**monumentet**	monewmehntert
museum	**museet**	mewssāyert
observatory	**observatoriet**	obsehrvahtōōriert
old town	**gamla stan**	gahmlah staan
opera house	**operan**	ōōperrahn
palace	**slottet**	slottert
park	**parken**	pahrkern
parliament building	**riksdagshuset**	riksdah(g)shewssert
planetarium	**planetariet**	plahnertaariert
royal palace	**Kungliga slottet**	kewngliggah slottert
ruins	**ruinerna**	reweener^rnah
shopping area	**affärscentrum**	ahfæ^rssehntrewm

square	**torget**	tor^ryert
stadium	**stadion**	staadion
statue	**statyn**	staht<u>ēw</u>n
stock exchange	**börsen**	bur^rsern
television studios	**TV-huset**	t<u>ā</u>yveh-h<u>ēw</u>ssert
theatre	**teatern**	t<u>ā</u>yaater^rn
tomb	**graven**	graavern
tower	**tornet**	t<u>ōō</u>^rnert
town hall	**rådhuset**	rawdh<u>ēw</u>ssert
university	**universitetet**	ewniv<u>æ</u>^rsitt<u>āy</u>tert
zoo	**djurparken**	y<u>ēw</u>rpahrkern

Admission *Inträde*

Is ... open on Sundays?	**Är ... öppet på söndagar?**	<u>æ</u>r ... urpert paw surndaagahr
When is it open?	**När är det öppet?**	n<u>æ</u>r <u>æ</u>r d<u>āy</u>(t) urpert
When does it close?	**När stänger det?**	n<u>æ</u>r stehngerr d<u>āy</u>(t)
What's the entrance fee?	**Vad kostar det i inträde?**	vaad kostahr d<u>āy</u>(t) ee intraider
Is there any reduction for (the) ...?	**Är det någon rabatt för ...?**	<u>æ</u>r d<u>āy</u>(t) nawgon rahbaht f<u>ū</u>rr
children	**barn**	baa^rn
disabled	**handikappade**	hahndikahpahder
groups	**grupper**	grewperr
pensioners	**pensionärer**	pahnshoon<u>æ</u>rerr
students	**studerande**	stewd<u>āy</u>rahnder
Do you have a guide-book (in English)?	**Har ni någon guide-bok (på engelska)?**	haar nee nawgon "guide"-b<u>ōō</u>k (paw ehngerlskah)
Can I buy a catalogue?	**Kan jag få köpa en katalog?**	kahn yaa(g) faw kh<u>ū</u>rpah ehn kahtahlawg
Is it all right to take pictures?	**Är det tillåtet att fotografera?**	<u>æ</u>r d<u>āy</u>(t) tillawtert aht footograhf<u>āy</u>rah

FRITT INTRÄDE	ADMISSION FREE
FOTOGRAFERING FÖRBJUDEN	NO CAMERAS ALLOWED

Who—What—When? *Vem – Vad – När?*

What's that building?	**Vad är det där för byggnad?**	vaad ӕr day(t) dӕr fürr bewgnahd
Who was the ...?	**Vem var ...?**	vehm vaar
architect	**arkitekten**	ahrkitehktern
artist	**konstnären**	konstnӕrern
painter	**konstnären**	konstnӕrern
sculptor	**skulptören**	skewlptürrern
Who built it?	**Vem har byggt den?**	vehm haar bewgt dehn
Who painted that picture?	**Vem har målat den där tavlan?**	vehm haar mawlaht dehn dӕr taavlahn
When did he live?	**När levde han?**	nӕr layvder hahn
When was it built?	**När byggdes det?**	nӕr bewgderss day(t)
Where's the house where ... lived?	**Var ligger huset där ... bodde?**	vaar liggerr hewssert dӕr ... booderr
We're interested in ...	**Vi är intresserade av ...**	vee ӕr intrehssayrahder aav
antiques	**antikviteter**	ahntikvitayterr
archaeology	**arkeologi**	ahrkehologgee
art	**konst**	konst
botany	**botanik**	bootahneek
ceramics	**keramik**	khehrahmeek
coins	**mynt**	mewnt
folk art	**allmogekonst**	ahlmoogerkonst
furniture	**möbler**	mürblerr
geology	**geologi**	yayologgee
handicrafts	**konsthantverk**	konsthahntværk
history	**historia**	histooriah
medicine	**medicin**	mehdisseen
modern art	**modern konst**	moodӕrn konst
music	**musik**	mewsseek
natural history	**naturhistoria**	nahtewrhistooriah
ornithology	**ornitologi**	or'nitologgee
painting	**måleri**	mawlerree
pottery	**lergods**	layrgoodss
religion	**religion**	rehliyoon
sculpture	**skulptur**	skewlptewr
wildlife	**djurliv**	yewrleev
zoology	**zoologi**	sologgee
Where's the ... department?	**Var ligger avdelningen för ...?**	vaar liggerr aavdaylningern fürr

It's ...	Det är ...	day(t) ār
amazing	fantastiskt	fahntahstiskt
awful	förskräckligt	fur^rskrehkli(g)t
beautiful	vackert	vahker^rt
gloomy	dystert	dewster^rt
impressive	imponerande	imponnäyrahnder
interesting	intressant	intrehssahnt
magnificent	storslaget	stoo^rslaagert
pretty	sött	surt
romantic	romantiskt	roomahntiskt
strange	konstigt	konsti(g)t
superb	utomordentligt	ewtomo^rdehntli(g)t
terrible	hemskt	hehmskt
tremendous	förfärligt	furrfärli(g)t
ugly	fult	fewlt

Churches — Religious services   *Kyrkor – Gudstjänster*

The Swedish state church is Lutheran. But freedom of religion is assured and other denominations have their own churches.

Most churches and cathedrals are open to the public to view except, of course, when a service is being conducted.

Is there a ... near here?	Finns det någon ... här i närheten?	finss day(t) nawgon ... hār ee nārhäytern
Catholic church	katolsk kyrka	kahtoolsk khewrkah
Protestant church	protestantisk kyrka	prooterstahntisk khewrkah
mosque	moské	moskäy
synagogue	synagoga	sewnahgoogah
At what time is ...?	Hur dags börjar ...?	hewr dahgss burryahr
mass	mässan	mehssahn
the service	gudstjänsten	gewdskhainstern
Where can I find a ... who speaks English?	Var kan jag få tag på en ... som talar engelska?	vaar kahn yaa(g) faw taag paw ehn ... som taalahr ehngerlskah
priest	katolsk präst	kahtoolsk prehst
minister	protestantisk präst	prootehstahntisk prehst
rabbi	rabbin	rahbeen
I'd like to visit the church.	Jag skulle vilja titta på kyrkan.	yaa(g) skewler vilyah tittah paw khewrkahn

In the countryside *På landet*

Is there a scenic route to ...?	**Finns det någon vacker väg till ...?**	finss dāy(t) nawgon vahkerr vaig til
How far is it to ...?	**Hur långt är det till ...?**	hēwr longt ǣr dāy(t) til
Can we walk there?	**Kan man gå dit?**	kahn mahn gaw deet
How high is that mountain?	**Hur högt är det där berget?**	hēwr hurgt ǣr dāy(t) dǣr bǣryert
What kind of ... is that?	**Vad är det där för ...?**	vaad ǣr dāy(t) dǣr fūrr
animal	**ett djur**	eht yēwr
bird	**en fågel**	ehn fawgerl
flower	**en blomma**	ehn bloomah
tree	**ett träd**	eht traid

Landmarks *Landmärken*

bridge	**en bro**	ehn brōō
cliff	**en klippa**	ehn klippah
farm	**en bondgård**	ehn boon(d)gawᵣd
field	**ett fält**	eht fehlt
footpath	**en stig**	ehn steeg
forest	**en skog**	ehn skōōg
garden	**en trädgård**	ehn trail(d)gawᵣd
hill	**en kulle**	ehn kewler
house	**ett hus**	eht hēwss
lake	**en sjö**	ehn shūr
meadow	**en äng**	ehn ehng
mountain	**ett berg**	eht bǣry
path	**en stig**	ehn steeg
peak	**en topp**	ehn top
pond	**en damm**	ehn dahm
river	**en flod**	ehn flōōd
road	**en väg**	ehn vaig
sea	**ett hav**	eht haav
spring	**en källa**	ehn khehlah
stream	**en å**	ehn aw
valley	**en dal**	ehn daal
village	**en by**	ehn bēw
wall	**en mur**	ehn mēwr
waterfall	**ett vattenfall**	eht vahternfahl
well	**en brunn**	ehn brewn
wood	**en skog**	ehn skōōg

ASKING THE WAY, see page 76

Relaxing

Cinema (movies)—Theatre *Bio – Teater*

To find out what's playing, consult the newspapers and bill-boards, or the weekly (monthly) tourist publication in Stockholm and other towns.

All films are shown in the original language with Swedish subtitles. Advance booking is essential for theatres and the opera.

What's on at the cinema tonight?	**Vad går det för filmer i kväll?**	vaad gawr dāȳ(t) fūrr filmerr ee kvehl
What's playing at the ... Theatre?	**Vad går det på ... teatern?**	vaad gawr dāȳ(t) paw ... tāȳaaterᶠn
What sort of play is it?	**Vad är det för slags pjäs?**	vaad ǣr dāȳ(t) fūrr slahgss pyaiss
Who's it by?	**Vem har skrivit den?**	vehm haar **skree**vit dehn
Can you recommend a ...?	**Kan ni rekommendera någon ...?**	kahn nee rehkommern-**dāȳ**rah **naw**gon
good film	**bra film**	braa film
comedy	**komedi**	kommer**dee**
musical	**musikal**	mewss**sikaal**
revue	**revy**	reh**vēw**
Where's that new film directed by ... being shown?	**Var går den nya filmen av ...?**	vaar gawr dehn **nēw**ah **film**ern aav
Who's in it?	**Vem spelar i den?**	vehm **spāȳ**lahr ee dehn
Who's playing the lead?	**Vem spelar huvudrollen?**	vehm **spāȳ**lahr **hēw**vew(d)-rollern
Who's the director?	**Vem har regisserat den?**	vehm haar rehhiss**sāȳ**raht dehn
At which theatre is that new play by ... being performed?	**På vilken teater går den nya pjäsen av ...?**	paw **vil**kern tāȳaaterr gawr dehn **nēw**ah **pyaiss**ern aav

What time does it begin?	**Hur dags börjar det?**	hewr dahgss **burry**ahr d$\overline{ay}$(t)
What time does it finish?	**Hur dags slutar det?**	hewr dahgss **slew**tahr d$\overline{ay}$(t)
Are there any tickets for tonight?	**Finns det några biljetter till i kväll?**	finss d$\overline{ay}$(t) **naw**grah bilyehterr til ee kvehl
How much are the tickets?	**Hur mycket kostar biljetterna?**	hewr **mew**ker(t) **kost**ahr bilyehter^{r}nah
I'd like to reserve 2 tickets for the show on Friday evening.	**Jag skulle vilja beställa 2 biljetter till föreställningen på fredag kväll.**	yaa(g) **skew**ler **vil**yah ber**steh**lah 2 bilyehterr til fürrerstehlningern paw fr$\overline{ay}$daa(g) kvehl
Can I have a ticket for the matinée on Tuesday?	**Kan jag få en biljett till matinén på tisdag?**	kahn yaa(g) faw ehn bilyeht til mahtin$\overline{ay}$n paw **tees**daa(g)
I'd like a seat in the stalls (orchestra).	**Jag skulle vilja ha en plats på parkett.**	yaa(g) **skew**ler **vil**yah haa ehn plahtss paw pahr**keht**
Not too far back.	**Inte för långt bak.**	inter fürr longt baak
Somewhere in the middle.	**Någonstans i mitten.**	**naw**gonstahnss ee **mit**tern
How much are the tickets for the circle (mezzanine)?	**Hur mycket kostar biljetterna på första raden?**	hewr **mew**ker(t) **kost**ahr bilyehter^{r}nah paw fur^{r}stah **raad**ern
May I have a programme, please?	**Kan jag få ett program, tack?**	kahn yaa(g) faw eht proo**grahm** tahk
Where's the cloakroom?	**Var är garderoben?**	vaar $\overline{æ}$r gah^{r}der**raw**bern

---

Tyvärr är det utsålt.	I'm sorry, we're sold out.
Det finns bara några få platser kvar på första raden.	There are only a few seats left in the circle (mezzanine).
Kan jag få se biljetten?	May I see your ticket?
Det här är er plats.	This is your seat.

DAYS OF THE WEEK, see page 150

Opera—Ballet—Concert   *Opera – Balett – Konsert*

Can you recommend a/an ...?	**Kan ni rekommendera någon ...?**	kahn nee rehkommern-dayrah nawgon
ballet	**balett**	bahleht
concert	**konsert**	konsær
opera	**opera**	ōōperrah
operetta	**operett**	ooperreht

| Where's the opera house/the concert hall? | **Var ligger Operan/Konserthuset?** | vaar liggerr ōōperrahn/konsærhēwssert |

| What's on at the opera tonight? | **Vad ger man på Operan i kväll?** | vaad yayr mahn paw ōōperrahn ee kvehl |

| Who's singing/dancing? | **Vem sjunger/dansar?** | vehm shewngerr/dahnsahr |

| Which orchestra is playing? | **Vilken orkester är det som spelar?** | vilkern orkehsterr ær day(t) som spaylahr |

| What are they playing? | **Vad spelar man?** | vaad spaylahr mahn |

| Who's the conductor/soloist? | **Vem är dirigent/solist?** | vehm ær dirrishehnt soolist |

Nightclubs   *Nattklubbar*

| Can you recommend a good nightclub? | **Kan ni rekommendera någon trevlig nattklubb?** | kahn nee rehkommern-dayrah nawgon trayvli(g) nahtklewb |

| Is there a floor show? | **Är det någon show?** | ær day(t) nawgon "show" |

| What time does the show start? | **Hur dags börjar showen?** | hēwr dahgss burryahr "show"ern |

| Do I have to wear a tie? | **Är det slipstvång?** | ær day(t) slipstvong |

Discos   *Diskotek*

| Where can we go dancing? | **Var kan man gå och dansa?** | vaar kahn mahn gaw ok dahnsah |

| Is there a discotheque in town? | **Finns det något diskotek i stan?** | finss day(t) nawgot diskotayk ee staan |

| Would you like to dance? | **Skall vi dansa?** | skah(l) vee dahnsah |

Sports *Sport*

In summer the most popular sports are golf, tennis, sailing and swimming, not to mention jogging, cycling, riding and hiking. In winter the Swedes are active skiers and skaters. Popular spectator sports are football, ice hockey and tennis.

Is there a football (soccer) match (anywhere) this Saturday?	**Är det någon fotbollsmatch (någonstans) nu på lördag?**	ǣr dāȳ(t) nawgon fōōtbolsmahtsh (nawgonstahnss) nēw paw lūr^rdaa(g)
Which teams are playing?	**Vilka lag spelar?**	vilkah laag spāȳlahr
Can you get me a ticket?	**Kan ni skaffa mig en biljett?**	kahn nee skahfah may ehn bilyeht
I'd like to see a tennis match.	**Jag skulle vilja se en tennismatch.**	yaa(g) skewler vilyah sāȳ ehn tehnismahtsh
What's the admission charge?	**Vad kostar det i inträde?**	vaad kostahr dāȳ(t) ee intraider

canoeing	**kanot**	kahnōōt
car racing	**biltävling**	beeltaivling
cycling	**cykel**	sewkerl
football (soccer)	**fotboll**	fōōtbol
horse racing	**hästkapplöpning**	hehstkahplūrpning
(horse-back) riding	**ridning**	reedning
hunting	**jakt**	yahkt
sailing	**segling**	sāȳgling
skiing	**skidåkning**	sheedawkning
swimming	**simning**	simning
table tennis	**bordtennis**	bōō^rdtehniss
team handball	**handboll**	hahndbol
tennis	**tennis**	tehniss

Where's the nearest golf course?	**Var ligger närmaste golfbana?**	vaar liggerr nærmahster golfbaanah
Where are the tennis courts?	**Var ligger tennisbanorna?**	vaar liggerr tehnisbaanoo^rnah
What's the charge per ...?	**Vad kostar det per ...?**	vaad kostahr dāȳ(t) pær
day/round/hour	**dag/runda/timme**	daa(g)/rewndah/timmer

Can I hire (rent) rackets?	**Kan man hyra racketar?**	kahn mahn **hew**rah **rah**kertahr
Where's the race course (track)?	**Var ligger häst-kapplöpningsbanan?**	vaar **lig**gerr **hehst**-kahpl**ur**pningsbaanahn
Is there any good fishing around here?	**Finns det något bra fiskevatten i närheten?**	finss **day**(t) **naw**got braa **fis**kervahtern ee **nær**haytern
Do I need a permit?	**Behöver jag fiskekort?**	ber**hur**verr yaa(g) **fis**kerkoo**r**t
Where can I get one?	**Var kan jag få tag på ett?**	vaar kahn yaa(g) faw taag paw eht
Can one swim in the lake/river/sea?	**Kan man bada i sjön/floden/havet?**	kahn mahn **baa**dah ee shurn/**floo**dern/**haa**vert
Is there a swimming pool here?	**Finns det någon swimmingpool här?**	finss **day**(t) **naw**gon "swimmingpool" hær
Is it open-air or indoor?	**Är den utomhus eller inomhus?**	ær dehn **ew**tomhewss **ehl**lerr **in**nomhewss
Is it heated?	**Är den uppvärmd?**	ær dehn **ewp**værmd
Is there a sandy beach?	**Finns det någon sandstrand?**	finss **day**(t) **naw**gon **sahnd**strahnd

On the beach *På stranden*

Is it safe to swim/ dive here?	**Är det riskfritt att bada/dyka här?**	ær **day**(t) **risk**frit aht **baa**dah/**dew**ka hær
Is there a lifeguard?	**Finns det någon badvakt?**	finss **day**(t) **naw**gon **baad**vahkt
Is it safe for children?	**Är det riskfritt för barn?**	ær **day**(t) **risk**frit fürr baa**r**n
Could I have swimming lessons?	**Kan man ta simlektioner?**	kahn mahn taa **sim**lehkshoonerr
What's the tempera-ture of the water?	**Hur många grader är det i vattnet?**	hewr **mong**ah **graa**derr ær **day**(t) ee **vaht**nert
Are there any dangerous currents?	**Finns det några farliga strömmar?**	finss **day**(t) **naw**grah faa**r**liggah **strur**mahr
How deep is it?	**Hur djupt är det?**	hewr **yewp**t ær **day**(t)
Is it shallow?	**Är det långgrunt?**	ær **day**(t) **long**grewnt

I want to hire a/an/ some ...	**Jag skulle vilja hyra ...**	yaa(g) skewler vilyah hewrah
bathing hut (cabana)	**en badhytt**	ehn baadhewt
deck chair	**en solstol**	ehn sōōlstōōl
motorboat	**en motorbåt**	ehn mōōtorbawt
rowing boat	**en roddbåt**	ehn roodbawt
sailing boat	**en segelbåt**	ehn saygerlbawt
skin-diving equipment	**en dykar- utrustning**	ehn dewkahr- ewtrewstning
sunshade (umbrella)	**ett parasoll**	eht pahrahsol
water-skis	**vattenskidor**	vahternsheedoor
windsurfer	**en windsurfingbräda**	ehn windsewrfingbraidah

| **BADNING FÖRBJUDEN** | NO SWIMMING |
| **ANKRING FÖRBJUDEN** | NO ANCHORAGE |

Winter sports *Vintersport*

I'd like to see an ice hockey match.	**Jag skulle vilja se en ishockeymatch.**	yaa(g) skewler vilyah say ehn eeshokkimahtsh
Is there a skating rink near here?	**Finns det en skrid- skobana i närheten?**	finss day(t) ehn skri(d)skoo- baanah ee nærhaytern
I'd like to ski.	**Jag skulle vilja åka skidor.**	yaa(g) skewler vilyah awkah sheedoor
downhill	**utförsåkning**	ewtfür'sawkning
cross-country skiing	**längdåkning**	lehngdawkning
Are there any ski runs for ...?	**Finns det några (skid)backar för ...?**	finss day(t) nawgrah (sheed)bahkahr fürr
beginners	**nybörjare**	newbürryahrer
average skiers	**medelgoda åkare**	mayderlgōōdah awkahrer
good skiers	**bra åkare**	braa awkahrer
Which way are the ski lifts?	**Åt vilket håll ligger skidliftarna?**	awt vilkert hol liggerr sheedliftah'nah
I'd like to hire ...	**Jag skulle vilja hyra ...**	yaa(g) skewler vilyah hewrah
poles	**stavar**	staavahr
skates	**ett par skridskor**	eht paar skri(d)skoor
ski boots	**pjäxor**	pyehksoor
skiing equipment	**skidutrustning**	sheedewtrewstning
skis	**skidor**	sheedoor

Making friends

Introductions *Presentation*

May I introduce ...?	**Får jag presentera ...?**	fawr yaa(g) prehssernt**ay**rah
John, this is ...	**John, det här är ...**	John d**ay**(t) h**ae**r **ae**r
My name is ...	**Mitt namn är ...**	mit nahmn **ae**r
Pleased to meet you!	**Trevligt att träffas!**	tr**ay**vli(g)t aht **treh**fahss
What's your name?	**Vad heter ni/du?***	vaad h**ay**terr nee/d**ew**
How are you?	**Hur står det till?**	h**ew**r stawr d**ay**(t) til
Fine, thanks. And you?	**Bra, tack. Och du?**	braa tahk. ok d**ew**

Follow up *Lära känna varandra*

How long have you been here?	**Hur länge har du varit här?**	h**ew**r **lehng**er haar d**ew** vaarit h**ae**r
I've been here a week.	**Jag har varit här en vecka.**	yaa(g) haar **vaa**rit h**ae**r ehn **veh**kah
Is this your first visit to Stockholm?	**Är det ditt första besök i Stockholm?**	**ae**r d**ay**(t) dit fur**r**stah bers**ew**k ee stokholm
How do you like Sweden?	**Vad tycker du om Sverige?**	vaad **tew**kerr d**ew** om sv**ae**ryer
What do you think of the country/people?	**Vad tycker du om landet/människorna?**	vaad **tew**kerr d**ew** om **lahn**dert/mehnishoo**r**nah
I love the landscape.	**Jag älskar naturen.**	yaa(g) **ehl**skahr naht**ew**rern
Where do you come from?	**Varifrån kommer du?**	**vaa**rifrawn **kom**mer d**ew**
I'm from ...	**Jag är från ...**	yaa(g) **ae**r frawn
What nationality are you?	**Vad har du för nationalitet?**	vaad haar d**ew** f**ur**r nahtshoonahlit**ay**(t)

---

* In this section we use *du*, the informal form for "you". If you want to use the polite form *ni*, the rest of the sentence does not change.

COUNTRIES, see page 146

I'm ...	Jag är ...	yaa(g) ær
American	amerikan	ahm(er)rikaan
British	britt	brit
Canadian	kanadensare	kahnahdehnsahrer
English	engelsman	ehngerlsmahn
Irish	irländare	irlehndahrer

Where are you staying?	Var bor du här?	vaar bōōr dew hær
Are you on your own?	Är du här ensam?	ær dew hær ehnsahm
I'm with my ...	Jag är här med ...	yaa(g) ær hær māyd

wife	min fru	min frew
husband	min man	min mahn
family	min familj	min fahmily
children	mina barn	minah baaᵣn
parents	mina föräldrar	minah furrehldrahr
boyfriend/girlfriend	min pojkvän/ flickvän	min poykvehn/ flikvehn

father/mother	far/mor	faar/mōōr
son/daughter	son/dotter	sawn/dotterr
brother/sister	bror/syster	brōōr/sewsterr
cousin	kusin	kewseen
uncle	farbror*/morbror**	fahrbroor/moorbroor
aunt	faster*/moster**	fahsterr/moosterr

* father's side ** mother's side

Are you married/ single?	Är du gift/ogift?	ær dew yeeft/ōōyeeft
Do you have children?	Har du barn?	haar dew baaᵣn
What do you do?	Vad har du för yrke?	vaad haar dew fürr ewrker
I'm a student.	Jag studerar.	yaa(g) stewdāyrahr
What are you studying?	Vad studerar du?	vaad stewdāyrahr dew
I'm here on a business trip.	Jag är här på affärsresa.	yaa(g) ær hær paw ahfæᵣsrāyssah
Do you travel a lot?	Reser du mycket?	rāysserr dew mewker(t)
Do you play cards/ chess?	Spelar du kort/ schack?	spāylahr dew kooᵣt/ shahk

The weather *Vädret*

What a lovely day!	**Vilken underbar dag!**	vilkern ewnderrbaar daa(g)
What awful weather!	**Ett sånt för-skräckligt väder!**	eht sont fur^r-skrehkli(g)t vaiderr
Isn't it cold/hot today?	**Är det inte kallt/varmt idag?**	ǟr dāy(t) inter kahlt/vahrmt ee daa(g)
Is it usually as warm as this?	**Brukar det vara så här varmt?**	brēwkahr dāy(t) vaarah saw hǟr vahrmt
Do you think it's going to ... tomorrow?	**Tror du att det kommer att ... i morgon?**	trōōr dēw aht dāy(t) kommerr aht ... ee morron
be a nice day	**bli vackert**	blee vahker^rt
rain	**regna**	rehngnah
snow	**snöa**	snūrah
What is the weather forecast?	**Vilka är väderleks-utsikterna?**	vilkah ǟr vaiderrlāyks-ēwtsikter^rnah

cloud	**molnet**	mawlnert
fog	**dimman**	dimmahn
frost	**frosten**	frostern
ice	**isen**	eessern
lightning	**blixten**	bleekstern
midnight sun	**midnattssolen**	meednahtsōōlern
moon	**månen**	mawnern
rain	**regnet**	rehngnert
sky	**himlen**	himlern
snow	**snön**	snurn
star	**stjärnan**	shǟ^rnahn
sun	**solen**	sōōlern
thunder	**åskan**	awskahn
thunderstorm	**åskvädret**	awskvaidrert
wind	**vinden**	vindern

Invitations *Inbjudan*

Would you like to have dinner with us on ...?	**Vill du äta middag med oss på ...?**	vil dēw aitah middah(g) māyd oss paw
May I invite you to lunch?	**Får jag bjuda på lunch?**	fawr yaa(g) byēwdah paw lewnsh

DAYS OF THE WEEK, see page 150

Can you come round for a drink this evening?	**Kan du komma på en drink i kväll?**	kahn dew kommah paw ehn drink ee kvehl
We are having a party. Can you come?	**Vi skall ha fest. Kan du komma?**	vee skah(l) haa fehst. kahn dew kommah
Great. I'd love to come.	**Tack, jag kommer gärna.**	tahk yaa(g) kommerr yæ̱ʳnah
What time shall I come?	**Hur dags skall jag komma?**	hewr dahgss skah(l) yaa(g) kommah
May I bring a friend?	**Får jag ta med en vän?**	fawr yaa(g) taa mäyd ehn vehn
I'm afraid we've got to leave now.	**Tyvärr måste vi gå nu.**	tewvær moster vee gaw new
Next time you (pl.) must come to visit us.	**Nästa gång måste ni komma och hälsa på oss.**	nehstah gong moster nee kommah ok hehlsah paw oss
Thanks for the evening.	**Tack för i kväll.**	tahk fürr ee kvehl
It was great.	**Det var verkligen trevligt.**	däy(t) vaar vehrkliggern träyvli(g)t

Dating *Träff*

Do you mind if I smoke?	**Har du något emot att jag röker?**	haar dew nawgot äymōōt aht yaa(g) rürkerr
Would you like a cigarette?	**Vill du ha en cigarrett?**	vil dew haa ehn siggahreht
Do you have a light, please?	**Har du eld?**	haar dew ehld
Why are you laughing?	**Varför skrattar du?**	vahrfurr skrahtahr dew
Is my Swedish that bad?	**Är min svenska så dålig?**	ær min svehnskah saw dawlig
Do you mind if I sit here?	**Har du något emot att jag sätter mig här?**	haar dew nawgot äymōōt aht yaa(g) sehterr may hær
Can I get you a drink?	**Kan jag hämta en drink åt dig?**	kahn yaa(g) hehmtah ehn drink awt day
Are you waiting for someone?	**Väntar du på någon?**	vehntahr dew paw nawgon

Are you free this evening?	**Är du ledig i kväll?**	ǟr dew **lay**di(g) ee kvehl
Would you like to go out with me tonight?	**Skall vi gå ut i kväll?**	skah(l) vee gaw ewt ee kvehl
Would you like to go dancing?	**Har du lust att gå ut och dansa?**	haar dew lewst aht gaw ewt ok **dahn**sah
I know a good discotheque.	**Jag vet ett bra diskotek.**	yaa(g) vāyt eht braa diskotāyk
Shall we go to the cinema (movies)?	**Skall vi gå på bio?**	skah(l) vee gaw paw **bee**oo
Would you like to go for a drive?	**Har du lust att göra en biltur?**	haar dew lewst aht **yurr**ah ehn **beel**tewr
Where shall we meet?	**Var skall vi träffas?**	vaar skah(l) vee **treh**fahss
I'll pick you up at your hotel.	**Jag kommer och hämtar dig på hotellet.**	yaa(g) **kom**merr ok **hehm**tahr day paw ho**tell**ert
I'll call for you at 8.	**Jag hämtar dig klockan 8.**	yaa(g) **hehm**tahr day **klok**kahn 8
May I take you home?	**Får jag följa dig hem?**	fawr yaa(g) **furl**yah day hehm
Can I see you again tomorrow?	**Skall vi ses i morgon igen?**	skah(l) vee **sāy**ss ee **mor**ron ee**yehn**
I hope we'll meet again.	**Jag hoppas vi ses igen.**	yaa(g) **hop**pahss vee **sāy**ss ee**yehn**

... and you might answer:

I'd love to, thank you.	**Mycket gärna, tack.**	**mew**ker(t) yǟ**r**nah tahk
That's very kind of you.	**Det var hemskt snällt av dig.**	dāy(t) vaar hehmskt snehlt aav day
Thank you, but I'm busy.	**Tack, men jag är tyvärr upptagen.**	tahk mehn yaa(g) ǟr tew**vǟr** **ewp**taagern
Leave me alone, please!	**Var snäll och lämna mig ifred.**	vaar snehl ok **lehm**nah may ee**frāy**(d)
Thank you, it's been a wonderful evening.	**Tack, det har varit en underbar kväll.**	tahk dāy(t) haar **vaa**rit ehn **ewn**derrbaar kvehl

Shopping Guide

This shopping guide is designed to help you find what you want with ease, accuracy and speed. It features:

1. A list of all major shops, stores and services (p. 98).
2. Some general expressions required when shopping to allow you to be specific and selective (p. 100).
3. Full details of the shops and services most likely to concern you. Here you'll find advice, alphabetical lists of items and conversion charts listed under the headings below.

Shops, stores and services *Affärer och service*

Most shops are open from 9 or 9.30 a.m. to 6 p.m., Monday to Friday, and on Saturdays closing time varies from 1 to 4 p.m. In larger cities certain supermarkets and the food sections of some of the main department stores remain open till 8 p.m. They open on Sundays, too, as do several corner shops.

Where can I find a (an) ...?	Var finns det ...?	vaar finss dāȳ(t)
antique shop	en antikvitetsaffär	ehn ahntikvittāȳtsahfǣr
art gallery	ett konstgalleri	eht konstgahlerree
baker's	ett bageri	eht baagerree
bank	en bank	ehn bahnk
barber's	en herrfrisör	ehn hehrfrissūrr
beauty salon	en skönhetssalong	ehn shūrnhāȳtssahlong
bookshop	en bokhandel	ehn bōōkhahnderl
butcher's	en slaktare/ ett charkuteri	ehn slahktahrer/ eht shahrkewterree
cake shop	ett konditori	eht kondittoree
camera shop	en fotoaffär	ehn fōōtooahfǣr
candy store	en godisaffär	ehn gōōdissahfǣr
chemist's	ett apotek	eht ahpootāȳk
dairy	en ostaffär	ehn oostahfǣr
delicatessen	en delikatessaffär	ehn dehlikkatehssahfǣr
dentist	en tandläkare	ehn tahn(d)laikahrer
department store	ett varuhus	eht vaarewhēwss
doctor	en läkare	ehn laikahrer
drugstore	ett apotek	eht ahpootāȳk
dry cleaner's	en kemtvätt	ehn khāȳmtveht
electricial goods shop	en elaffär	ehn āȳlahfǣr
fishmonger's	en fiskaffär	ehn fiskahfǣr
flea market	en loppmarknad	ehn lopmahrknahd
florist's	en blomsteraffär	ehn blomsterrahfǣr
furrier's	en körsnär	ehn khur'snǣr
glass and china shop	en glas- och porslinsaffär	ehn glaass- ok poo'sleensahfǣr
greengrocer's	en grönsaksaffär	ehn grūrnsaaksahfǣr
grocer's	en livsmedelsaffär	ehn livsmāȳderlsahfǣr
hairdresser's (ladies/men)	en frisör (dam-/herr-)	ehn frisūrr (daam-/hehr-)
hardware store	en järnhandel	ehn yǣ'nhahnderl
health food shop	en hälsokostaffär	ehn hehlsookostahfǣr

hospital	ett sjukhus	eht shēwkhēwss
ironmonger's	en järnhandel	ehn yǣ'nhahnderl
jeweller's	en juvelerare/	ehn yēwverlāÿrahrer/
	guldsmedsaffär	gewldsmāÿdsahfǣr
launderette	en snabbtvätt	ehn snahbtveht
laundry	en tvättinrättning	ehn tvehtinrehtning
library	ett bibliotek	eht bibliotāÿk
liquor store	ett systembolag	eht sewstāÿmboolaag
market	en marknad/	ehn mahrknahd
	en torghandel	ehn toryhahnderl
newsstand	en tidningskiosk	ehn tee(d)ningskhiosk
optician	en optiker	ehn optikkerr
pastry shop	ett konditori	eht kondittoree
perfumery	ett parfymeri	eht pahrfewmerree
photographer	en fotograf	ehn footoograaf
police station	en polisstation	ehn pooleesstahshōōn
post office	ett postkontor	eht postkontōōr
second-hand shop	en andrahandsaffär	ehn ahndrahhahndsahfǣr
shoemaker's (repairs)	en skomakare	ehn skōōmaakahrer
shoe shop	en skoaffär	ehn skōōahfǣr
shopping centre	ett shoppingcenter	eht shoppingsehnterr
silversmith	en silversmed	ehn silver'smāÿd
souvenir shop	en souvenirbutik	ehn sooverneerbewteek
sporting goods shop	en sportaffär	ehn spo'tahfǣr
stationer's	en pappershandel	ehn pahper'shahnderl
supermarket	ett snabbköp	eht snahbkhürp
sweet shop	en godisaffär	ehn gōōdissahfǣr
tailor's	en skräddare	ehn skrehdahrer
telegraph office	en telegraf	ehn tehlehgraaf
tobacconist's	en tobaksaffär	ehn tōōbahksahfǣr
toy shop	en leksaksaffär	ehn lāÿksaaksahfǣr
travel agency	en resebyrå	ehn rāÿsserbēwraw
vegetable store	en grönsaksaffär	ehn grürnsaaksahfǣr
veterinarian	en veterinär	ehn vehterrinnǣr
watchmaker's	en urmakare	ehn ēwrmaakahrer
wine merchant	ett systembolag	eht sewstāÿmboolaag

INGÅNG	ENTRANCE
UTGÅNG	EXIT
UTNöd	EMERGENCY EXIT

General expressions   *Allmänna uttryck*

Where?   *Var?*

Where's there a good ...?	**Var finns det någon bra ...?**	vaar finss dā͞y(t) nawgon braa
Where can I find a ...?	**Var hittar jag en ...?**	vaar hittahr yaa(g) ehn
Where's the main shopping area?	**Var ligger affärscentrum?**	vaar liggerr ahfæ͞rssehntrewm
Is it far from here?	**Är det långt härifrån?**	æ͞r dā͞y(t) longt hæ͞rifrawn
How do I get there?	**Hur kommer jag dit?**	hē͞wr kommerr yaa(g) deet

REA   SALE

Service   *Betjäning*

Can you help me?	**Kan ni hjälpa mig?**	kahn nee yehlpah may
I'm just looking.	**Jag tittar bara.**	yaa(g) tittahr baarah
Do you sell ...?	**Säljer ni ...?**	sehlyerr nee
I'd like to buy ...	**Jag skulle vilja köpa ...**	yaa(g) skewler vilyah khū͞rpah
Can you show me some ...?	**Kan ni visa mig några ...?**	kahn nee veessah may nawgrah
Do you have any ...?	**Har ni några ...?**	haar nee nawgrah
Where's the ... department?	**Var ligger ... -avdelningen?**	vaar liggerr ... -aavdā͞ylningern
Where is the lift (elevator)/escalator?	**Var är hissen/ rulltrappan?**	vaar æ͞r hissern/ rewltrahpahn
Where do I pay?	**Var betalar man?**	vaar bertaalahr mahn

That one   *Den där*

Can you show me ...?	**Kan ni visa mig ...?**	kahn nee veessah may
this/that the one in the window/in the display case	**det här/det där den i skyltfönstret/ i montern**	dā͞y(t) hæ͞r/dā͞y(t) dæ͞r/ dehn ee shewltfurnstrert/ ee monter͞rn

Defining the article *Beskrivning av varan*

I'd like a ... one.	**Jag skulle vilja ha en ...**	yaa(g) **skew**ler **vil**yah haa ehn
big	**stor**	stoor
cheap	**billig**	**bil**lig
dark	**mörk**	murrk
good	**bra**	braa
heavy	**tung**	tewng
large	**stor**	stoor
light (weight)	**lätt**	leht
light (colour)	**ljus**	yewss
oval	**oval**	oo**vaal**
rectangular	**rektangulär**	rehktang**gew**lær
round	**rund**	rewnd
small	**liten**	**lee**tern
square	**kvadratisk**	kvah**draa**tisk
sturdy	**kraftig**	**krahf**tig
I don't want anything too expensive.	**Jag vill inte ha någonting för dyrt.**	yaa(g) vil **in**ter haa **naw**gonting fūr dēw^r t

Preference *Jag föredrar ...*

Can you show me some others?	**Kan ni visa mig några andra?**	kahn nee **vee**ssah may **naw**grah **ahn**drah
Don't you have anything ...?	**Har ni inte någonting ...?**	haar nee **in**ter **naw**gonting
cheaper/better	**billigare/bättre**	**bil**liggahrer/**beh**trer
larger/smaller	**större/mindre**	**stur**rer/**min**drer

How much? *Hur mycket?*

How much is this?	**Hur mycket kostar det här?**	hēwr **mew**ker(t) **kos**tahr dāy(t) hǟr
How much are they?	**Hur mycket kostar de där?**	hēwr **mew**ker(t) **kos**tahr dom dǟr
I don't understand.	**Jag förstår inte.**	yaa(g) fur^r **stawr in**ter
Please write it down.	**Kan ni skriva det?**	kahn nee **skree**vah dāy(t)
I don't want to spend more than ... crowns.	**Jag vill inte lägga ut mer än ... kronor.**	yaa(g) vil **in**ter **leh**gah ēwt māyr ehn ... **krōō**noor

COLOURS, see page 113

Decision   *Beslut*

It's not quite what I want.	**Det är inte riktigt vad jag vill ha.**	dāy(t) ǣr inter rikti(g)t vaad yaa(g) vil haa
No, I don't like it.	**Nej, jag tycker inte om det.**	nay yaa(g) tewkerr inter om dāy(t)
I'll take it.	**Jag tar det.**	yaa(g) taar dāy(t)

Ordering   *Beställning*

| Can you order it for me? | **Kan ni beställa det åt mig?** | kahn nee berstehlah dāy(t) awt may |
| How long will it take? | **Hur lång tid tar det?** | hēwr long teed taar dāy(t) |

Delivery   *Leverans*

I'll take it with me.	**Jag tar det med mig.**	yaa(g) taar dāy(t) māyd may
Deliver it to the ... Hotel.	**Kan ni leverera det till hotell ...?**	kahn nee lehverrāyrah dāy(t) til hotehl
Please send it to this address.	**Skulle ni kunna skicka det till den här adressen?**	skewler nee kewnah shikkah dāy(t) til dehn hǣr ahdrehssern
Will I have any difficulty with the customs?	**Kommer jag att få problem i tullen?**	kommerr yaa(g) aht faw prooblāym ee tewlern

Paying   *Betalning*

How much is it?	**Hur mycket kostar det?**	hēwr mewker(t) kostahr dāy(t)
Can I pay by traveller's cheque?	**Kan jag betala med resecheck?**	kahn yaa(g) bertaalah māyd rāysserkhehk
Do you accept dollars/pounds?	**Tar ni emot dollar/pund?**	taar nee āymōōt dollahr/pewnd
Do you accept credit cards?	**Tar ni kreditkort?**	taar nee krehdeetkoo^rt
Can I get the VAT (sales tax) back?	**Får jag tillbaka momsen?**	fawr yaa(g) tilbaakah momsern
I think there's a mistake in the bill.	**Jag tror att det är ett fel på räkningen.**	yaa(g) trōōr aht dāy(t) ǣr eht fāyl paw raikningern

Anything else? *Något annat?*

No, thanks, that's all.	**Nej tack. Det var allt.**	nay tahk dāȳ(t) vaar ahlt
Yes, I'd like ...	**Ja, jag skulle vilja ha ...**	yaa yaa(g) skewler vilyah haa
May I have a bag, please?	**Kan jag få en kasse, tack?**	kahn yaa(g) faw ehn kahsser tahk
Could you wrap it up for me, please?	**Kan ni slå in det åt mig, tack?**	kahn nee slaw in dāȳ(t) awt may tahk

Dissatisfied? *Missnöjd?*

Can you exchange this, please?	**Kan jag få byta det här, tack?**	kahn yaa(g) faw bēwtah dāȳ(t) hǣr tahk
I want to return this.	**Jag vill lämna tillbaka det här.**	yaa(g) vil lehmnah tilbaakah dāȳ(t) hǣr
Could I have a refund? Here's the receipt.	**Kan jag få pengarna tillbaka? Här är kvittot.**	kahn yaa(g) faw pehngahᶦnah tilbaakah. hǣr ǣr kvittot

Kan jag hjälpa er?	Can I help you?
Vad önskar ni?	What would you like?
Vilken ... önskar ni?	What ... would you like?
färg/form	colour/shape
kvalitet	quality
Jag är ledsen, vi har inga.	I'm sorry, we don't have any.
Det är slut på lagret.	We're out of stock.
Skall vi beställa det åt er?	Shall we order it for you?
Tar ni det med er eller skall vi skicka det?	Will you take it with you or shall we send it?
Något annat?	Anything else?
Det blir ... kronor, tack.	That's ... crowns, please.
Kassan är där borta.	The cash desk is over there.

Bookshop—Stationer's   *Bokhandel – Pappershandel*

In Sweden, books and stationery are usually sold in the same shop. Newspapers, magazines and paperbacks are sold at newsstands and tobacconist's.

Where's the nearest ...?	**Var ligger närmaste ...?**	vaar liggerr nærmahster
bookshop	**bokhandel**	bōōkhahnderl
stationer's	**pappershandel**	pahper^rshahnderl
newsstand	**tidningskiosk**	tee(d)ningskhiosk
Where can I buy an English-language newspaper?	**Var kan jag köpa en engelskspråkig tidning?**	vaar kahn yaa(g) khūrpah ehn ehngerlsksprawki(g) tee(d)ning
Where's the guide-book section?	**Var finns guideböckerna?**	vaar finns "guide"burker^rnah
Where do you keep the English books?	**Var har ni engelska böcker?**	vaar haar nee ehngerlskah burkerr
Do you have any of ...'s books in English?	**Har ni någon av ...s böcker på engelska?**	haar nee nawgon aav ...s burkerr paw ehngerlskah
Do you have second-hand books?	**Har ni antikvariska böcker?**	haar nee ahntikvaariskah burkerr
I want to buy a/an/some ...	**Jag skulle vilja köpa ...**	yaa(g) skewler vilyah khūrpah
address book	**en adressbok**	ehn ahdrehsbōōk
adhesive tape	**tejp**	"tape"
ball-point pen	**en kulspetspenna**	ehn kēwlspehtspehnah
book	**en bok**	ehn bōōk
calendar	**en kalender**	ehn kahlehnderr
carbon paper	**karbonpapper**	kahrbawnpahperr
crayons	**färgkritor**	færykreetoor
dictionary	**en ordbok**	ehn ōō^rdbōōk
pocket	**fick-**	fik-
Swedish-English	**Svensk-Engelsk**	svehnsk-ehngerlsk
drawing pad	**ett ritblock**	eht reetblok
drawing pins	**häftstift**	hehftstift
envelopes	**några kuvert**	nawgrah kewvær
eraser	**ett radergummi**	eht rahdāyrgewmi
exercise book	**en skrivbok**	ehn skreevbōōk
felt-tip pen	**en filtpenna**	ehn filtpehnah
fountain pen	**en reservoarpenna**	ehn rehsserrvaarpehnah

glue	**klister**	klisterr
grammar book	**en grammatik**	ehn grahmahteek
guidebook	**en reseguide**	ehn rāysser"guide"
ink	**bläck**	blehk
black/red/blue	**svart/rött/blått**	svah‹r›t/rurt/blot
(adhesive) labels	**(självhäftande)**	(shehlvhehftahnder)
	etiketter	ehtikehterr
magazine	**en veckotidning**	ehn vehkootee(d)ning
map	**en karta**	ehn kaa‹r›tah
street map of ...	**en karta över ...**	ehn kaa‹r›tah ūrverr
road map of ...	**en vägkarta över ...**	ehn vaigkaa‹r›tah ūrverr
mechanical pencil	**en stiftpenna**	ehn stiftpehnah
newspaper	**en dagstidning**	ehn dahgstee(d)ning
American/English	**amerikansk/**	ahm(eh)rikaansk/
	engelsk	engerlsk
notebook	**en anteckningsbok**	ehn ahntehkningsbōōk
note paper	**brevpapper**	brāyvpahperr
paintbox	**en färglåda**	ehn færylawdah
paper	**papper**	pahperr
paperback	**en pocketbok**	ehn pokkertbōōk
paperclips	**gem**	gāym
paper napkins	**pappersservetter**	pahper‹r›ssehrvehterr
pen	**en penna**	ehn pehnah
pencil	**en blyertspenna**	ehn blēwer‹r›tspehnah
pencil sharpener	**en pennvässare**	ehn pehnvehssahrer
picture-book	**bilderbok**	bilderrbōōk
playing cards	**spelkort**	spāylkoo‹r›t
pocket calculator	**en fickräknare**	ehn fikræknahrer
postcard	**ett vykort**	eht vēwkoo‹r›t
propelling pencil	**en stiftpenna**	ehn stiftpehnah
refill (for a pen)	**en refill**	ehn rehfil
rubber	**ett radergummi**	eht rahdāyrgewmi
rubber bands	**gummisnoddar**	gewmisnooddahr
ruler	**en linjal**	ehn linyaal
stapler	**häftapparat**	hehftahpahraat
staples	**häftklammer**	hehftklahmerr
string	**ett snöre**	eht snūrrer
thumbtacks	**häftstift**	hehftstift
tissue paper	**silkespapper**	silkerspahperr
travel guide	**en reseguide**	ehn rāysser"guide"
typewriter ribbon	**ett skrivmaskins-**	eht skreevmahsheens-
	band	bahnd
typing paper	**skrivmaskins-**	skreevmahsheens-
	papper	pahperr
wrapping paper	**omslagspapper**	omslagspahperr
writing pad	**ett skrivblock**	eht skreevblok
writing paper	**brevpapper**	brāyvpahperr

Camping equipment *Campingutrustning*

I'd like a/an/some …	Jag skulle vilja ha …	yaa(g) **skewl**er **vil**yah haa
air bed	en luftmadrass	ehn **lewft**mahdrahss
backpack	en ryggsäck	ehn **rewg**sehk
bottle-opener	en flasköppnare	ehn **flahsk**urpnahrer
bucket	en hink	ehn hink
butane gas	butangas	bew**taan**gaass
camp bed	en tältsäng	ehn **tehlt**sehng
candles	några ljus	**nawg**rah **yēw**ss
can opener	en konservöppnare	ehn kon**sær**vurpnahrer
chair	en stol	ehn st**ōō**l
folding chair	en fällstol	ehn **fehl**st**ōō**l
charcoal	träkol (briketter)	**trai**kawl (bri**keht**terr)
clothes pegs	klädnypor	**klai**(d)**nēw**poor
compass	en kompass	ehn kom**pahss**
cool bag	en kylväska	ehn **khēw**lvehskah
cool box	en kylbox	ehn **khēw**lbokss
corkscrew	en korkskruv	ehn **kork**skr**ēw**v
crockery	porslin	poo**r**s**leen**
cutlery	bestick	ber**stik**
deck chair	en solstol	ehn **sōōl**st**ōō**l
first-aid kit	en förbandslåda	ehn furr**bahnds**lawdah
fishing tackle	fiskeredskap	**fisk**err**āy**dskaap
flashlight	en ficklampa	ehn **fik**lahmpah
food box	en matlåda	ehn **maat**lawdah
frying pan	en stekpanna	ehn **stāyk**pahnah
groundsheet	ett tältunderlag	eht **tehlt**ewnder**r**laag
hammer	en hammare	ehn **hah**mahrer
hammock	en hängmatta	ehn **hehng**mahtah
ice packs	några frysklampar	**nawg**rah **frēw**sklahmpahr
kerosene	fotogen	footoo**shāy**n
knapsack	en ryggsäck	ehn **rewg**sehk
lamp	en lampa	ehn **lahm**pah
lantern	en lykta	ehn **lewk**tah
mallet	en träklubba	ehn **trai**klewbah
matches	tändstickor	**tehn**(d)stikkoor
mattress	en madrass	ehn mah**drahss**
methylated spirits	rödsprit	**rūr**(d)spreet
mosquito net	ett myggnät	eht **mewg**nait
pail	en hink	ehn hink
paper napkins	pappersservetter	**pahper**r**ss**ehrvehterr
paraffin	fotogen	footoo**shāy**n
penknife	en pennkniv	ehn **pehn**kneev
picnic basket	en picknickkorg	ehn **pik**nikkory

CAMPING, see page 32

plastic bags	**plastpåsar**	**plahst**pawssahr
pliers	**en tång**	ehn tong
pump	**pump**	pewmp
rope	**ett rep**	eht rāyp
rucksack	**en ryggsäck**	ehn **rewg**sehk
saucepan	**en kastrull**	ehn kah**strewl**
scissors	**en sax**	ehn sahkss
screwdriver	**en skruvmejsel**	ehn skrēwvmayserl
sleeping bag	**en sovsäck**	ehn **sawv**sehk
stew pot	**en gryta**	ehn grēwtah
table	**ett bord**	eht bōōʳd
folding table	**ett fällbord**	eht fehlbōōʳd
tent	**ett tält**	eht tehlt
tent pegs	**tältpinnar**	**tehlt**pinnahr
tent pole	**en tältstång**	ehn **tehlt**stawng
tinfoil	**aluminiumfolie**	ahlewmeenyewmfōōlyer
tin opener	**en konservöppnare**	ehn konsærvurpnahrer
torch	**en ficklampa**	ehn **fik**lahmpah
vacuum flask	**en termosflaska**	ehn **tær**mosflahskah
washing powder	**tvättmedel**	tvehtmāyderl
washing-up liquid	**diskmedel**	diskmāyderl
water flask	**en fältflaska**	ehn **fehlt**flahskah
wood alcohol	**rödsprit**	rūīʳ(d)spreet

Crockery *Porslin*

cups	**koppar**	koppahr
mugs	**muggar**	mewgahr
plates	**tallrikar**	**tahl**rikkahr
saucers	**tefat**	tāyfaat
tumblers	**dricksglas**	**driks**glaass

Cutlery *Bestick*

forks	**gafflar**	gahflahr
knives	**knivar**	kneevahr
spoons	**skedar**	shāydahr
teaspoons	**teskedar**	tāyshāydahr
(made of) plastic	**(av) plast**	(aav) plahst
(made of) stainless steel	**(av) rostfritt stål**	(aav) rostfrit stawl

Chemist's (drugstore)   *Apotek*

Swedish chemists' normally don't stock the great range of goods that you'll find in Britain or the U.S.A. For example, they don't sell photographic equipment or books. And for perfume, cosmetics, etc. you must go to a *parfymeri* (**pahr**fewmerree). Note that you need a prescription for most medicines.

In the window you'll see a notice telling you where the nearest all-night chemist's is.

This section is divided into two parts:

1. Pharmaceutical—medicine, first-aid, etc.
2. Toiletry—toilet articles, cosmetics

General   *Allmänt*

Where's the nearest (all-night) chemist's?	**Var ligger närmaste (jour)apotek?**	vaar liggerr **nær**mahster (shoor)ahpootāyk
What time does the chemist's open/ close?	**Hur dags öppnar/ stänger apoteket?**	hewr dahgss **urp**nahr/ **steh**ngerr ahpootāykert

1—Pharmaceutical   *Medicin – Förbandsartiklar*

I'd like something for ...	**Jag skulle vilja ha något mot ...**	yaa(g) skewler **vil**yah haa **naw**got moot
a cold	**förkylning**	fur'khewlning
a cough	**hosta**	hoostah
a hangover	**baksmälla**	baaksmehlah
hay fever	**hösnuva**	hursnewvah
insect bites	**insektsbett**	insehktsbeht
sunburn	**solsveda**	soolsvāydah
travel sickness	**åksjuka**	awkshewkah
an upset stomach	**orolig mage**	ooroolig maager
Can you prepare this prescription for me?	**Kan ni göra i ordning det här receptet åt mig?**	kahn nee yurrah ee o'dning det här rehsehptert awt may
Can I get it without a prescription?	**Kan jag få det utan recept?**	kahn yaa(g) faw dāy(t) ewtahn rehsehpt
Shall I wait?	**Skall jag vänta?**	skah(l) yaa(g) vehntah

DOCTOR, see page 137

Can I have a/an/some ...?	Skulle jag kunna få ...?	skewler yaa(g) kewnah faw
analgesic	något smärt-stillande	nawgot smæ'tstillahnder
antiseptic cream	en antiseptisk salva	ehn ahntissehptisk sahlvah
aspirin	aspirin	ahspireen
bandage	ett förband	eht fur'bahnd
elastic bandage	en elastisk binda	ehn ehlahstisk bindah
Band-Aids	plåster	plosterr
charcoal tablets	koltabletter	kawltahblehterr
condoms	kondomer	kondawmerr
contraceptives	preventivmedel	prehvehnteevmayderl
corn plasters	liktornsplåster	leektoo'nsplosterr
cotton wool (absorbent cotton)	ett paket bomull	eht pahkayt boomewl
cough drops	några halstabletter	nawgrah hahlstahblehterr
disinfectant	desinficeringsmedel	dehssinfissayrings-mayderl
ear drops	örondroppar	urrondroppahr
Elastoplast	plåster	plosterr
eye drops	ögondroppar	urgondroppahr
(roll of) gauze	en gasbinda	ehn gaasbindah
insect repellent/insect spray	ett insektsmedel/insektsspray	eht insehktsmayderl/insehkts"spray"
iodine	jod	yod
laxative	ett laxermedel	eht lahksayrmayderl
mouthwash	ett munvatten	eht mewnvahtern
nose drops	näsdroppar	naisdroppahr
painkiller	något smärt-stillande	nawgot smæ'tstillahnder
sanitary towels (napkins)	ett paket dambindor	eht pahkayt daambindoor
suppositories	några stolpiller	nawgrah stoolpillerr
... tablets	... tabletter	... tahblehterr
tampons	tamponger	tahmpongerr
thermometer	en termometer	ehn tehrmoomayterr
throat lozenges	några halstabletter	nawgrah hahlstahblehterr
vitamin pills	vitamintabletter	vittahmeentahblehterr

GIFT	POISON
ENDAST FÖR UTVÄRTES BRUK	FOR EXTERNAL USE ONLY

2 — Toiletry   *Toalettartiklar*

I'd like a/an/some ...	Jag skulle vilja ha ...	yaa(g) **skew**ler **vil**yah haa
after-shave lotion	**ett rakvatten**	eht **raak**vahtern
bath salts	**ett badsalt**	eht **baad**sahlt
blusher (rouge)	**rouge**	rōōsh
bubble bath	**ett skumbad**	eht **skewm**baad
cream	**en kräm/crème**	ehn kraim
cleansing cream	**en rengöringskräm**	ehn rāȳnyürringskraim
foot cream	**en fotkräm**	ehn **fōōt**kraim
foundation cream	**ett puderunderlag**	eht **pēw**derrewnderrlaag
hand cream	**en handkräm**	ehn **hahn(d)**kraim
moisturizing cream	**en fuktighets-bevarande kräm**	ehn **fewk**tighāȳts-bervaarahnder kraim
night cream	**en nattkräm**	ehn **naht**kraim
sun-tan cream	**en solkräm**	ehn **sōōl**kraim
cuticle remover	**nagelbandsvatten**	**naa**gerlbahndsvahtern
deodorant	**deodorant**	dāȳodo**rahnt**
emery boards	**sandpappersfilar**	sahnd**pahper**ʳsfeelahr
eyebrow pencil	**en ögonbrynspenna**	ehn ūrgonbrēwnspehnah
eye liner	**en eyeliner**	ehn "eye liner"
eye shadow	**en ögonskugga**	ehn ūrgonskewgah
face flannel	**en tvättlapp**	ehn **tveht**lahp
face powder	**puder**	**pēw**derr
lipbrush	**en läppstiftpensel**	ehn **lehp**stiftpehnserl
lipsalve	**ett cerat**	eht seh**raat**
lipstick	**ett läppstift**	eht **lehp**stift
make-up bag	**en sminkväska**	ehn **smink**vehskah
make-up remover pads	**make-up remover pads**	"make-up remover pads"
mascara	**en mascara**	ehn mahs**kaa**rah
nail brush	**en nagelborste**	ehn **naa**gerlboʳster
nail clippers	**en nageltång**	ehn **naa**gerltong
nail file	**en nagelfil**	ehn **naa**gerlfeel
nail polish	**ett nagellack**	eht **naa**gerllahk
nail polish remover	**nagellacks-borttagningsmedel**	eht **naa**gerllahks-boʳttaagningsmāȳderl
nail scissors	**en nagelsax**	ehn **naa**gerlsahkss
perfume	**en parfym**	ehn pahr**fēwm**
powder	**puder**	**pēw**derr
powder puff	**en pudervippa**	ehn **pēw**derrvippah
razor	**en rakhyvel**	ehn **raak**hēwverl
razor blades	**rakblad**	**raak**blaad
rouge	**rouge**	rōōsh
safety pins	**säkerhetsnålar**	**sai**kerrhāȳtsnawlahr

shaving brush	**en rakborste**	ehn raakbo^{r}ster
shaving cream	**en rakkräm**	ehn raakkraim
soap	**en tvål**	ehn tvawl
sponge	**en tvättsvamp**	ehn tvehtsvahmp
sponge bag	**en necessär**	ehn nehssers**æ**r
sun-tan oil	**sololja**	ehn s$\overline{oo}$lolyah
talcum powder	**talkpuder**	tahlkp$\overline{ew}$derr
tissues	**pappersnäsdukar**	pahper^{r}snaisd$\overline{ew}$kahr
toilet paper	**toalettpapper**	tooahleht pahperr
toilet water	**eau de toilette**	aw der tooahleht
toothbrush	**en tandborste**	ehn tahn(d)bo^{r}ster
toothpaste	**en tandkräm**	ehn tahn(d)kraim
towel	**en handduk**	ehn hahn(d)d$\overline{ew}$k
tweezers	**en pincett**	ehn pinseht

For your hair   *För håret*

bobby pins	**hårklämmor**	hawrklehmoor
colour shampoo	**tonande schampo**	t$\overline{oo}$nahnder **shahm**poo
comb	**en kam**	ehn kahm
curlers	**papiljotter**	pahpil**y**otterr
dry shampoo	**torrschampo**	torshahmpoo
hairbrush	**en hårborste**	ehn hawrbo^{r}ster
hair dye	**hårfärgnings-**	hawrfæryenings-
	medel	m$\overline{ay}$derl
hair gel	**frisyrgelé**	friss$\overline{ew}$rshehl$\overline{ay}$
hair mousse	**mousse**	mooss
hairgrips	**hårklämmor**	hawrklehmoor
hair lotion	**hårvatten**	hawrvahtern
hairpins	**hårnålar**	haw^{r}nawlahr
hair slide	**ett hårspänne**	eht haw^{r}spehner
hair spray	**hårspray**	haw^r"spray"
setting lotion	**en läggningsvätska**	ehn lehgningsvehtskah
shampoo	**ett shampo**	eht shahmpoo
for dry/greasy	**för torrt/**	f$\overline{u}$rr to^{r}t/
(oily) hair	**fett hår**	feht hawr
tint	**ett toningsmedel**	eht t$\overline{oo}$ningsm$\overline{ay}$derl
wig	**en peruk**	ehn pehr$\overline{ew}$k

For the baby   *För babyn*

baby food	**barnmat**	baa^{r}nmaat
dummy (pacifier)	**en napp**	ehn nahp
feeding bottle	**en nappflaska**	ehn nahpflahskah
nappies (diapers)	**blöjor**	blur**y**oor

Clothing *Kläder*

If you want to buy something specific, prepare yourself in advance. Look at the list of clothing on page 116. Get some idea of the colour, material and size you want. They're all listed on the next few pages.

General *Allmänt*

I'd like ...	**Jag skulle vilja ha ...**	yaa(g) **skewler vilyah** haa
I'd like ... for a 10-year-old boy/girl.	**Jag skulle vilja ha ... till en 10-årig pojke/flicka.**	yaa(g) **skewler vilyah** haa ... til ehn 10-**awri**(g) **poyker/flikkah**
I'd like something like this.	**Jag skulle vilja ha något som det här.**	yaa(g) **skewler vilyah** haa **nawg**ot som dā̄y(t) hǣr
I like the one in the window.	**Jag tycker om den i fönstret.**	yaa(g) **tewkerr** om dehn ee **furn**strert
How much is that per metre?	**Hur mycket kostar det där per meter?**	hēw̄r **mewk**er(t) kostahr dā̄y(t) dǣr pǣr **mā̄y**terr

1 centimetre (cm.)	= 0.39 in.	1 inch = 2.54 cm.
1 metre (m.)	= 39.37 in.	1 foot = 30.5 cm.
10 metres	= 32.81 ft.	1 yard = 0.91 m.

Colour *Färg*

I want something in ...	**Jag skulle vilja ha något i ...**	yaa(g) **skewler vilyah** haa **nawg**ot ee
I'd like a darker/lighter shade.	**Jag skulle vilja ha en nyans mörkare/ljusare.**	yaa(g) **skewler vilyah** haa ehn nēw̄**ahngss murr**kahrer/yēw̄**ss**sahrer
I want something to match this.	**Jag vill ha något som passar till det här.**	yaa(g) vil haa **naw**got som **pahss**ahr til dā̄y(t) hǣr
I don't like the colour/pattern.	**Jag tycker inte om färgen/mönstret.**	yaa(g) **tewkerr inter** om **fær**yern/**murn**strert

beige	**beige**	baish
black	**svart**	svah^{r}t
blue	**blå**	blaw
brown	**brun**	brewn
fawn	**gulbrun**	gewlbrewn
golden	**guldfärgad**	gewldfæryahd
green	**grön**	grurn
grey	**grå**	graw
mauve	**lila**	leelah
orange	**orange**	orahnsh
pink	**rosa**	rawssah
purple	**violett**	veeooleht
red	**röd**	rurd
scarlet	**scharlakansröd**	shah^{r}laakahnsrurd
silver	**silverfärgad**	silverrfæryahd
turquoise	**turkos**	tewrkooss
white	**vit**	veet
yellow	**gul**	gewl
light ...	**ljus ...**	yewss
dark ...	**mörk ...**	murrk

enfärgad
(aynfæryahd)

randig
(rahndig)

prickig
(prikkig)

rutig
(rewtig)

mönstrad
(murnstrahd)

Fabric *Tyg*

Do you have anything in ...?	**Har ni någonting i ...?**	haar nee nawgonting ee
Is that ...?	**Är det där ...?**	ær day(t) dær
handmade	**handgjort**	hahn(d)yoo^{r}t
imported	**importerat**	impo^{r}tayraht
made in Sweden	**svensktillverkat**	svehnsktilvehrkaht
I'd like something thinner.	**Jag skulle vilja ha någonting tunnare.**	yaa(g) skewler vilyah haa nawgonting tewnaher
Do you have anything of better quality?	**Har ni någon bättre kvalitet?**	haar nee nawgon behtrer kvahlitay(t)

What's it made of?	Vad är det gjort av?	vaad ǣr dāy(t) yōoͬt aav
cambric	batist	bahtist
camelhair	kamelhår	kahmāylhawr
chiffon	chiffon	shiffong
corduroy	manchester	mahnkhehsterr
cotton	bomull	boomewl
crepe	crêpe	krehp
denim	denim	dehneem
felt	filt	filt
flannel	flanell	flahnehl
gabardine	gabardin	gahbahrdeen
lace	spets	spehtss
leather	läder/skinn	laider/shin
linen	linne	linner
poplin	poplin	popleen
satin	satin	sahtehng
silk	siden/silke	seedern/silker
suede	mocka	mokkah
towelling	frotté	frottāy
velvet	sammet	sahmert
velveteen	bomullssammet	boomewlssahmert
wool	ylle	ewler
worsted	kamgarn	kahmgaaͬn

Is it ...?	Är det ...?	ǣr dāy(t)
pure cotton/wool	ren bomull/ull	rāyn boomewl/ewl
synthetic	syntetiskt	sewntāytiskt
colourfast	färgäkta	færyehktah
crease (wrinkle) resistant	skrynkelfritt	skrewnkerlfrit
Is it hand washable/ machine washable?	Skall det tvättas för hand/i maskin?	skah(l) dāy(t) tvehtahss fūrr hahnd/ee mahsheen
Will it shrink?	Krymper det?	krewmperr dāy(t)

Size *Storlek*

I take size 38.	Jag har storlek 38.	yaa(g) haar stōoͬlāyk 38
Could you measure me?	Kan ni ta mina mått?	kahn nee taa meenah mot
I don't know the Swedish sizes.	Jag känner inte till de svenska storlekarna.	yaa(g) khehnerr inter til dom svehnskah stōoͬlāykahͬnah

Sizes vary from country to country and from one manufacturer to another, so be sure to try on the clothes before you buy.

Women *Damer*

Dresses/Suits					
American	8	10	12	14	16	18
British	10	12	14	16	18	20
Continental	36	38	40	42	44	46

Stockings						Shoes			
American ⎫	8	8½	9	9½	10	10½	5½	6½	7½	8½
British ⎭							4	5	6	7
Continental	1		2		3		37	38	39	40

Men *Herrar*

Suits/Overcoats							Shirts			
American ⎫	36	38	40	42	44	46	15	16	17	18
British ⎭										
Continental	46	48	50	52	54	56	38	40	42	44

Shoes							
American ⎫	6½	7	7½	8	8½	9	11
British ⎭	5	6	7	8	9	10	12
Continental	38	39	40	41	42	43	44

A good fit? *Passar det?*

Can I try it on?	**Kan jag få prova den?**	kahn yaa(g) faw **prōō**vah dehn
Where's the changing room?	**Var är provhytten?**	vaar ær **prōō**vhewtern
Is there a mirror?	**Finns det någon spegel?**	finss dāy(t) **naw**gon **spāy**gerl
It fits very well.	**Den sitter mycket bra.**	dehn sitterr **mew**ker(t) braa
It doesn't fit.	**Den passar inte.**	dehn **pahss**ahr inter

NUMBERS, see page 147

It's too ...	**Den är för ...**	dehn ær fûrr
short/long	**kort/lång**	ko^{r}t/long
tight/loose	**trång/vid**	trong/veed
How long will it take to alter it?	**Hur lång tid tar det att ändra den?**	hewr long teed taar dāȳ(t) aht ehndrah dehn

Clothes and accessories *Kläder och accessoarer*

I would like a/an/some ...	**Jag skulle vilja ha ...**	yaa(g) skewler vilyah haa
anorak	**en anorak**	ehn ahnorahk
bathing cap	**en badmössa**	ehn baadmurssahr
bathrobe	**en badrock**	ehn baadrok
blouse	**en blus**	ehn blewss
bow tie	**en fluga**	ehn flewgah
bra	**en behå**	ehn bāȳhaw
braces	**ett par hängslen**	eht paar hengslehn
cap	**en mössa**	ehn murssah
cardigan	**en kofta**	ehn koftah
coat (man's)	**en rock**	ehn rok
coat (woman's)	**en kappa**	ehn kahpah
dress	**en klänning**	ehn klehning
with long sleeves	**med lång ärm**	māȳd long ærm
with short sleeves	**med kort ärm**	māȳd ko^{r}t ærm
sleeveless	**utan ärm**	ewtahn ærm
dressing gown	**en morgonrock**	ehn morronrok
evening dress (woman's)	**en aftonklänning**	ehn ahftonklehning
fur coat	**en päls**	ehn pehlss
girdle	**en höfthållare**	ehn hurfthollahrer
gloves	**ett par handskar**	eht paar hahn(d)skahr
handbag	**en handväska**	ehn hahn(d)vehskah
handkerchief	**en näsduk**	ehn naisdewk
hat	**en hatt**	ehn haht
jacket	**en kavaj**	ehn kahvahy
jeans	**ett par jeans**	eht paar yeenss
jersey	**en jumper/tröja**	ehn jewmperr/truryah
kneesocks	**ett par knästrumpor**	eht paar knaistrewmpoor
nightdress	**ett par nattlinne**	eht nahtlinner
overalls	**en overall**	ehn ovverrawl
pair of ...	**ett par ...**	eht paar
panties	**ett par trosor**	eht paar trōōssoor
pants (Am.)	**ett par (lång)byxor**	eht paar (long)bewksoor
panty girdle	**en byxgördel**	ehn bewksyûr^{r}derl

panty hose	ett par strump-byxor	eht paar strewmp-bewksoor
parka	en anorak	ehn ahnorahk
pullover	en jumper/tröja	ehn yewmperr/truryah
polo (turtle)-neck	med polokrage	māyd pōōlookraager
round-neck	rundringad	rewndringahd
V-neck	V-ringad	vāy-ringahd
pyjamas	en pyjamas	ehn pewyaamahss
raincoat (man's)	en regnrock	ehn rehngnrok
raincoat (woman's)	en regnkappa	ehn rehngnkahpah
scarf	en scarf	ehn skaarf
shirt	en skjorta	ehn shoo'tah
shorts	ett par shorts	eht paar sho'tss
skirt	en kjol	ehn khōōl
slip	en underklänning	ehn ewnderrklehnning
socks	ett par sockor	eht paar sokkoor
stockings	ett par strumpor	eht paar strewmpoor
suit (man's)	en kostym	ehn kostēwm
suit (woman's)	en dräkt	ehn drehkt
suspenders (Am.)	ett par hängslen	eht paar hengslern
sweater	en tröja	ehn truryah
sweatshirt	en sweatshirt	ehn "sweatshirt"
swimming trunks	ett par badbyxor	eht paar baadbewksoor
swimsuit	en baddräkt	ehn baa(d)drehkt
T-shirt	en T-shirt	ehn "T-shirt"
tie	en slips	ehn slipss
tights	ett par strump-byxor	eht paar strewmp-bewksoor
tracksuit	en träningsoverall	ehn trainingsovverrawl
trousers	ett par (lång)byxor	eht paar (long)bewksoor
umbrella	ett paraply	eht pahrahplēw
underpants	ett par kalsonger	eht paar kahlsongerr
undershirt	en undertröja	ehn ewnderrtruryah
vest (Am.)	en väst	ehn vehst
vest (Br.)	en undertröja	ehn ewnderrtruryah
waistcoat	en väst	ehn vehst

belt	ett bälte/skärp	eht behlter/shairp
buckle	ett spänne	eht spehner
button	en knapp	ehn knahp
collar	en krage	ehn kraager
pocket	en ficka	ehn fikkah
press stud (snap fastener)	en tryckknapp	ehn trewkknahp
zip (zipper)	ett blixtlås	bliks(t)lawss

Shoes *Skor*

I'd like a pair of ...	**Jag skulle vilja ha ett par ...**	yaa(g) skewler vilyah haa eht paar
boots	**stövlar**	sturvlahr
moccasins	**loafers**	"loafers"
plimsolls (sneakers)	**tenniskor**	tehnisskoor
sandals	**sandaler**	sahndaalerr
shoes	**skor**	skoor
flat	**platta**	plahtah
with a heel	**med klack**	māyd klahk
with leather soles	**med lädersula**	māyd laider^rsēwlaw
with rubber soles	**med gummisula**	māyd gewmissēwlah
slippers	**tofflor**	tofloor
These are too ...	**De här är för ...**	dom hǟr ǟr fūrr
narrow/wide	**smala/breda**	smaalah/brāydah
big/small	**stora/små**	stōōrah/smaw
Do you have a smaller/larger size?	**Har ni en storlek mindre/större**	haar nee ehn stōō^rlāyk mindrer/sturrer
Do you have the same in black?	**Har ni samma i svart?**	haar nee sahmah ee svah^rt
cloth	**tyg**	tēwg
leather	**läder/skinn**	laiderr/shin
rubber	**gummi**	gewmi
suede	**mocka**	mokkah
Is it real leather?	**Är det äkta läder?**	ǟr dāy(t) ehktah laiderr
I need some ...	**Jag behöver ...**	yaa(g) berhūrverr
shoe polish	**skokräm**	skōōkraim
shoelaces	**skosnören**	skōōsnūrrern

Shoes worn out? Here's the way to get them mended:

Can you repair these shoes?	**Kan ni laga de här skorna?**	kahn nee laagah dom hǟr skōō^rnah
Can you stitch this?	**Kan ni sy ihop det här?**	kahn nee sēw eehoop dāy(t) hǟr
I want new soles and heels.	**Jag vill ha nya sulor och klackar.**	yaa(g) vil haa nēwah sēwloor ok klahkahr
When will they be ready?	**När blir de klara?**	nǟr bleer dom klaarah

COLOURS, see page 113

Electrical appliances   *Elektriska artiklar*

220-volt, 50-cycle A.C. is used almost everywhere in Sweden.

Do you have a battery for this?	**Har ni ett batteri till den här?**	haar nee eht bahterree til dehn hær
This is broken. Can you repair it?	**Den här har gått sönder. Kan ni laga den?**	dehn hær haar got surnderr. kahn nee laagah dehn
Can you show me how it works?	**Kan ni visa mig hur den fungerar?**	kahn nee veessah may hewr dehn fewnggāȳrahr
How do I switch it on?	**Hur sätter jag på den?**	hewr sehterr yaa(g) paw dehn
I'd like to buy/hire a video cassette.	**Jag skulle vilja köpa/hyra en videokassett.**	yaa(g) skewler vilyah khūrpah/hewrah ehn veedyokahsseht
I'd like a/an/ some ...	**Jag skulle vilja ha ...**	yaa(g) skewler vilyah haa
adaptor	**en adapter**	ehn ahdahpterr
amplifier	**en förstärkare**	ehn fur^rstærkahrer
bulb	**en glödlampa**	ehn glūrdlahmpah
clock-radio	**en klockradio**	ehn klokraadyo
electric toothbrush	**en elektrisk tandborste**	ehn ehlehktrisk tahn(d)bo^rster
extension lead (cord)	**en förlängnings-sladd**	ehn fur^rlehngningsslahd
hair dryer	**en hårtork**	ehn haw^rtork
headphones	**ett par hörlurar**	eht paar hur^rlewrahr
(travelling) iron	**ett (rese)strykjärn**	eht (rāysser)strewkyæ^rn
lamp	**en lampa**	ehn lahmpah
plug	**en stickkontakt**	ehn stikkontahkt
portable ...	**en bärbar ...**	ehn bærbaar
radio	**en radio**	ehn raadyo
car radio	**en bilradio**	ehn beelraadyo
(cassette) recorder	**en (kassett)-bandspelare**	ehn (kahsseht)-bahndspāȳlahrer
record player	**en skivspelare**	ehn sheevspāȳlahrer
shaver	**en rakapparat**	ehn raakahpahraat
speakers	**högtalare**	hūrgtaalahrer
(colour) television	**en (färg)TV**	ehn (færy)tāȳvāȳ
transformer	**en transformator**	ehn trahnsformaator
video recorder	**en videoband-spelare**	ehn veedyobahnd-spāȳlahrer

Grocer's   *Livsmedelsaffär*

I'd like some bread, please.	**Jag skulle vilja ha lite bröd, tack.**	yaa(g) **skew**ler **vil**yah haa **lee**ter brǖrd tahk
crispbread	**hårt bröd**	haw^rt brǖrd
sliced bread	**skivat bröd**	**shee**vaht brǖrd
white bread	**vitt bröd**	vit brǖrd
What sort of cheese do you have?	**Vad har ni för sorts ostar?**	vaad haar nee fǖrr so^rtss **oos**tahr
A piece of that one, please.	**En bit av den där, tack.**	ehn beet aav dehn dǟr tahk
I'll have one of those, please.	**Kan jag få en av de där, tack?**	kahn yaa(g) faw ehn aav dom dǟr tahk
May I help myself?	**Kan jag ta själv?**	kahn yaa(g) taa shehlv
I'd like ...	**Jag skulle vilja ha ...**	yaa(g) **skew**ler **vil**yah haa
a kilo of apples	**ett kilo äpplen**	eht **kee**loo **ehp**lern
half a kilo of tomatoes	**ett halvt kilo tomater**	eht hahlft **kee**loo too**maa**terr
250 grams of butter	**¼ kg smör**	eht kvah^rtss **kee**loo smǖrr
3 hg. (300 g.) of pâté	**3 hekto paté**	3 **hehk**too pah**tāy**
a litre of milk	**en liter mjölk**	ehn **lee**terr myurlk
4 slices of ham	**4 skivor skinka**	4 **shee**voor **shin**kah
a packet of tea	**ett paket te**	eht pah**kāyt** tāy
a jar of jam	**en burk sylt**	ehn bewrk sewlt
a tin (can) of peaches	**en burk persikor**	ehn bewrk **pæ**^rsikkor
a tube of mustard	**en tub senap**	ehn tēwb **sāy**nahp
a box of chocolates	**en ask choklad**	ehn ahsk shook**laa(d)**

Weights and measures
1 kilogram or kilo (kg.) = 1000 grams (g.)

100 g. = 3.5 oz.	½ kg. = 1.1 lb.
200 g. = 7.0 oz.	1 kg. = 2.2 lb.

1 oz. = 28.35 g.
1 lb. = 453.60 g.

1 litre (l.) = 0.88 imp. qt. or 1.06 U.S. qt.

1 imp. qt. = 1.14 l.	1 U.S. qt. = 0.95 l.
1 imp. gal. = 4.55 l.	1 U.S. gal. = 3.8 l.

FOOD, see also page 64

Jeweller's — Watchmaker's *Juvelerare – Urmakare*

Jeweller's are also known as *guldsmedsaffär*.

I want a present for ...	**Jag skulle vilja ha en present till ...**	yaa(g) skewler vilyah haa ehn prehsehnt til
Could I see that, please?	**Kan jag få se på det där?**	kahn yaa(g) faw sāy paw dāy(t) dǣr
Do you have anything in gold?	**Har ni någonting i guld?**	haar nee nawgonting ee gewld
How many carats is this?	**Hur många karat är det?**	hēwr mongah kahraat ǣr dāy(t)
Is this real silver?	**Är det här äkta silver?**	ǣr dāy(t) hǣr ehktah silverr
Can you engrave these initials on it?	**Kan ni gravera in de här initialerna?**	kahn nee grahvāyrah in dom hǣr initsiaaler^rnah
Can you repair this watch?	**Kan ni laga den här klockan?**	kahn nee laagah dehn hǣr klokkahn
I'd like a/an/some ...	**Jag skulle vilja ha ...**	yaa(g) skewler vilyah haa
alarm clock	**en väckarklocka**	ehn vehkahrklokkah
bangle	**en armring**	ehn ahrmring
battery	**ett batteri**	eht bahterree
bracelet	**ett armband**	eht ahrmbahnd
chain bracelet	**en armlänk**	ehn ahrmlehnk
charm bracelet	**ett berlockarmband**	eht ber^rlokkahrmbahnd
brooch	**en brosch**	ehn brawsh
chain	**en kedja**	ehn khāydyah
charm	**en berlock**	ehn ber^rlok
cigarette case	**ett cigarrettetui**	eht siggahrehtehtewee
cigarette lighter	**en cigarrettändare**	ehn siggahrehttehndahrer
clock	**en klocka**	ehn klokkah
cross	**ett kors**	eht ko^rss
cuff links	**ett par manschett-knappar**	eht paar mahnsheht-knahpahr
cutlery	**ett bestick**	eht berstik
earrings	**ett par örhängen**	eht paar ūrrhehngern
gem	**en ädelsten**	ehn aiderlstāyn
jewel box	**ett smyckeskrin**	eht smewkerskreen
mechanical pencil	**en stiftpenna**	ehn stiftpehnah
music box	**en speldosa**	ehn spāyldōōssah
necklace	**ett halsband**	eht hahlsbahnd
pendant	**ett hängsmycke**	eht hehngsmewker
pocket watch	**ett fickur**	eht fikēwr

powder compact	en puderdosa	ehn pewder'dōōssah
propelling pencil	en stiftpenna	ehn stiftpehnah
ring	en ring	ehn ring
engagement ring	en förlovningsring	ehn fur'lawvningsring
signet ring	en signetring	ehn signaytring
wedding ring	en vigselring	ehn vigserlring
silverware	något i silver	nawgot ee silverr
tie clip	en slipshållare	ehn slipshollahrer
tie pin	en kravattnål	ehn krahvahtnawl
watch	en klocka	ehn klokkah
automatic	automatisk	aa(ew)toomaatisk
digital	digital	diggitaal
quartz	quartz	kvah'tss
with a second hand	med sekundvisare	mayd sehkewndveessahrer
waterproof	vattentät	vahterntait
watchstrap	ett klockarmband	eht klokkahrmbahnd
wristwatch	ett armbandsur	eht ahrmbahndsewr

amber	bärnsten	bæ'nstayn
amethyst	ametist	ahmertist
chromium	krom	krawm
copper	koppar	koppahr
coral	korall	koorahl
crystal	kristall	kristahl
cut glass	slipat glas	sleepaht glaass
diamond	diamant	diahmahnt
emerald	smaragd	smahrahgd
enamel	emalj	ehmahly
gold	guld	gewld
gold plate	gulddoublé	gewl(d)doblay
ivory	elfenben	ehlfernbayn
jade	jade	yehyd
onyx	onyx	ōōnewkss
mother-of-pearl	pärlemor	pæ'lermōōr
pearl	pärla	pæ'lah
pewter	tenn	tehn
platinum	platina	plahteenah
ruby	rubin	rewbeen
sapphire	safir	sahfeer
silver	silver	silverr
silver plate	nysilver	newsilverr
stainless steel	rostfritt stål	rostfrit stawl
topaz	topas	toopaass
turquoise	turkos	tewrkōōss

Optician *Optiker*

I've broken my glasses.	**Mina glasögon har gått sönder.**	meenah **glaass**ūrgon haar got **surn**derr
Can you repair them for me?	**Kan ni laga dem åt mig?**	kahn nee **laa**gah dom awt may
When will they be ready?	**När är de klara?**	nǣr ǣr dom **klaa**rah
Can you change the lenses?	**Kan ni byta ut glasen?**	kahn nee **bēw**tah ēwt **glaa**ssern
I'd like tinted lenses.	**Jag skulle vilja ha färgade glas.**	yaa(g) **skew**ler **vil**yah haa **fær**yahder glaass
The frame is broken.	**Bågen har gått sönder.**	**baw**gern haar got **surn**derr
I'd like a glasses case.	**Jag skulle vilja ha ett glasögon-fodral.**	yaa(g) **skew**ler **vil**yah haa eht **glaass**ūrgon-**food**raal
I'd like to have my eyesight checked.	**Jag skulle vilja få min syn kontrollerad.**	yaa(g) **skew**ler **vil**yah faw min sēwn kontroll**ā**yrahd
I'm short-sighted/long-sighted.	**Jag är närsynt/långsynt.**	yaa(g) ǣr nǣ**ʳ**sēwnt/**long**sēwnt
I'd like some contact lenses.	**Jag skulle vilja ha kontaktlinser.**	yaa(g) **skew**ler **vil**yah haa kon**tahkt**linserr
I've lost one of my contact lenses.	**Jag har tappat en kontaktlins.**	yaa(g) haar **tah**paht ehn kon**tahkt**linss
Could you give me another one?	**Skulle jag kunna få en ny?**	**skew**ler yaa(g) **kew**nah faw ehn nēw
I have hard/soft lenses.	**Jag har hårda/mjuka linser.**	yaa(g) haar **haw**ʳdah/**myēw**kah linserr
Do you have any contact-lens fluid?	**Har ni någon kontaktlinsvätska?**	haar nee **naw**gon kon**tahkt**linsvehtskah
I'd like to buy a pair of sunglasses.	**Jag skulle vilja köpa ett par solglasögon.**	yaa(g) **skew**ler **vil**yah **khūr**pah eht paar **sool**glaassūrgon
May I look in the mirror?	**Får jag se i spegeln?**	fawr yaa(g) sāy ee **spāy**gerln
I'd like to buy a pair of binoculars.	**Jag skulle vilja köpa en kikare.**	yaa(g) **skew**ler **vil**yah **khūr**pah ehn **khee**kahrer

Photography   *Fotografering*

I'd like a(n) ... camera.	**Jag skulle vilja köpa en ... kamera.**	yaa(g) **skewl**er vi**lyah** kh**ūr**pah ehn ... **kaam**(er)rah
automatic	**automatisk**	aa(ew)too**maat**isk
inexpensive	**billig**	**bill**i(g)
simple	**enkel**	**ehn**kerl
Can you show me some ..., please?	**Kan jag få se på ...?**	kahn yaa(g) faw s**ā**y paw
cine (movie) cameras	**en filmkamera**	ehn **film**kaam(eh)rah
video cameras	**en videokamera**	ehn **veed**yokaam(eh)rah
I'd like to have some passport photos taken.	**Jag skulle vilja ha ett passfoto taget.**	yaa(g) **skewl**er vi**lyah** haa eht pahsf**ōō**too **taa**gert

Film   *Film*

I'd like a film for this camera.	**Jag skulle vilja ha film till den här kameran.**	yaa(g) **skewl**er vi**lyah** haa film til dehn h**ǣ**r **kaam**(er)rahn
black and white	**svart-vit**	svah**ʳ**t-veet
colour	**färg**	f**ǣ**ry
colour negative	**färgnegativ**	f**ǣ**ry**neh**gahteev
colour slide	**färgdiapositiv**	f**ǣ**ry**dee**ahpoositteev
cartridge	**en kassett**	ehn kah**sseh**t
disc film	**en disc**	ehn disk
roll film	**en filmrulle**	ehn **film**rewler
video cassette	**en videokassett**	ehn **veed**yokahsseht
24/36 exposures	**tjugofyra/trettiosex bilder**	kh**ēw**goof**ēw**rah/trehti-**sseh**ks **bild**err
this size	**det här formatet**	d**ā**y(t) h**ǣ**r for**maat**ert
this ASA/DIN number	**det här ASA/DIN numret**	d**ā**y(t) h**ǣ**r **aass**ah/deen **newm**rert
artificial light type	**för inomhusljus**	f**ū**rr innomh**ēw**sy**ēw**ss
daylight type	**för dagsljus**	f**ū**rr **dahgs**y**ēw**ss
fast (high-speed)	**snabb**	snahb
fine grain	**finkornig**	feenk**ōō**ʳnig

Processing   *Framkallning*

Does the price include processing?	**Ingår framkallning i priset?**	**in**gawr **frahm**kahlning ee **pree**sert

How much do you charge for processing?	**Hur mycket kostar framkallning?**	hewr mewker(t) kostahr frahmkahlning
I'd like ... prints of each negative.	**Jag skall be att få ... kopior av varje negativ.**	yaa(g) skahl bay aht faw ... koopeeoor aav vahryer nehgahteev
with a mat finish	**med matt yta**	mayd maht ewtah
with a glossy finish	**med glansig yta**	mayd glahnsi(g) ewtah
Will you enlarge this, please?	**Kan ni förstora det här?**	kahn nee fur'stoorah day(t) hær
When will the photos be ready?	**När blir korten klara?**	nær bleer koo'tern klaarah

Accessories and repairs   *Tillbehör och reparationer*

I'd like a/an/ some ...	**Jag skulle vilja ha ...**	yaa(g) skewler vilyah haa
battery	**ett batteri**	eht bahterree
cable release	**en trådutlösare**	ehn trawdewtlurssahrer
camera case	**ett kamerafodral**	eht kaam(er)rahfoodraal
(electronic) flash	**en (elektronisk) blixt**	ehn (ehlehktrawnisk) blikst
filter	**ett filter**	eht filterr
for black and white	**för svart-vit**	fürr svah't-vit
for colour	**för färg**	fürr færy
lens	**ett objektiv**	eht obyehkteev
telephoto lens	**ett teleobjektiv**	eht taylerobyehkteev
wide-angle lens	**ett vidvinkel-objektiv**	eht veedvinkerl-obyehkteev
lens cap	**ett linsskydd**	eht linsshewd
Can you repair this camera?	**Kan ni laga den här kameran?**	kahn nee laagah dehn hær kaam(er)rahn
The film is jammed.	**Filmen har fastnat.**	filmern haar fahsnaht
There's something wrong with the ...	**Det är något fel på ...**	day(t) ær nawgot fayl paw
exposure counter	**exponeringsmätaren**	ehkspoonnayrings-maitahrern
film winder	**frammatningen**	frahmmaatningern
flash attachment	**blixtaggregatet**	blikstahgrergaatert
lens	**objektivet**	obyehkteevert
light meter	**ljusmätaren**	yewsmaitahrern
rangefinder	**avståndsväljaren**	aavstondsvehlyahrern
shutter	**slutaren**	slewtahrern

NUMBERS, see page 147

126

Tobacconist's   *Tobaksaffär*

Tobacco is a state monopoly in Sweden. Virtually all international brands are available in tobacco shops, kiosks, supermarkets and so on. Sweden is especially known for its quality pipe tobaccos and snuff.

A packet of cigarettes, please.	**Ett paket cigarretter, tack.**	eht pahkāȳt siggahrehterr tahk
Do you have any American/English cigarettes?	**Har ni några amerikanska/engelska cigarretter?**	haar nee nawgrah ahm(er)rikaanskah/ehngerlskah siggahrehterr
Could I have a carton, please?	**Kan jag få en limpa, tack?**	kahn yaa(g) faw ehn limpah tahk
I'd like a/some …	**Jag skall be att få …**	yaa(g) skah(l) bāȳ aht faw
candy	**lite godis**	leeter gōōdiss
chewing gum	**ett tuggummi**	eht tewgewmi
chewing tobacco	**lite tuggtobak**	leeter tewgtōōbahk
chocolate bar	**en chokladkaka**	shooklaa(d)kaakah
cigarette case	**ett cigarrettetui**	eht siggahrehtehtēwee
cigarette holder	**ett cigarrettmunstycke**	eht siggahrehtmewnstewker
cigarettes	**cigarretter**	siggahrehterr
filter-tipped	**med filter**	māȳd filterr
without filter	**utan filter**	ēwtahn filterr
light/dark tobacco	**ljus/mörk tobak**	yēwss/murrk tōōbahk
mild/strong	**svaga/starka**	svaagah/stahrkah
menthol	**mentol-**	mehntawl
king-size	**king-size**	"king-size"
cigars	**några cigarrer**	nawgrah siggahrerr
lighter	**en tändare**	ehn tehndahrer
lighter fluid/gas	**bensin/gas till en tändare**	behnseen/gaass til ehn tehndahrer
matches	**tändstickor**	tehn(d)stikkoor
pipe	**en pipa**	ehn peepah
pipe cleaners	**piprensare**	peeprehnsahrer
pipe tobacco	**piptobak**	peeptōōbahk
pipe tool	**pipverktyg**	peepvǣrktēwg
postcard	**ett vykort**	eht vēwkoo͡rt
snuff	**en dosa snus**	ehn dōōssah snēwss
stamps	**några frimärken**	nawgrah freemǣrkern
sweets	**lite godis**	leeter gōōdiss
wick	**en veke**	ehn vāȳker

Miscellaneous *Diverse*

Souvenirs *Souvenirer*

Finding something typically Swedish to take home is not a problem. If anything, the choice is daunting. You'll find colourful textiles, modern pottery and silverware, leather goods, wood- and horncarvings. And, of course, beautiful glassware, even more tempting after seeing the glassblowers at work in "The Kingdom of Crystal", the glassmaking district near Växjö in southeastern Sweden.

And don't forget the wide range of edible souvenirs: sausages and salmon, smoked reindeer meat, caviar, canned herring, crispbread, not to mention aquavit.

I'd like a souvenir from ...	**Jag skulle vilja ha en souvenir från ...**	yaa(g) **skewler vil**yah haa ehn sooverneer frawn
Something typically Swedish, please.	**Något typiskt svenskt.**	nawgot tewpiskt svehnskt
ceramics	**keramik**	khehrahmeek
clogs	**träskor**	trǣskoor
Dala horse	**en dalahäst**	ehn daalahhehst
glassware	**glas**	glaass
bowl	**en skål**	ehn skawl
vase	**en vas**	ehn vaass
Lapp handicrafts	**sameslöjd**	saamersluryd
birch-bark work	**något i näver**	nawgot ee nǣverr
horn work	**något i horn**	nawgot ee hoōʳn
knife	**en kniv**	ehn kneev
silverware	**något i silver**	nawgot ee silverr
jewellery	**ett smycke**	eht smewker
textiles	**textilvaror**	tehksteelvaaroor
woodwork	**något i trä**	nawgot ee trǣ
butter knife	**en smörkniv**	ehn smǖrrkneev
candlestick	**en ljusstake**	ehn yēwsstaaker

Records — Cassettes *Skivor – Kassetter*

I'd like a ...	**Jag skulle vilja ha ...**	yaa(g) **skew**ler vilyah haa
cassette	**en kassett**	ehn kahsseht
video cassette	**en videokassett**	ehn veedyokahsseht
compact disc	**en CD-skiva**	ehn sāy-dāy sheevah

L.P. (33 rpm)	**LP (33 varvs)**	ehlpāy (trehtitrāy vahrvss)
E.P. (45 rpm)	**EP (45 varvs)**	āypāy (fur'tifehm vahrvss)
single	**singel**	singerl

Do you have any records by ...?	**Har ni några skivor med ...?**	haar nee nawgrah sheevoor māyd
Can I listen to this record?	**Kan jag få lyssna på den här skivan?**	kahn yaa(g) faw lewssnah paw dehn hār sheevahn
chamber music	**kammarmusik**	kahmahrmewsseek
classical music	**klassisk musik**	klahssisk mewsseek
folk music	**folkmusik**	folkmewsseek
folk songs	**folksånger**	folksawngerr
instrumental music	**instrumentalmusik**	instrewmehntaalmewsseek
jazz	**jazz**	yahss
light music	**lätt musik**	leht mewsseek
orchestral music	**orkestermusik**	orkehsterrmewsseek
pop music	**pop**	pop

Toys *Leksaker*

I'd like a toy/ game ...	**Jag skulle vilja ha en leksak/ ett spel ...**	yaa(g) skewler vilyah haa ehn lāyksaak/ eht spāyl
for a boy	**till en pojke**	til ehn poyker
for a 5-year-old girl	**till en 5-årig flicka**	til ehn 5-awrig flikkah
(beach) ball	**en (bad)boll**	ehn (baad)bol
bucket and spade (pail and shovel)	**hink och spade**	hink ok spaader
building blocks (bricks)	**byggklotsar**	bewgklossahr
card game	**ett kortspel**	eht koo'tspāyl
chess set	**ett schackspel**	eht shahkspāyl
doll	**en docka**	ehn dokkah
electronic game	**ett elektroniskt spel**	eht ehlehktrawniskt spāyl
roller skates	**ett par rull- skridskor**	eht paar rewl- skri(d)skōōr
snorkel	**en snorkel**	ehn snorkerl

Your money: banks—currency

At most banks there's sure to be someone who speaks English. You'll find small currency-exchange offices in most tourist centres, especially during the summer season. Remember to take your passport along with you, as you may need it for identification.

Traveller's cheques and credit cards are widely accepted in tourist-oriented shops, hotels, restaurants, etc. However, if you're exploring way off the beaten track, you'll probably come across village stores where they are not taken. The same goes for garages and filling stations—generally, only the main agency garages in the large cities will accept payment in traveller's cheques or by credit card.

Opening hours: Banks are closed all day Saturday, Sunday and on public holidays. Opening hours are from 9.30 a.m. to 3 p.m. Monday to Friday; some banks also open between 4.30 and 6 p.m. one day a week. At the main railway station in Stockholm and at Arlanda airport, the currency exchange offices are open all day, including weekends.

Monetary unit: The crown (*krona—kroo*nah, plural *kronor—kroo*noor), is the monetary unit of Sweden, Norway and Denmark, but its value differs in each country. The krona (abbreviation *kr*) is divided into 100 *öre* (ūrrer).

Coins: 10 and 50 öre, 1 and 5 kronor.
Banknotes: 10, 50, 100, 500, 1,000 and 10,000 kronor.

Where's the nearest bank?	**Var ligger närmaste bank?**	vaar liggerr nærmahster bahnk
Where's the nearest currency exchange office?	**Var ligger närmaste växelkontor?**	vaar liggerr nærmahster vehkserlkontōōr
When is it open?	**När är det öppet?**	nær ær dāy(t) urpert

At the bank   *På banken*

| I'd like to change some dollars/pounds. | **Jag skulle vilja växla några dollar/ pund.** | yaa(g) **skew**ler **vil**yah **vehk**slah **naw**grah **dol**lahr/ pewnd |

I'd like to change some dollars/pounds. — **Jag skulle vilja växla några dollar/pund.** — yaa(g) **skew**ler **vil**yah **vehk**slah **naw**grah **dol**lahr/pewnd

I'd like to cash a traveller's cheque. — **Jag skulle vilja lösa in en resecheck.** — yaa(g) **skew**ler **vil**yah **lūr**ssah in ehn **rāy**sserkhehk

What's the exchange rate? — **Vilken är växelkursen?** — **vil**kern ǣr **vehk**serlkew**r**sern

How much commission do you charge? — **Hur stor är expeditionsavgiften?** — hēwr stōōr ǣr ehks-pehdish**ōōn**saavyiftern

Can you cash a personal cheque? — **Kan ni lösa in en personlig check?** — kahn nee **lūr**ssah in ehn pǣ**r**sh**ōō**nlig khehk

Can you telex my bank in London? — **Kan ni skicka ett telex till min bank i London?** — kahn nee **shik**kah eht **tāy**lehks til min bahnk ee **lon**don

I have a/an/some ... — **Jag har ...** — yaa(g) haar

credit card — **kreditkort** — kreh**deet**koo**r**t
Eurocheques — **Eurochecker** — ehew**rook**hehkerr
letter of credit — **en remburs** — ehn rehm**bew**r**s**

I'm expecting some money from New York. Has it arrived? — **Jag väntar pengar från New York. Har de kommit?** — yaa(g) **vehn**tahr **pehng**ahr frawn new york. haar dom **kom**mit

Please give me ... in notes (bills) and some small change. — **Kan jag få ... i sedlar och lite växel, tack?** — kahn yaa(g) faw ... ee **sāy**dlahr ok **lee**ter **vehk**serl tahk

Give me ... in large notes and the rest in small notes. — **Kan jag få ... i stora sedlar och resten i små sedlar?** — kahn yaa(g) faw ... ee st**ōō**rah **sāy**dlahr ok **reh**stern ee smaw **sāy**dlahr

Deposits — Withdrawals   *Insättning – Uttag*

I'd like to ... — **Jag skulle vilja ...** — yaa(g) **skew**ler **vil**yah

open an account — **öppna ett konto** — **urp**nah eht **kon**too
withdraw ... crowns — **ta ut ... kronor** — taa ēwt ... **krōō**noor

Where should I sign? — **Var skall jag skriva under?** — vaar skah(l) yaa(g) **skree**vah **ewn**derr

NUMBERS, see page 147

| I'd like to pay this into my account. | **Jag skulle vilja sätta in det här på mitt konto.** | yaa(g) skewler vilyah sehtah in dāȳ(t) hǣr paw mit kontoo |

Business terms *Affärstermer*

My name is ...	**Mitt namn är ...**	mit nahmn ǣr
Here's my card.	**Här är mitt kort.**	hǣr ǣr mit koorʳt
I have an appointment with ...	**Jag har avtalat ett möte med ...**	yaa(g) haar aavtaalaht eht mūrter māȳd
Can you give me an estimate of the cost?	**Kan ni ge mig en uppskattning av kostnaden?**	kahn nee yāȳ may ehn ewpskahtning aav kostnahdern
What's the rate of inflation?	**Hur hög är inflationen?**	hēwr hūrg ǣr inflahshōōnern
Can you provide me with an interpreter/ a secretary?	**Kan ni skaffa mig en tolk/ en sekreterare?**	kahn nee skahffah may ehn tolk/ ehn sehkrertāȳrahrer
Where can I make photocopies?	**Var kan jag göra fotokopior?**	vaar kahn yaa(g) yūrrah fōōtookoopeeor

amount	**en summa**	ehn sewmah
balance	**en balansräkning**	ehn bahlahnsraikning
capital	**ett kapital**	eht kahpitaal
cheque book	**ett checkhäfte**	eht khehkhehfter
contract	**ett kontrakt**	eht kontrahkt
discount	**en rabatt**	ehn rahbaht
expenses	**omkostnader**	omkostnahderr
interest	**en ränta**	ehn rehntah
investment	**en investering**	ehn invehstāȳring
invoice	**en faktura**	ehn fahktēwrah
loss	**en förlust**	ehn furʳlewst
mortgage	**ett hypotek**	eht hewpootāȳk
payment	**en betalning**	ehn bertaalning
percentage	**en procentsats**	ehn proosehntsahtss
profit	**en vinst**	ehn vinst
purchase	**ett köp**	eht khūrp
sale	**en försäljning**	ehn furʳsehlyning
share	**en aktie**	ehn ahktsier
transfer	**en överföring**	ehn ūrverrfurring
value	**ett värde**	eht vǣʳder

At the post office

The post office only handles mail; for telephone and telegram or telex services you have to go to a *Tele* office.

Post offices are indicated by a yellow sign with a blue horn, and mailboxes are also bright yellow except those for local mail which are blue. Business hours are generally from 9 a.m. to 6 p.m., Monday to Friday, but they might change in the summer months. The main post office in Stockholm is open from 7 a.m. to 9 p.m., Monday to Friday, and 10 a.m. to 1 p.m. on Saturdays.

In bigger post offices there's a queue system: you take a number when you enter. It will come up on a screen together with the number of the free window when it's your turn (there's a beep every time the number changes).

Where's the nearest post office?	**Var ligger närmaste postkontor?**	vaar liggerr nærmahster postkontōōr
What time does the post office open/close?	**Hur dags öppnar/ stänger posten?**	hēwr dahgss urpnahr/ stehngerr postern
A stamp for this letter/postcard, please.	**Ett frimärke till det här brevet/ kortet, tack.**	eht freemærker til dāȳ(t) hær brāȳvert/ kooᶠtert tahk
A ...-öres stamp, please.	**Ett ... -öres frimärke, tack.**	eht ... -ūrrerss freemærker tahk
What's the postage for a letter to England?	**Vad är portot för ett brev till England?**	vaad ær poᶠtot fūr eht brāȳv til englahnd
What's the postage for a postcard to the U.S.A.?	**Vad är portot för ett vykort till USA?**	vaad ær poᶠtot fūr eht vēwkooᶠt til ēwehssaa
Where's the letter box (mailbox)?	**Var är brevlådan?**	vaar ær brāȳvlawdahn
I want to send this parcel.	**Jag vill skicka det här paketet.**	yaa(g) vil shikkah dāȳ(t) hær pahkāȳtert

I'd like to send this by ...	**Jag vill skicka det här ...**	yaa(g) vil **shikkah** d$\overline{ay}$(t) h$\overline{æ}$r
airmail	**med flyg**	m$\overline{ay}$d fl$\overline{ew}$g
express (special delivery)	**express**	ehk**sprehss**
registered mail	**rekommenderat**	rehkommernd$\overline{ay}$raht
At which counter can I cash an international money order?	**I vilken lucka kan jag lösa in en internationell postanvisning?**	ee **vilkern lewkah** kahn yaa(g) **lurssah** in ehn interrnahtshoo**nehl** postahnveesning
Where's the poste restante (general delivery)?	**Var är poste restanteluckan?**	vaar $\overline{æ}$r post rehstahnterlewkahn
Is there any post (mail) for me?	**Finns det någon post till mig?**	finss d$\overline{ay}$(t) **naw**gon post til may
My name is ...	**Mitt namn är ...**	mit nahmn $\overline{æ}$r

FRIMÄRKEN	STAMPS
PAKET	PARCELS
POSTANVISNINGAR	MONEY ORDERS

Telegrams *Telegram*

Where's the nearest telegraph office?	**Var ligger närmaste telegraf?**	vaar **liggerr nærmahster** tehleh**graaf**
I'd like to send a ...	**Jag skulle vilja skicka ett ...**	yaa(g) **skewler vilyah** shikkah eht
fax/telegram/telex	**telefax/telegram/telex**	tehleh**fahkss**/tehleh**grahm**/t$\overline{ay}$lehks
May I have a form, please?	**Kan jag få en blankett, tack?**	kahn yaa(g) faw ehn blahn**keht** tahk
How much is it per word?	**Vad kostar det per ord?**	vaad **kostahr** d$\overline{ay}$(t) p$\overline{æ}$r $\overline{oo}^r$d
How long will a cable to Boston take?	**Hur lång tid tar ett telegram till Boston?**	h$\overline{ew}$r long teed taar eht tehleh**grahm** til boston
How much will this telex cost?	**Hur mycket kostar det här telexet?**	h$\overline{ew}$r **mewkert kostahr** d$\overline{ay}$(t) h$\overline{æ}$r **t$\overline{ay}$lehks**ert

Post

Telephoning *Telefon*

The telephone system in Sweden is entirely automatic. International or long-distance calls can be made from phone booths, but if you need help in making a call, go to the special telegraph offices marked *Tele* or *Telebutik*. Dialling instructions in foreign languages, including English, are posted inside the booth or can be found at the front of every telephone directory.

To call Britain from Sweden dial 00944, wait for a second dialling tone and then dial the number minus the initial 0 in the dialling (area) code. For the U.S.A. the prefix is 0091.

Where's the telephone?	**Var är telefonen?**	vaar ǣr tehlehfawnern
Where's the nearest telephone booth?	**Var finns närmaste telefonkiosk?**	vaar finss nærmahster tehlehfawnkhiosk
May I use your phone?	**Får jag låna telefonen?**	fawr yaa(g) lawnah tehlehfawnern
Do you have a telephone directory for Uppsala?	**Har ni en telefonkatalog över Uppsala?**	haar nee ehn tehlehfawnkahtahlawg ūrverr ewpsaalah
I'd like to call someone in England.	**Jag vill ringa någon i England.**	yaa(g) vil ringah nawgon ee ehnglahnd
What's the dialling (area) code for ...?	**Vad är riktnumret till ...?**	vaad ǣr riktnewmrert til
How do I get the international operator?	**Vilket nummer är det till utlands-telefonisten?**	vilkert newmerr ǣr dāȳ(t) til ēwtlahn(d)stehlehfonnistern

Operator *Telefonist*

I'd like Lund 23 45 67.	**Jag vill ha ett samtal till Lund, nummer 23 45 67.**	yaa(g) vil haa eht sahmtaal til lewnd newmerr 23 45 67
Can you help me get this number?	**Kan ni hjälpa mig att komma till det här numret?**	kahn nee yehlpah may aht kommah til dāȳ(t) til hǣr newmrert
I'd like to place a personal (person-to-person) call.	**Jag vill beställa ett personligt samtal.**	yaa(g) vil berstehlah eht pæ^rshōōnli(g)t sahmtaal

NUMBERS, see page 147

| I'd like to reverse the charges (call collect). | **Jag skulle vilja beställa ett Ba-samtal.** | yaa(g) **skew**ler vilyah ber**steh**lah eht **bā**yaa-sahmtaal |

Telephone alphabet *Bokstaveringsalfabet*

A	**Adam**	aadahm	P	**Petter**	**peh**terr
B	**Bertil**	bǣ{'}til	Q	**Qvintus**	**kvin**tewss
C	**Cesar**	**sāy**ssahr	R	**Rudolf**	**rēw**dolf
D	**David**	**daa**vid	S	**Sigurd**	**see**gew{'}d
E	**Erik**	**āy**rik	T	**Tore**	**tōo**rer
F	**Filip**	**fee**lip	U	**Urban**	**ewr**bahn
G	**Gustav**	**gew**stahv	V	**Viktor**	viktor
H	**Helge**	**heh**lger	W	**Wilhelm**	vil**heh**lm
I	**Ivar**	**ee**vahr	X	**Xerxes**	**ksehrk**sehss
J	**Johan**	**yōo**(h)ahn	Y	**Yngve**	**ewng**ver
K	**Kalle**	**kah**ler	Z	**Zäta**	**sai**tah
L	**Ludvig**	**lewd**vig	Å	**Åke**	**aw**ker
M	**Martin**	**mah**{'}tin	Ä	**Ärlig**	**ǣ**{'}lig
N	**Niklas**	**nik**lahss	Ö	**Östen**	**ur**stern
O	**Olof**	**ōo**lof			

Speaking *Samtal*

Hello. This is ...	**Hallå, det här är ...**	hah**law** dāy(t) hǣr ǣr
I'd like to speak to ...	**Kan jag få tala med ...?**	kahn yaa(g) faw **taa**lah māyd
Extension ...	**Anknytning ...**	**ahn**knēwtning
Speak louder/more slowly, please.	**Kan ni tala lite högre/långsammare, tack?**	kahn nee **taa**lah **lee**ter **hū**grer/**long**sahmahrer tahk

Bad luck *Otur*

| Would you try again later, please? | **Kan ni försöka igen lite senare?** | kahn nee fur{'}**sū**rkah ee**yehn leeter sāy**nahrer |
| Operator, you gave me the wrong number. | **Jag tror ni gav mig fel nummer.** | yaa(g) trōor nee gaav may fāyl **new**merr |

Operator, we were cut off. — **Hallå, vi blev avbrutna.** — hahlaw vee blāȳv aavbrēw̄tnah

Not there *Inte inne*

When will he/she be back? — **När kommer han/ hon tillbaka?** — nǣr kommerr hahn/ hoon tilbaakah

Will you tell him/her I called? — **Kan ni tala om för honom/henne att jag har ringt?** — kahn nee taalah om fū̄r honnom/hehner aht yaa(g) haar ringt

My name is ... — **Mitt namn är ...** — mit nahmn ǣr

Would you ask him/her to phone me? — **Skulle ni kunna be honom/henne ringa mig?** — skewler nee kewnah bāȳ honnom/hehner ringah may

Would you take a message, please? — **Skulle ni kunna lämna ett meddelande?** — skewler nee kewnah lehmnah eht māȳdāȳlahnder

Charges *Avgifter*

How much did the call cost? — **Hur mycket kostade samtalet?** — hēw̄r mewkert kostahder sahmtaalert

I'd like to pay for the call. — **Jag skulle vilja betala samtalet.** — yaa(g) skewler vilyah bertaalah sahmtaalert

---

Det är telefon till er.	There's a telephone call for you.
Vilket nummer ringer ni?	What number are you calling?
Det är upptaget.	The line's engaged.
Det är ingen som svarar.	There's no answer.
Ni har slagit fel nummer.	You've got the wrong number.
Telefonen är trasig.	The phone is out of order.
Ett ögonblick.	Just a moment.
Var god dröj.	Hold on, please.
Han/hon är ute för ögonblicket.	He's/She's out at the moment.

Doctor

British subjects are covered by Sweden's national health insurance plan. Other nationalities should check to see if their health insurance policy covers medical treatment in Sweden before leaving home.

General *Allmänt*

Can you get me a doctor?	**Kan ni skaffa mig en läkare?**	kahn nee skahfah may ehn laikahrer
Is there a doctor here?	**Finns det någon läkare här?**	finss dāy(t) nawgon laikahrer hǣr
I need a doctor, quickly.	**Jag behöver en läkare fort.**	yaa(g) berhūrverr ehn laikahrer foo^rt
Where can I find a doctor who speaks English?	**Var kan jag få tag på en läkare som talar engelska?**	vaar kahn yaa(g) faw taag paw ehn laikahrer som taalahr engerlskah
Where's the surgery (doctor's office)?	**Var ligger läkarmottagningen?**	vaar liggerr laikahr-mōōtaagningern
What are the surgery (office) hours?	**Vilka är mottagningstiderna?**	vilkah ǣr mōōtaagnings-teeder^rnah
Could the doctor come to see me here?	**Kan doktorn komma hit och undersöka mig?**	kahn dokto^rn kommah heet ok ewnder^rsūrkah may
What time can the doctor come?	**Hur dags kan doktorn komma?**	hēwr dahgss kahn dokto^rn kommah
Can you recommend a/an ...?	**Kan ni rekommendera en ...?**	kahn nee rehkom-merndāyrah ehn
general practitioner	**allmänpraktiker**	ahlmehnprahktikkerr
children's doctor	**barnläkare**	baa^rnlaikahrer
eye specialist	**ögonspecialist**	ūrgonspehssiahlist
gynaecologist	**gynekolog**	yewnerkoolawg
Can I have an appointment ...?	**Kan jag få en tid ...?**	kahn yaa(g) faw ehn teed
tomorrow	**i morgon**	ee morron
as soon as possible	**så snart som möjligt**	saw snaa^rt som muryli(g)t

CHEMIST'S, see page 108

Parts of the body *Kroppsdelar*

appendix	**blindtarmen**	blin(d)tahrmern
arm	**armen**	ahrmern
artery	**pulsådern**	pewlsawder^{r}n
back	**ryggen**	rewgern
bladder	**urinblåsan**	ēwreenblawssahn
bone	**benen (i kroppen)**	bāȳnern (ee kroppern)
bowel	**tarmen**	tahrmern
breast	**bröstet**	brurstert
chest	**bröstkorgen**	brurstkoryern
ear	**örat**	ūrraht
face	**ansiktet**	ahnsiktert
finger	**fingret**	fingrert
foot	**foten**	fōōtern
genitals	**könsorganen**	khūrnsorgaanern
gland	**körteln**	khur^{r}terln
hand	**handen**	hahndern
head	**huvudet**	hēwv(ewd)ert
heart	**hjärtat**	yæ^{r}taht
jaw	**käken**	khaikern
joint	**leden**	lāȳdern
kidney	**njuren**	nyēwrern
knee	**knä(e)t**	knai(e)t
leg	**benet**	bāȳnert
lip	**läppen**	lehpern
liver	**levern**	lāȳver^{r}n
lung	**lungan**	lewngahn
mouth	**munnen**	mewnern
muscle	**muskeln**	mewskerln
neck	**nacken**	nahkern
nerve	**nerven**	nærvern
nervous system	**nervsystemet**	nærvsewstāȳmert
nose	**näsan**	naissahn
rib	**revbenet**	rāȳvbāȳnert
shoulder	**skuldran/axeln**	skewldrahn/ahkserln
skin	**huden**	hēwdern
spine	**ryggraden**	rewgraadern
stomach	**magen**	maagern
tendon	**senan**	sāȳnahn
thigh	**låret**	lawrert
throat	**halsen**	hahlsern
thumb	**tummen**	tewmern
toe	**tån**	tawn
tongue	**tungan**	tewngahn
tonsils	**mandlarna**	mahndlah^{r}nah
vein	**venen/ådern**	vāȳnern/awder^{r}n

Accident—Injury   *Olycksfall – Skada*

There's been an accident.	**Det har hänt en olycka.**	dāȳ(t) haar hehnt ehn ōōlewkah
My child has had a fall.	**Mitt barn har ramlat.**	mit baaʳn haar rahmlaht
He/She has hurt his/her head.	**Han/Hon har slagit sig i huvudet.**	hahn/hoon haar slaagit say ee hēwv(ewd)ert
He's/She's unconscious.	**Han/Hon är medvetslös.**	hahn/hoon ǣr māȳdvāȳtslūrss
He's/She's bleeding (heavily).	**Han/Hon blöder (kraftigt).**	hahn/hoon blūrderr (krahftigt)
He's/She's (seriously) injured.	**Han/Hon är (allvarligt) skadad.**	hahn/hoon ǣr (ahlvaaʳligt) skaadahd
His/Her ankle is swollen.	**Hans/Hennes vrist är svullen.**	hahnss/hehnerss vrist ǣr svewlern
I've broken my arm.	**Jag har brutit armen.**	yaa(g) haar brēwtit ahrmern
I've been stung.	**Jag har blivit biten.**	yaa(g) haar bleevit beetern
I've got something in my eye.	**Jag har fått något i ögat.**	yaa(g) haar fot nawgot ee ūrgaht
I've got a/an ...	**Jag har (fått) ...**	yaa(g) haar (fot)
blister	**en blåsa**	ehn blawssah
boil	**en böld**	ehn burld
bruise	**ett blåmärke**	eht blawmærker
bump	**en bula**	ehn bēwlah
burn	**ett brännsår**	eht brehnsawr
cut	**ett skärsår**	eht shæʳsawr
graze	**ett skrubbsår**	eht skrewbsawr
insect bite	**ett insektsbett**	eht insehktsbeht
lump	**en knöl**	ehn knūrl
rash	**ett utslag**	eht ēwtslaag
sting	**ett stick**	eht stik
swelling	**en svullnad**	ehn svewlnahd
wound	**ett sår**	eht sawr
Could you have a look at it?	**Skulle ni kunna titta på det?**	skewler nee kewnah tittah paw dāȳ(t)
I can't move my ...	**Jag kan inte röra ...**	yaa(g) kahn inter rūrrah
It hurts.	**Det gör ont.**	dāȳ(t) yūrr oont

Var gör det ont?	Where does it hurt?
Vad för slags smärta är det?	What kind of pain is it?
dov/intensiv/ pulserande/konstant/ kommer och går	dull/sharp/ throbbing/constant/ on and off
Det är ...	It's ...
brutet/vrickat/ur led	broken/sprained/dislocated
Ni har ett avslitet ligament.	You have a torn ligament.
Vi måste ta en röntgenbild.	I'd like you to have an X-ray.
Vi måste gipsa det.	We'll have to put it in plaster.
Det är infekterat.	It's infected.
Har ni vaccinerats mot stelkramp?	Have you been vaccinated against tetanus?
Jag skall ge er något smärtstillande.	I'll give you a painkiller.

Illness *Sjukdom*

I'm not feeling well.	**Jag mår inte bra.**	yaa(g) mawr inter braa
I'm ill.	**Jag är sjuk.**	yaa(g) ær shēwk
I feel ...	**Jag känner mig ...**	yaa(g) khehnerr may
dizzy	**yr**	ēwr
nauseous	**illamående**	illahmawehnder
weak	**svag**	svaag
I feel shivery.	**Jag har frossbrytningar.**	yaa(g) haar frosbrēwtningahr
I have a temperature (fever).	**Jag har feber.**	yaa(g) haar fāyberr
I've been vomiting.	**Jag har kräkts.**	yaa(g) haar kraiktss
I'm constipated.	**Jag har förstoppning.**	yaa(g) haar furᵣstopning
I've got diarrhoea.	**Jag har diarré.**	yaa(g) haar diahrāy
My ... hurt(s).	**Jag har ont i ...**	yaa(g) haar oont ee

I've got (a/an) ...	Jag har ...	yaa(g) haar
asthma	**astma**	**ahst**mah
backache	**ont i ryggen**	oont ee **rew**gern
cough	**hosta**	**hoo**stah
cramps	**kramp**	krahmp
earache	**ont i örat**	oont ee u**r̄r̄**aht
hay fever	**hösnuva**	**hūr**snēwvah
headache	**huvudvärk**	**hēw**vew(d)værk
indigestion	**dålig matsmältning**	**dawl**i(g) **maats**mehltning
nosebleed	**näsblod**	**nais**blōōd
palpitations	**hjärtklappning**	**yæᵣt**klahpning
rheumatism	**reumatism**	**reh**mah**tism**
sore throat	**ont i halsen**	oont ee **hahl**sern
stiff neck	**stel nacke**	**stāyl nah**ker
stomach ache	**ont i magen**	oont ee **maa**gern
sunstroke	**solsting**	**sōōl**sting

I've got a cold.	**Jag är förkyld.**	yaa(g) ær fur**ᵣkhēw**ld
I have difficulties breathing.	**Jag har svårt att andas.**	yaa(g) haar svaw**ᵣ**t aht **ahn**dahss
I have chest pains.	**Jag har ont i bröstet.**	yaa(g) haar oont ee **brur**stert
I had a heart attack ... years ago.	**Jag hade en hjärt-attack för ... år sedan.**	yaa(g) **hah**der ehn **yæᵣt**-ah**tahk** fū**r̄r̄** ... awr **seh**n
My blood pressure is too high/too low.	**Mitt blodtryck är för högt/för lågt.**	mit **blōō(d)**trewk ær fū**r̄r̄** hurgt/lawgt
I'm allergic to ...	**Jag är allergisk mot ...**	yaa(g) ær ah**lær**gisk mōōt
I'm diabetic.	**Jag är diabetiker.**	yaa(g) ær diah**bāȳ**tikkerr

Women's section *För kvinnor*

I have period pains.	**Jag har mens-(truations)smärtor.**	yaa(g) haar **mehns**-(trewah**shōōns**)smæ**ᵣ**toor
I have a vaginal infection.	**Jag har en infektion i underlivet.**	yaa(g) haar ehn infehk-**shōōn** ee ewnderr**lee**vert
I'm on the pill.	**Jag tar p-piller.**	yaa(g) taar **pāȳ**-pillerr
I haven't had a period for 2 months.	**Jag har inte haft mens(truation) på 2 månader.**	yaa(g) haar **in**terr hahft mehns(trewah**shōōn**) paw 2 **maw**nahderr
I'm pregnant.	**Jag är gravid.**	yaa(g) ær grah**veed**

Hur länge har ni känt er så här?	How long have you been feeling like this?
Är det första gången ni har det här?	Is this the first time you've had this?
Jag skall ta temperaturen/ blodtrycket.	I'll take your temperature/ blood pressure.
Kavla upp ärmen, tack.	Roll up your sleeve, please.
Var snäll och klä av er (på överkroppen).	Please undress (down to the waist).
Var snäll och lägg er här.	Please lie down over here.
Öppna munnen.	Open your mouth.
Andas djupt.	Breathe deeply.
Hosta.	Cough, please.
Var gör det ont?	Where does it hurt?
Ni har ...	You've got (a/an) ...
en allergi	allergy
blindtarmsinflammation	appendicitis
gulsot	jaundice
en inflammation i ...	inflammation of ...
influensa	flu
en könssjukdom	venereal disease
lunginflammation	pneumonia
en magförgiftning	food poisoning
en magkatarr	gastritis
mässling	measles
urinvägsinfektion	cystitis
Det smittar (inte).	It's (not) contagious.
Jag skall ge er en spruta.	I'll give you an injection.
Jag vill ha ett blodprov/ avföringsprov/urinprov.	I want a specimen of your blood/stools/urine.
Ni bör ligga till sängs i ... dagar.	You must stay in bed for ... days.
Jag vill att ni vänder er till en specialist.	I want you to see a specialist.
Jag vill att ni gör en allmän hälsokontroll på sjukhuset.	I want you to go to the hospital for a general check-up.

Prescription—Treatment   *Ordination – Behandling*

This is my usual medicine.	**Det här är min vanliga medicin.**	dāy(t) hǣr ǣr min **vaanliggah mehdisseen**
Can you give me a prescription for this?	**Kan ni ge mig ett recept på det här?**	kahn nee yāy māy eht **rehsehpt** paw dāy(t) hǣr
Can you prescribe a/an/some ...?	**Kan ni skriva ut ...**	kahn nee **skreevah ēwt**
antidepressant	**något mot depression**	nawgot mōōt dehprershōōn
sleeping pills	**några sömntabletter**	nawgrah **surmntahblehterr**
tranquillizer	**något nervlugnande**	nawgot **nærvlewngnahnder**
I'm allergic to certain antibiotics/ penicillin.	**Jag är allergisk mot viss antibiotika/ penicillin.**	yaa(g) ǣr ahlehrgisk mōōt viss ahntibiawtikkah/ pehnissileen
I don't want anything too strong.	**Jag vill inte ha någonting för starkt.**	yaa(g) vil inter haa nawgonting fūrr stahrkt
How many times a day should I take it?	**Hur många gånger om dagen skall jag ta det?**	hēwr mongah gongerr om daa(ger)n skah(l) yaa(g) taa dāy(t)
Must I swallow them whole?	**Måste jag svälja dem hela?**	moster yaa(g) svehlyah dom hāylah

---

 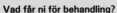

Vad får ni för behandling?	What treatment are you having?
Vilken medicin tar ni?	What medicine are you taking?
Intravenöst eller oralt?	By injection or orally?
Ta ... teskedar av den här medicinen ...	Take ... teaspoons of this medicine ...
Ta en tablett med ett glas vatten ...	Take one pill with a glass of water ...
var ... timme	every ... hours
... gånger om dagen	... times a day
före/efter varje måltid	before/after each meal
på morgonen/på kvällen	in the morning/at night
vid smärta	if there is any pain
i ... dagar	for ... days

CHEMIST'S, see page 108

Fee *Arvode*

How much do I owe you?	**Hur mycket är jag skyldig?**	hewr mewker(t) ǣr yaa(g) shewldig
May I have a receipt for my health insurance?	**Kan jag få ett kvitto för min sjukförsäkring?**	kahn yaa(g) faw eht kvitto fūrr min shewkfur^rsaikring
Can I have a medical certificate?	**Kan jag få ett läkarintyg?**	kahn yaa(g) faw eht laikahrintēwg
Would you fill in this health insurance form, please?	**Skulle ni kunna fylla i den här sjukförsäkrings-blanketten?**	skewler nee kewnah fewlah ee dehn hǣr shewkfur^rsaikrings-blahnkehtern

Hospital *Sjukhus*

Please notify my family.	**Var snäll och under-rätta min familj.**	vaar snehl ok ewnder-rehtah min fahmily
What are the visiting hours?	**När är det besöks-tid?**	nǣr ǣr dāy(t) bāysūrks-teed?
When can I get up?	**När får jag stiga upp?**	nǣr fawr yaa(g) steegah ewp
When will the doctor come?	**När kommer doktorn?**	nǣr kommer dokto^rn
I'm in pain.	**Jag har ont.**	yaa(g) haar oont
I can't eat/sleep.	**Jag kan inte äta/sova.**	yaa(g) kahn inter aitah/sawvah
Where is the bell?	**Var är ringklockan?**	vaar ǣr ringklokkahn

nurse	**en sköterska**	ehn shūrter^rskah
patient	**en patient**	ehn pahssiehnt
anaesthetic	**en narkos**	ehn nahrkawss
blood transfusion	**en blodtransfusion**	ehn blōōdtrahnsfewshōōn
injection	**en injektion**	ehn inyehkshōōn
operation	**en operation**	ehn ooperrahshōōn
bed	**en säng**	ehn sehng
bedpan	**ett bäcken**	eht behkehn
thermometer	**en termometer**	ehn tehrmomāyterr

Dentist   *Tandläkare*

Can you recommend a good dentist?	**Kan ni rekommendera en bra tandläkare?**	kahn nee rehkommerndāȳrah ehn braa tahn(d)laikahrer
Can I make an (urgent) appointment to see Dr...?	**Kan jag få en tid (så fort som möjligt) hos doktor ...?**	kahn yaa(g) faw ehn teed (saw foo^rt som muryli(g)t) hooss doktor
Couldn't you make it earlier?	**Går det inte tidigare?**	gawr dāȳ(t) inter teediggahrer
I have a broken tooth.	**Jag har bitit av en tand.**	yaa(g) haar beetit aav ehn tahnd
I have a loose tooth.	**Jag har en lös tand.**	yaa(g) haar ehn lūrss tahnd
I have a toothache.	**Jag har tandvärk.**	yaa(g) haar tahn(d)værk
Is it an abscess?	**Är det en varbildning?**	ǣr dāȳ(t) ehn vaarbildning
This tooth hurts.	**Den här tanden gör ont.**	dehn hǣr tahndern yūrr oont
at the top/bottom at the front/back	**där uppe/nere där framme/bak**	dǣr ewper/nāȳrer dǣr frahmer/baak
Can you fix it temporarily?	**Kan ni laga den provisoriskt?**	kahn nee laagah dehn proovissōōriskt
I don't want it taken out.	**Jag vill inte ha den utdragen.**	yaa(g) vil inter haa dehn ēwtdraagern
Could you give me an anaesthetic?	**Kan jag få bedövning?**	kahn yaa(g) faw berdūrvning
I've lost a filling.	**Jag har tappat en plomb.**	yaa(g) haar tahphaht ehn plomb
The gums ...	**Tandköttet ...**	tahn(d)khurtert
are very sore are bleeding	**är mycket ömt blöder**	ǣr mewker(t) urmt blūrderr
I've broken my dentures.	**Min tandprotes har gått sönder.**	min tahn(d)prootāȳss haar got surnderr
Can you repair my dentures?	**Kan ni laga min tandprotes?**	kahn nee laagah min tahn(d)prootāȳss
When will they be ready?	**När blir den klar?**	nǣr bleer dehn klaar

Reference section

Where do you come from?   *Varifrån kommer ni?*

I'm from …	Jag är från …	yaa(g) ær frawn
Africa	**Afrika**	aafrikkah
Asia	**Asien**	aassiern
Australia	**Australien**	aaewstraaliern
Europe	**Europa**	ehewrōōpah
North America	**Nordamerika**	nōō^rdahmāyrikkah
South America	**Sydamerika**	sēwdahmāyrikkah
Austria	**Österrike**	ursterreeker
Belgium	**Belgien**	behlgiern
Canada	**Kanada**	kahnahdah
China	**Kina**	kheenah
Denmark	**Danmark**	dahnmahrk
England	**England**	englahnd
Finland	**Finland**	finlahnd
France	**Frankrike**	frahnkrikker
Germany	**Tyskland**	tewsklahnd
Great Britain	**Storbritannien**	stōōrbrittahniern
Greece	**Grekland**	grāyklahnd
Hungary	**Ungern**	ewngerrn
Iceland	**Island**	eeslahnd
India	**Indien**	indiern
Ireland	**Irland**	irlahnd
Israel	**Israel**	eesraherl
Italy	**Italien**	itaaliern
Japan	**Japan**	yaapahn
Luxembourg	**Luxemburg**	lewksermbewry
Netherlands	**Nederländerna/**	nāyderrlehnder^rnah/
	Holland	hollahnd
New Zealand	**Nya Zealand**	nēwah sāylahnd
Norway	**Norge**	noryer
Poland	**Polen**	polern
Portugal	**Portugal**	po^rtewgahl
Russia	**Ryssland**	rewsslahnd
Scotland	**Skottland**	skotlahnd
South Africa	**Sydafrika**	sēwdaafrikkah
Spain	**Spanien**	spahniern
Sweden	**Sverige**	sværyer
Switzerland	**Schweiz**	shvehytss
Turkey	**Turkiet**	tewrkeeert
United States	**USA**	ēwehssaa
Wales	**Wales**	"wales"

Numbers *Räkneord*

0	**noll**	nol
1	**ett**	eht
2	**två**	tvaw
3	**tre**	trāy
4	**fyra**	fēwrah
5	**fem**	fehm
6	**sex**	sehks
7	**sju**	shēw
8	**åtta**	ottah
9	**nio**	neeoo
10	**tio**	teeoo
11	**elva**	ehlvah
12	**tolv**	tolv
13	**tretton**	trehton
14	**fjorton**	fyōōʳton
15	**femton**	fehmton
16	**sexton**	sehkston
17	**sjutton**	shewton
18	**arton**	aaʳton
19	**nitton**	nitton
20	**tjugo**	khēwgoo
21	**tjugoett**	khēwgoeht
22	**tjugotvå**	khēwgotvaw
23	**tjugotre**	khēwgotrāy
24	**tjugofyra**	khēwgofēwrah
25	**tjugofem**	khēwgofehm
26	**tjugosex**	khēwgossehks
27	**tjugosju**	khēwgoshēw
28	**tjugoåtta**	khēwgoottah
29	**tjugonio**	khēwgoneeoo
30	**trettio**	trehti
31	**trettioett**	trehtieht
32	**trettiotvå**	trehtitvaw
33	**trettiotre**	trehtitrāy
40	**fyrtio**	furʳti
50	**femtio**	fehmti
60	**sextio**	sehksti
70	**sjuttio**	shewti
80	**åttio**	otti
90	**nittio**	nitti
100	**(ett)hundra**	(eht)hewndrah
101	**hundraett**	hewndraheht
102	**hundratvå**	hewndrahtvaw
110	**hundratio**	hewndrahteeoo
120	**hundratjugo**	hewndrahkhēwgoo

200	**tvåhundra**	tvawhewndrah
300	**trehundra**	trāyhewndrah
400	**fyrahundra**	fēwrahhewndrah
500	**femhundra**	fehmhewndrah
600	**sexhundra**	sehkshewndrah
700	**sjuhundra**	shēwhewndrah
800	**åttahundra**	ottahhewndrah
900	**niohundra**	neeoohewndrah
1000	**(ett)tusen**	(eht)tēwssern
1100	**ettusenetthundra**	ehttēwssernehthewndrah
1200	**ettusentvåhundra**	ehttēwsserntvawhewndrah
2000	**tvåtusen**	tvawtēwssern
10,000	**tiotusen**	teeootēwssern
50,000	**femtiotusen**	fehmtitēwssern
100,000	**(ett)hundratusen**	(eht)hewndrahtēwssern
1,000,000	**en miljon**	ehn milyōōn
1,000,000,000	**en miljard**	ehn milyaaʳd

first	**första**	furʳstah
second	**andra**	ahndrah
third	**tredje**	trāydyer
fourth	**fjärde**	fyāēʳder
fifth	**femte**	fehmter
sixth	**sjätte**	shehter
seventh	**sjunde**	shewnder
eighth	**åttonde**	ottonder
ninth	**nionde**	neeonder
tenth	**tionde**	teeonder

once/twice	**en gång/två gånger**	ehn gong/tvaw gongerr
three times	**tre gånger**	trāy gongerr

a half	**en halva**	ehn hahlvah
half a ...	**en halv ...**	ehn hahlv
half of ...	**hälften av ...**	hehlftern aav
half (adj.)	**halv**	hahlv
a quarter	**en fjärdedel**	ehn fyāēʳderdāyl
a third	**en tredjedel**	ehn trāydyerdāyl
a pair of	**ett par**	eht paar
a dozen	**ett dussin**	eht dewssin
3.4%	**3,4 procent**	trāy kommah fēwrah proosehnt

1981	**nittonhundra-åttioett**	nittonhewndrah-ottieht
1992	**nittonhundra-nittiotvå**	nittonhewndrah-nittitvaw
2003	**tvåtusentre**	tvawtēwsserntrāy

Year and age *År och ålder*

year	**året**	awrert
leap year	**skottåret**	skotawrert
decade	**årtiondet**	aw'teeondert
century	**århundradet**	awrhewndrahdert

this year	**det här året**	day(t) hær awrert
last year	**förra året**	furrah awrert
next year	**nästa år**	nehstah awr
each year	**varje år**	vahryer awr

2 years ago	**för 2 år sedan**	fūrr tvaw awr sehn
in one year	**om ett år**	om eht awr
in the eighties	**på åttiotalet**	paw ottitaalert
the 17th century	**1600-talet**	sehkstonhewndrahtaalert
in the 20th century	**på 1900-talet**	paw nittonhewndrahtaalert

| old/young | **gammal/ung** | gahmahl/ewng |
| old/new | **gammal/ny** | gahmahl/new |

| How old are you? | **Hur gammal är du?** | hewr gahmahl ær dew |

| I'm 30 years old. | **Jag är 30 år.** | yaa(g) ær trehti awr |

| At my age ... | **Vid min ålder ...** | veed min awlderr |

| He/She was born in 1960. | **Han/Hon är född 1960.** | hahn/hon ær furd nittonhewndrahsehksti |

| Children under 16 are not admitted. | **Barn under 16 år äger ej tillträde.** | baa'n ewnderr sehkston awr aigerr ay tiltraider |

Seasons *Årstider*

spring	**vår**	vawr
summer	**sommar**	sommahr
autumn	**höst**	hurst
winter	**vinter**	vinterr

in spring	**på våren**	paw vawrern
during the summer	**under sommaren**	ewnderr sommahrern
in autumn	**på hösten**	paw hurstern
during the winter	**under vintern**	ewnderr vinterrn

| high season | **högsäsong** | hūrgsaissong |
| low season | **lågsäsong** | lawgsaissong |

Months *Månader*

January	**januari***	yahnewaari
February	**februari**	fehbrewaari
March	**mars**	mah^{r}ss
April	**april**	ahpril
May	**maj**	mahy
June	**juni**	yēwni
July	**juli**	yēwli
August	**augusti**	ahgewsti
September	**september**	sehptehmberr
October	**oktober**	oktōōberr
November	**november**	noovehmberr
December	**december**	dehssehmberr

after June	**efter juni**	ehfterr yēwni
before July	**före juli**	fürrer yēwli
during the month of August	**under augusti månad**	ewnderr ahgewsti mawnahd
in September	**i september**	ee sehptehmberr
until October	**till oktober**	til oktōōberr
not until November	**inte före november**	inter fürrer noovehmberr
since December	**sedan december**	sehn dehssehmberr
last month	**förra månaden**	furrah mawnahdern
next month	**nästa månad**	nehstah mawnahd
the month before	**månaden innan**	mawnahdern innahn
the month after	**följande månad**	furlyahnder mawnahd
the beginning of January	**början av januari**	burryahn aav yahnewaari
the middle of February	**mitten av februari**	mittern aav fehbrewaari
the end of March	**slutet av mars**	slēwtert aav mah^{r}ss

Days and Date *Dagar och datum*

What day is it today?	**Vad är det för dag idag?**	vaad ǣr dāy(t) fürr daa(g) eedaa(g)
Sunday	**söndag***	surndaa(g)
Monday	**måndag**	mondaa(g)
Tuesday	**tisdag**	teesdaa(g)
Wednesday	**onsdag**	oonsdaa(g)
Thursday	**torsdag**	too^{r}sdaa(g)
Friday	**fredag**	frāydaa(g)
Saturday	**lördag**	lür^{r}daa(g)

---

* The names of months and days aren't capitalized in Swedish.

What's the date today?	**Vad är det för datum idag?**	vaad **ǣ**r d**ā**y(t) f**ū**rr **daa**tewm ee**daa**(g)
It's ...	**Det är ...**	d**ā**y(t) **ǣ**r
July 1	**den 1 juli**	dehn **fur**ˈstah **yē**wli
March 31	**den 31 mars**	dehn trehti**fur**ˈstah mah**ˈ**ss
When's your birthday?	**När är det din födelsedag?**	n**ǣ**r **ǣ**r d**ā**y(t) din **fū**r(deh)lserdaa(g)
August 3rd.	**3 augusti.**	**trā**ydyer ah**gew**sti
in the morning	**på morgonen**	paw **mor**ronern
during the day	**under dagen**	**ewn**derr **daa**gern
in the afternoon	**på eftermiddagen**	paw **ehf**terrmiddahn
in the evening	**på kvällen**	paw **kveh**lern
at night	**på natten**	paw **nah**tern
the day before yesterday	**i förrgår**	ee **fur**rgawr
yesterday	**i går**	ee gawr
today	**idag**	ee**daa**(g)
tomorrow	**i morgon**	ee **mor**ron
the day after tomorrow	**i övermorgon**	ee **ū**rverrmorron
the day before	**dagen innan**	**daa**(ger)n **in**nahn
the next day	**nästa dag**	**neh**stah daa(g)
two days ago	**för två dagar sedan**	f**ū**rr tvaw **daa**(gah)r sehn
in three days' time	**om tre dagar**	om tr**ā**y **daa**(gah)r
last week	**förra veckan**	**fur**rah **veh**kahn
next week	**nästa vecka**	**neh**stah **veh**kah
for a fortnight (two weeks)	**i fjorton dagar**	ee **fyō**ōˈton **daa**(gah)r
day off	**en ledig dag**	ehn **lā**ydig daa(g)
holiday	**en helgdag**	ehn **hehly**daa(g)
holidays/vacation	**en semester**	ehn seh**meh**sterr
school holidays	**ett skollov**	eht **skō**ōlawv
week	**en vecka**	ehn **veh**kah
weekend	**en weekend**	ehn **vee**kehnd
working day	**en arbetsdag**	ehn **ahr**bāytsdaa(g)

Greetings and wishes *Hälsningar och gratulationer*

| Merry Christmas! | **God jul!** | good y**ē**wl |
| Happy New Year! | **Gott nytt år!** | got newt awr |

Happy Easter!	**Glad påsk!**	glaad pawsk
Happy birthday!	**Gratulerar på födelsedagen!**	grahtewlāȳrahr paw fūr(deh)lserdaa(ger)n
Best wishes!	**Bästa välgångs-önskningar!**	behstah vailgongs-urnskningahr
Congratulations!	**Gratulerar!**	grahtewlāȳrahr
Good luck/ All the best!	**Lycka till!**	lewkah til
Have a good trip!	**Trevlig resa!**	trāȳvli(g) rāȳssah
Have a good holiday!	**Trevlig semester!**	trāȳvli(g) sehmehsterr
Regards from ...	**Hälsningar från ...**	hehlsningahr frawn
My regards to ...	**Hälsa till ...**	hehlsah til

Public holidays   *Allmänna helgdagar*

Note that on the days before most public holidays, offices, banks, post offices and shops usually observe shorter working hours.

January 1	**Nyårsdagen**	New Year's Day
January 6	**Trettondagen**	Epiphany
May 1	**Första maj**	May Day
Saturday that falls between June 20 and 26	**Midsommardagen**	Midsummer Day
Saturday that falls between Oct. 31 and Nov. 6	**Allhelgonadagen**	All Saints' Day
December 25	**Juldagen**	Christmas Day
December 26	**Annandag jul**	Boxing Day
Movable Dates:	**Långfredagen**	Good Friday
	Påskdagen	Easter Sunday
	Annandag påsk	Easter Monday
	Kristi himmelsfärds-dag	Ascension
	Pingstdagen	Whit Sunday
	Annandag pingst	Whit Monday

What time is it?   *Hur mycket är klockan?*

Excuse me. Can you tell me the time?	**Ursäkta. Kan ni säga vad klockan är?**	ēwʳsehktah. kahn nee sehyah vaad klokkahn ǣr
It's ...	**Den är ...**	dehn ǣr
five past one	**fem över ett***	fehm ūrverr eht
ten past two	**tio över två**	teeoo ūrverr tvaw
a quarter past three	**kvart över tre**	kvahʳt ūrverr trāy
twenty past four	**tjugo över fyra**	khēwgoo ūrverr fēwrah
twenty-five past five	**fem i halv sex**	fehm ee hahlv sehks
half past six	**halv sju**	hahlv shēw
twenty-five to seven	**fem över halv sju**	fehm ūrverr hahlv shēw
twenty to eight	**tjugo i åtta**	khēwgoo ee ottah
a quarter to nine	**kvart i nio**	kvahʳt ee neeoo
ten to ten	**tio i tio**	teeoo ee teeoo
five to eleven	**fem i elva**	fehm ee ehlvah
twelve o' clock	**tolv**	tolv
noon	**klockan tolv (på dagen)**	klokkahn tolv (paw daagern)
midnight	**midnatt**	meednaht
in the morning	**på morgonen**	paw morronern
in the afternoon	**på eftermiddagen**	paw ehfterrmiddahn
in the evening	**på kvällen**	paw kvehlern
What time does the train leave?	**Hur dags går tåget?**	hēwr dahgss gawr tawgert
It leaves at ...	**Det går klockan ...**	dāy(t) gawr klokkahn
13.04 (1.04 p.m.)	**tretton noll fyra**	trehton nol fēwrah
0.40 (0.40 a.m.)	**noll fyrtio**	nol furʳti
in five minutes	**om fem minuter**	om fehm minēwterr
in a quarter of an hour	**om en kvart**	om ehn kvahʳt
half an hour ago	**för en halvtimme sedan**	fūr ehn hahlvtimmer sehn
about two hours	**cirka två timmar**	sirkah tvaw timmahr
more than 10 minutes	**över tio minuter**	ūrverr teeoo minēwterr
a few seconds	**ett par sekunder**	eht paar sehkewnderr
The clock is fast/ slow.	**Klockan går före/ efter.**	klokkahn gawr fūrer/ ehfterr

---

* In everyday conversation, time is expressed as shown here. However, official time uses a 24-hour clock which means that after noon hours are counted from 13 to 24.

Common abbreviations *Vanliga förkortningar*

AB	aktiebolag	Ltd.
av.	aveny	avenue
avd.	avdelning	department
avs.	avsändare	sender
ca	cirka	around
Co.	kompani	company
D	Damer	Ladies
dir.	direktör	manager/(Am.) president
e.Kr.	efter Kristus	A.D.
e.m.	eftermiddagen	p.m.
f.Kr.	före Kristus	B.C.
FN	Förenta Nationerna	United Nations
f.m.	förmiddagen	a.m.
f.n.	för närvarande	at present
g	gram	gram
g.	gata	street
H	Herrar	Gentlemen
hg	hekto(gram)	hectogram
Hr	Herr	Mr.
KAK	Kungliga Automobil- klubben	Royal Automobile Club
kg	kilo(gram)	kilogram
kl.	klockan	o' clock
km	kilometer	kilometer
kr	kronor	crowns
moms	mervärdeskatt	value added tax
nr	nummer	number
n.b.	nedre botten	ground floor
obs.	observera	N.B.
o.s.a.	om svar anhålles	R.S.V.P.
osv.	och så vidare	etc.
SJ	Statens Järnvägar	Swedish State Railways
SR	Sveriges Radio	Swedish Radio
STF	Svenska Turist- föreningen	Swedish Touring Club
STTF	Svenska Turisttrafik- förbundet	Swedish Tourist Transport Association
t.ex.	till exempel	e.g. (for example)
tfn	telefon	telephone
t.o.m.	till och med	up to, including
tr.	trappor	stairs
UD	Utrikes- departementet	Ministry for Foreign Affairs
v.	vägen	road
VD	verkställande direktör	managing director

Signs and notices *Skyltar och anslag*

Att hyra	For hire/For rent/To let
Damer	Ladies
Drag	Pull
Ej ingång	No entrance
Ej tillträde	No trespassing
Fara	Danger
Fritt inträde	Admission free
Får ej vidröras	Do not touch
... förbjuden	... forbidden
Herrar	Gentlemen
Hiss	Lift (elevator)
Högspänningsledning	High voltage
Icke rökare	Nonsmoker
Ingång	Entrance
Kallt	Cold
Kassa	Cash desk
Ledigt	Free (vacant)
Livsfara	Danger of death
Nymålat	Wet paint
Nödutgång	Emergency exit
Privat	Private
Privat väg	Private road
Rea(lisation)	Sale
Reserverat	Reserved
Rökare	Smoker
Rökning förbjuden	No smoking
Rökning tillåten	Smoking allowed
Skjut	Push
Stängt	Closed
Stör ej	Do not disturb
Till salu	For sale
Tillträde förbjudet	No trespassing
Upplysningar	Information
Upptaget	Occupied
Ur funktion	Out of order
Utgång	Exit
Utsålt	Sold out
Var god ring	Please ring
Var god stäng dörren	Close the door
Var god vänta	Please wait
Varmt	Hot
Varning	Caution
Varning för hunden	Beware of the dog
Öppet	Open
Öppettider	Opening hours

Emergency *Nödsituation*

Call the police	**Ring polisen**	ring poo**lee**ssern
Consulate	**Konsulat**	konsew**laat**
DANGER	**FARA**	**faa**rah
Embassy	**Ambassad**	ahmbah**ssaad**
FIRE	**DET BRINNER**	dāy(t) **brinn**err
Gas	**Gas**	gaass
Get a doctor	**Hämta en läkare**	**hehm**tah ehn **lai**kahrer
Go away	**Ge er i väg**	yāy āyr ee vaig
HELP	**HJÄLP**	yehlp
Get help quickly	**Skaffa hjälp fort**	**skah**fah yehlp foo^{r}t
I'm ill	**Jag är sjuk**	yaa(g) ār **shēw**k
I'm lost	**Jag har gått vilse**	yaa(g) haar got **vil**ser
Leave me alone	**Lämna mig ifred**	**lehm**nah may eefrāy(d)
LOOK OUT	**SE UPP**	sāy ewp
Poison	**Gift**	yift
POLICE	**POLIS**	poo**leess**
Stop that man/ woman	**Stoppa den där mannen/kvinnan**	**stopp**ah dehn dār **mahn**ern/**kvinn**ahn
STOP THIEF	**STOPPA TJUVEN**	**stopp**ah **khēw**vern

Emergency telephone numbers *I nödsituation ring ...*

Fire Ambulance Police	90 000

Lost property—Theft *Borttappat – Stöld*

Where's the ...?	**Var ligger ...?**	vaar **ligg**err
lost property (lost and found) office	**hittegods- expeditionen**	**hitt**egoods- ehkspehdi**shoo**nern
police station	**polisstationen**	poo**leess**tahsh**oo**nern
I want to report a theft.	**Jag vill anmäla en stöld.**	yaa(g) vil **ahn**mailah ehn sturld
My ... has been stolen.	**... har stulits.**	... haar **stēw**litss
I've lost my ...	**Jag har tappat ...**	yaa(g) haar **tahp**aht
handbag	**min handväska**	min **hahn(d)**vehskah
passport	**mitt pass**	mit pahss
wallet	**min plånbok**	min **plawn**bōōk

CAR ACCIDENTS, see page 78

Conversion tables

Centimetres and inches

To change centimetres into inches, multiply by .39.

To change inches into centimetres, multiply by 2.54.

	in.	feet	yards
1 mm.	0.039	0.003	0.001
1 cm.	0.39	0.03	0.01
1 dm.	3.94	0.32	0.10
1 m.	39.40	3.28	1.09

	mm.	cm.	m.
1 in.	25.4	2.54	0.025
1 ft.	304.8	30.48	0.305
1 yd.	914.4	91.44	0.914

(32 metres = 35 yards)

Temperature

To convert centigrade into degrees Fahrenheit, multiply centigrade by 1.8 and add 32.

To convert degrees Fahrenheit into centigrade, subtract 32 from Fahrenheit and divide by 1.8.

Kilometres into miles

1 kilometre (km.) = 0.62 miles

km.	10	20	30	40	50	60	70	80	90	100	110	120	130
miles	6	12	19	25	31	37	44	50	56	62	68	75	81

Miles into kilometres

1 mile = 1.609 kilometres (km.)

miles	10	20	30	40	50	60	70	80	90	100
km.	16	32	48	64	80	97	113	129	145	161

Fluid measures

1 litre (l.) = 0.88 imp. quart or 1.06 U.S. quart

1 imp. quart = 1.14 l.	1 U.S. quart = 0.95 l.
1 imp. gallon = 4.55 l.	1 U.S. gallon = 3.8 l.

litres	5	10	15	20	25	30	35	40	45	50
imp. gal.	1.1	2.2	3.3	4.4	5.5	6.6	7.7	8.8	9.9	11.0
U.S. gal.	1.3	2.6	3.9	5.2	6.5	7.8	9.1	10.4	11.7	13.0

Weights and measures

1 kilogram or kilo (kg.) = 1000 grams (g.)

100 g. = 3.5 oz.	½ kg. = 1.1 lb.
200 g. = 7.0 oz.	1 kg. = 2.2 lb.

1 oz. = 28.35 g.
1 lb. = 453.60 g.

CLOTHING SIZES, see page 115/YARDS AND INCHES, see page 112

Allmänt

Basic grammar

Articles

All Swedish nouns are either common or neuter in gender.

1. Indefinite article (a/an)

common:	**en** man	a man
neuter:	**ett** barn	a child

2. Definite article (the)

Where we, in English, say "the house", the Swedes say the equivalent of "house-the", i.e. they tag the definite article onto the end of the noun. Common nouns take an **-(e)n** ending, neuter nouns an **-(e)t** ending.

common:	**mannen**	*the* man
neuter:	**barnet**	*the* child

Nouns

1. As already noted, nouns are either common or neuter. There are no easy rules for determining gender. Learn each new word with its accompanying article.

2. The plural is formed according to one of five declensions.

	singular		indefinite plurals	
Declension 1	**flicka**	girl	**flickor**	girls
2	**bil**	car	**bilar**	cars
3	**dam**	lady	**damer**	ladies
	sko	shoe	**skor**	shoes
4	**äpple**	apple	**äpplen**	apples
5	**hus**	house	**hus**	houses
			definite plurals	
			flickorna	the girls
			äpplena	the apples
			husen	the houses

There are also various irregular plurals.

3. Possession is shown by adding **-s** (singular and plural).
Note: There is no apostrophe.

Görans **bror**	George's brother
hotellets **ägare**	the owner of the hotel
veckans **första dag**	the first day of the week
den resandes **väska**	the traveller's suitcase
barnens **rum**	the children's room

Adjectives

1. Adjectives agree with the noun in gender and number.
For the indefinite form, the neuter is formed by adding **-t**;
the plural by adding **-a.**

(en) stor hund	(a) big dog	**stor***a* **hundar**	big dogs
(ett) stor*t* **hus**	(a) big house	**stor***a* **hus**	big houses

2. For the definite declension of the adjective, add the ending **-a** (common, neuter and plural). This form is used when the adjective is preceded by **den, det, de** (the definite article used with adjectives) or by a demonstrative or a possessive adjective.

den stor*a* **hunden**	the big dog
de stor*a* **hundarna**	the big dogs
det stor*a* **huset**	the big house
de stor*a* **husen**	the big houses

3. Demonstrative adjectives:

	common	neuter	plural
this/these	**den här/ denna**	**det här/ detta**	**de här/ dessa**
that/those	**den där/ den**	**det där/ det**	**de där/ de**

4. Possessive adjectives agree in number and gender with the noun they modify, i.e. with the thing possessed and not the possessor.

	common	neuter	plural
my	**min**	**mitt**	**mina**
your	**din**	**ditt**	**dina**
his			
her }	**sin**	**sitt**	**sina**
its			
our	**vår**	**vårt**	**våra**
your	**er**	**ert**	**era**
their	**sin**	**sitt**	**sina**

The forms **er, ert, era** correspond to the personal pronoun **ni** and refer to one or several possessors.

The forms **sin, sitt, sina** always refer back to the subject:

Han har sin bok.	He has his (own) book.
De har sina böcker.	They have their (own) books.

The genitive forms of the personal pronouns (see p. 162) are also used to show possession, however, the meaning changes:

Han har hans bok.	He has his (another person's) book.

5. Comparative and superlative:

The comparative and superlative are normally formed either by adding the endings **-(a)re** and **-(a)st**, respectively, to the adjective or by putting **mer** and **mest** (more, most) before the adjective.

Hans arbete är lätt.	His work is easy.
Hans arbete är lätt*are*.	His work is easier.
Hans arbete är lätt*ast*.	His work is easiest.

Er bil är stor.	Your car is big.
Er bil är stör*re*.	Your car is bigger.
Er bil är stör*st*.	Your car is the biggest.

Det är imponerande.	It's impressive.
Det är *mer* imponerande.	It's more impressive.
Det är *mest* imponerande.	It's most impressive.

Adverbs

Adverbs are generally formed by adding **-t** to the corresponding adjective.

Hon går snabbt.   She walks quickly.

Personal pronouns

	subject	object	genitive
I	**jag**	**mig**	—
you	**du/ni**	**dig/er**	—
he	**han**	**honom**	**hans**
she	**hon**	**henne**	**hennes**
it	**den/det**	**den/det**	**dess**
we	**vi**	**oss**	—
you	**ni**	**er**	—
they	**de**	**dem**	**deras**

Like many other languages, Swedish has two forms for "you". The formal word **ni,** traditionally the correct form of address between all but close friends and children, is now giving way to the informal **du.**

Verbs

Here we are concerned only with the infinitive, imperative, and present tense. The present tense is simple, because it has the same form for all persons. The infinitive of most Swedish verbs ends in **-a** (a few verbs of one syllable end in other vowels). Here are three useful auxiliary verbs:

	to be	to have	to be able to
Infinitive	**(att) vara**	**(att) ha**	**(att) kunna**
Present tense (same form for all persons)	**är**	**har**	**kan**
Imperative	**var**	**ha**	—

The present tense of Swedish verbs ends in **-r**:

	to ask	to buy	to believe	to do/make
Infinitive	(att) fråga	(att) köpa	(att) tro	(att) göra
Present tense (same form for all persons)	frågar	köper	tror	gör
Imperative	fråga	köp	tro	gör

There is no equivalent to the English present continuous tense. Thus:

Jag reser.   I travel/I am travelling.

Negatives

Negation is expressed by using the adverb **inte** (not). It is usually placed immediately after the verb in a main clause. In compound tenses **inte** comes between the auxiliary and the main verb.

Jag talar svenska.   I speak Swedish.
Jag talar inte svenska. I do not speak Swedish.
Hon har inte skrivit.   She has not written.

Questions

Questions are formed by reversing the order of the subject and the verb:

Bussen stannar här.   The bus stops here.
Stannar bussen här?   Does the bus stop here?

Jag kommer i kväll.   I am coming tonight.
Kommer ni i kväll?   Are you coming tonight?

Dictionary
and alphabetical index

English–Swedish

c common	nt neuter	pl plural

a en, ett 159
abbreviation förkortning c 154
able, to be kunna 162
about (approximately) cirka 78, 153
above ovanför 15, 62
abscess varbildning c 145
absorbent cotton bomull c 109
accept, to ta emot 61, 102
accessories accessoarer c/pl 116;
tillbehör nt 125
accident olycka c 78, 139;
olycksfall nt 139
accommodation logi nt 22
account konto nt 130, 131
ache värk c 141
adaptor adapter c 119
address adress c 21, 76, 79, 102
address book adressbok c 104
adhesive självhäftande 105
adhesive tape tape c 104
admission inträde nt 82, 89, 155
admitted, to be äga tillträde 149
Africa Afrika (nt) 146
after efter 15, 77, 150; följande
150
afternoon eftermiddag c 151, 153
after-shave lotion rakvatten nt
110
age ålder c 149
ago för ... sedan 149, 153
air bed luftmadrass c 106
air conditioning
luftkonditionering c 23, 28
airmail med flyg 133
airplane flyg nt 65
airport flygplats c 16, 21, 65
alarm clock väckarklocka c 121
alcohol alkohol c 37, 59
alcoholic alkoholhaltig 56

all allt 103
allergic allergisk 141, 143
allowed tillåten 155
almond mandel c 54
alphabet alfabet nt 9
also också 15
alter, to ändra 116
amazing fantastisk 84
amber bärnsten c 122
ambulance ambulans c 79, 156
American amerikansk 105, 126
American amerikan c 93
American plan helpension c 24
amount summa c 61, 131
amplifier förstärkare c 119
anaesthetic narkos c 144;
bedövning c 145
analgesic något smärtstillande 109
anchovy sardell c 46
and och 15
animal djur nt 85
ankle vrist c 139
anorak anorak c 116
answer, to svara 136
antibiotic antibiotika nt/pl 143
antidepressant något mot
depression 143
antique antikvitet c 83
antique shop antikvitetsaffär c 98
antiseptic antiseptisk 109
any några 15
anyone någon 12
anything något 17, 25, 103;
någonting 101, 113
anywhere någonstans 89
apartment våning c 19
aperitif aperitif c 58
appendicitis blindtarms-
inflammation c 142

appendix blindtarm c 138
appetizer förrätt c 43
apple äpple nt 54, 120
apple juice äppeljuice c 59
appointment tid c 30, 137, 145; möte nt 131
apricot aprikos c 54
April april (c) 150
aquavit brännvin nt 56
archaeology arkeologi c 83
architect arkitekt c 83
area code riktnummer nt 134
arm arm c 138, 139
around i närheten 35; cirka 154
arrival ankomst c 16, 65
arrive, to vara framme 65, 68; komma fram 68
art konst c 83
artery pulsåder c 138
art gallery konstgalleri nt 98
art museum konstmuseum nt 81
artichoke kronärtskocka c 51
article vara c 101
artificial sweetener sötningsmedel nt 37
artist konstnär c 81, 83
ashtray askkopp c 27, 36
Asia Asien (nt) 146
ask, to fråga 76, 163; (beg) be 136
ask for, to be om 25, 60
asparagus sparris c 51
aspirin aspirin c 109
asthma astma c 141
at vid 15
at least minst 24
at once genast 31
aubergine äggplanta c 51
August augusti (c) 150
aunt faster c, moster c 93
Australia Australien (nt) 146
Austria Österrike (nt) 146
automatic automatisk 122, 124; (car) med automatlåda 20
autumn höst c 149
average medelgod 91
awful förskräcklig 84, 94

B

baby baby c 24, 111
baby food barnmat c 111
babysitter barnvakt c 27
back rygg c 138
backache ont i ryggen 141
backpack ryggsäck c 106
bacon bacon nt 38

bacon and eggs bacon och ägg 38
bad dålig 14, 95
bag bag c 17, 18; kasse c 103
baggage bagage nt 18, 26, 31, 71; (registered) resgods nt/pl 71
baggage cart bagagekärra c 18, 71
baggage check effektförvaring c 67, 71
baked bakad 52; ugnstekt 46
baker's bageri nt 98
balance (account) balansräkning c 131
balcony balkong c 23
ball (inflated) boll c 128
ballet balett c 88
ball-point pen kulspetspenna c 104
banana banan c 54
bandage förband nt; (elastic) binda c 109
Band-Aid plåster nt 109
bangle armring c 121
bank (finance) bank c 98, 129, 130
banknote sedel c 130
bar bar c 33; (chocolate) kaka c 64
barber's herrfrisör c 30, 98
bath (hotel) bad nt 23, 25, 27
bathing cap badmössa c 116
bathing hut badhytt c 91
bathrobe badkappa c 116
bathroom badrum nt 27
bath salts badsalt nt 110
bath towel badlakan nt 27
battery batteri nt 75, 78, 121, 125
be, to vara 162
beach strand c 90
beach ball badboll c 128
bean böna c 49, 51
bear björn c 50
beard skägg nt 31
beautiful vacker 14, 84
beauty salon skönhetssalong c 30, 98
bed säng c 24, 144
bed and breakfast rum med frukost 24
bedpan bäcken nt 144
beef oxkött nt 48, 49
beef steak biff c 48, 49
beer öl c 56, 64
beet(root) rödbeta c 51
before (place) framför 15; (time) före 15, 143, 149; innan 15, 150, 151
begin, to börja 87, 88; starta 80
beginner nybörjare c 91

beginning början c 150
behind bakom 15, 77
beige beige 113
believe, to tro 163
bell *(electric)* ringklocka c 144
bellboy pickolo c 26
below nedanför 15, 62
belt *(man's)* bälte nt; *(woman's)* skärp nt 117
bend *(road)* kurva c 79
berth bädd c 69, 71; sovplats c 69, 70
better bättre 14, 25, 101
between mellan 15
bicycle cykel c 74
bidet bidé c 28
big stor 14, 25, 101, 118
bilberry blåbär nt 54
bill nota c 61; räkning c 31, 102; *(banknote)* sedel c 130
billion *(Am.)* miljard c 148
binoculars kikare c 123
bird fågel c 85
birthday födelsedag c 151, 152
biscuit *(Br.)* kex nt 64
bitter besk 60
black svart 113
black and white svart-vit 124, 125
blackberry björnbär nt 54
bladder urinblåsa c 138
blanket filt c 27
bleed, to blöda 139, 145
blind *(window)* rullgardin c 29
blister blåsa c 139
blood blod nt 142
blood pressure blodtryck nt 141, 142
blood transfusion blodtransfusion c 144
blouse blus c 116
blow-dry, to föna 30
blue blå 113
blueberry blåbär nt 54
blusher rouge nt 110
boat båt c 73, 74
bobby pin hårklämma c 111
body kropp c 138
boil böld c 139
boiled kokt 49, 51, 52
bone ben nt 138
book bok c 12, 104
booking office biljettexpedition c 67; biljettkassa c 19
booklet *(of tickets)* biljetthäfte nt 72

bookshop bokhandel c 98, 104
boot stövel c 118
born född 149
botanical gardens botanisk trädgård c 81
botany botanik c 83
bottle flaska c 17, 57
bottle-opener flasköppnare c 106
bowel tarm c 138
bow tie fluga c 116
bowl skål c 127
box ask c 120
boy pojke c 112, 128
boyfriend pojkvän c 93
bra behå c 121
bracelet armband nt 121
braces *(suspenders)* hängslen nt/pl 116
braised bräserad 49
brake broms c 78
brake fluid bromsvätska c 75
brandy cognac c 58
bread bröd nt 36, 38, 64, 120
break, to bryta 139; gå sönder 123
break down, to gå sönder 78
breakdown motorstopp nt 78
breakdown van bärgningsbil c 78
breakfast frukost c 24, 34, 38
breast bröst nt 138
breathe, to andas 141, 142
bridge bro c 81, 85
bring, to ge 13; ta med 95
bring down, to ta ner 31
British britt c 93
broiled grillad 49
broken trasig 29; gått sönder 119; bruten 140
brooch brosch c 121
brother bror c 93
brown brun 113
bruise blåmärke nt 139
brush borste c 111
Brussels sprouts brysselkål c/pl 51
bubble bath skumbad nt 110
bucket hink c 106, 128
buckle spänne nt 117
buffet car cafévagn c 71
build, to bygga 83
building byggnad c 81, 83
building blocks/bricks byggklotsar c/pl 128
bulb glödlampa c 28, 75, 119
bump bula c 139
bun bulle c 63

burn brännsår *nt* 139
burned out *(bulb)* trasig 28
bus buss *c* 18, 19, 65, 66, 72, 80
business affär *c* 16, 131
business district affärskvarter *nt* 81
business trip affärsresa *c* 93
bus stop busshållplats *c* 72
busy upptagen 96
butane gas butangas *c* 32, 106
butcher's slaktare *c*, charkuteri *nt* 98
butter smör *nt* 36, 38, 64
button knapp *c* 29, 117
buy, to köpa 100, 104, 123, 163

C

cabana badhytt *c* 91
cabbage kål *c* 51
cabin *(ship)* hytt *c* 74
cable telegram *nt* 133
cable car linbana *c* 74
cable release trådutlösare *c* 125
café kafé *nt* 33
cake kaka *c* 55, 63
cake shop konditori *nt* 98
calculator räknare *c* 105
calendar kalender *c* 104
call *(phone)* samtal *nt* 134, 135, 136
call, to *(give name)* heta 11; *(phone)* ringa 78, 79, 134, 136, 156
camera kamera *c* 124, 125
camera case kamerafodral *nt* 125
camera shop fotoaffär *c* 98
camp, to campa 32
camp bed tältsäng *c* 106
camping camping *c* 32
camping equipment camping utrustning *c* 106
camp site campingplats *c* 32
can *(of peaches)* burk *c* 120
can *(to be able)* kunna 12, 162
Canada Kanada *(nt)* 146
Canadian kanadensare *c* 93
cancel, to annullera, avbeställa 65
candle ljus *nt* 106
candlestick ljusstake *c* 127
candy godis *nt* 126
candy store godisaffär *c* 99
canoe kanot *c* 74
can opener konservöppnare *c* 106
cap mössa *c* 116
capital *(finance)* kapital *nt* 131

car bil *c* 19, 20, 32, 75, 76, 78; *(train)* vagn *c* 70, 71
carafe karaff *c* 57
carat karat *c* 121
caravan husvagn *c* 32
carbon paper karbonpapper *nt* 104
carbonated med kolsyra 59
carburettor förgasare *c* 78
card kort *nt* 93, 131
card game kortspel *nt* 128
car hire biluthyrning *c* 20
car park parkering *c* 77
car racing biltävling *c* 89
car radio bilradio *c* 119
car rental biluthyrning *c* 20
carrot morot *c* 51
carry, to bära 21
cart kärra *c* 18, 71
carton *(of cigarettes)* limpa *c* 17, 126
cartridge *(camera)* kassett *c* 124
case fodral *c* 123, 125; *(cigarettes)* étui *nt* 121, 126
cash, to lösa in 130, 133
cash desk kassa *c* 103, 155
cassette kassett *c* 119, 127
castle slott *nt* 81
catalogue katalog *c* 82
cathedral domkyrka *c* 81
Catholic katolsk 84
cauliflower blomkål *c* 51
caution varning *c* 155
cave grotta *c* 81
cemetery kyrkogård *c* 81
centimetre centimeter *c* 112
centre centrum *nt* 19, 21, 76, 81
century århundrade *nt* 149
ceramics keramik *c* 83, 127
cereal flingor *c/pl* 38
chain *(jewellery)* kedja *c* 121
chain bracelet armlänk *c* 121
chair stol *c* 106
change *(money)* växel *c* 61, 77, 130
change, to ändra 65; *(replace, train)* byta 60, 68, 69, 73, 75, 123; *(money)* växla 18, 130
changing room provhytt *c* 115
chapel kapell *nt* 81
charcoal träkol *c* 106
charcoal tablets koltabletter *c/pl* 109
charge avgift *c* 77, 136; kostnad *c* 20, 40;
charge, to kosta 20, 24, 32, 89
charm *(trinket)* berlock *c* 121

charm bracelet berlockarmband *nt* 121

cheap billig 14, 24, 25, 101

check check *c* 130; *(restaurant)* nota *c* 61

check, to kontrollera 75, 123; *(luggage)* pollettera 71

checkbook checkhäfte *nt* 131

check-in *(airport)* incheckning *c* 65

check in, to *(airport)* checka in 65

check out, to checka ut 31

check-up *(medical)* hälsokontroll *c* 142

cheers! skål! 58

cheese ost *c* 38, 53, 62, 64, 120

chef kökschef *c* 40

chemist's apotek *nt* 98, 108

cheque check *c* 130

cheque book checkhäfte *nt* 131

cherry körsbär *nt* 54

chess schack *nt* 93

chess set schackspel *nt* 128

chest bröstkorg *c* 138; bröst *nt* 141

chewing gum tuggummi *c* 126

chewing tobacco tuggtobak *c* 126

chicken kyckling *c* 50

child barn *nt* 24, 60, 82, 93, 139, 149

children's doctor barnläkare *c* 137

chilled kyld 58

China Kina *(nt)* 146

china porslin *nt* 98

chips pommes frites *c/pl* 52, 62; *(Am.)* chips *c/pl* 64

chives gräslök *c* 53

chocolate choklad *c* 38, 55, 59, 120

chocolate bar chokladkaka *c* 64, 126

choice val *nt* 40

chop kotlett *c* 48

Christmas jul *c* 151, 152

church kyrka *c* 81, 84

cigar cigarr *c* 126

cigarette cigarrett *c* 17, 95, 126

cigarette case cigarrettetui *nt* 121, 126

cigarette holder cigarrett-munstycke *nt* 126

cigarette lighter cigarrettändare *c* 121

cine camera filmkamera *c* 124

cinema bio *c* 86, 96

cinnamon kanel *c* 53

circle *(theatre)* första raden 87

citizen medborgare *c* 25

city stad *c* 81

city hall stadshus *nt* 81

classical klassisk 128

clean ren 61

clean, to tvätta 29; *(wipe)* torka av 76

cleansing cream rengöringskräm *c* 110

cliff klippa *c* 85

cloakroom garderob *c* 87

clock klocka *c* 121, 153

clock-radio klockradio *c* 119

clog träsko *c* 127

close *(near)* nära 78, 132

close, to stänga 11, 82, 108, 132

closed stängt 155

cloth tyg *nt* 118

clothes kläder *pl* 29, 116

clothes peg klädnypa *c* 106

clothing kläder *pl* 112

cloud moln *nt* 94

coach *(bus)* expressbuss *c* 66

coach station busstation *c* 67

coat *(man's)* rock *c* 116; *(woman's)* kappa *c* 116

cod torsk *c* 46

coffee kaffe *c* 38, 59, 64

coin mynt *nt* 83

cold kall 14, 25, 60, 94, 155

cold *(illness)* förkylning *c* 108, 141

collar krage *c* 117

collect call Ba-samtal *nt* 135

colour färg *c* 103, 112, 124, 125

colour chart färgkarta *c* 30

colourfast färgäkta 114

colour rinse färgsköljning *c* 30

colour shampoo tonande shampo *nt* 111

colour slide färgdiapositiv *nt* 124

comb kam *c* 111

come, to komma 36, 92, 95, 137, 146

comedy komedi *c* 86

commission expeditionsavgift *c* 130

compact disc CD-skiva *c* 127

company kompani *nt* 154

compartment kupé *c* 70

compass kompass *c* 106

complaint klagomål *nt* 60

concert konsert *c* 88

concert hall konserthus *nt* 81, 88

condom kondom c 109
conductor (orchestra) dirigent c 88
conference room konferensrum nt 23
confirm, to bekräfta 65
confirmation bekräftelse c 23
congratulation gratulation c 151
connection (train) anslutning c 65, 68
consommé buljong c 44
constipation förstoppning c 140
consulate konsulat nt 156
contact lens kontaktlins c 123
contagious, to be smitta 142
contain, to innehålla 37
contraceptive preventivmedel nt 109
contract kontrakt nt 131
control kontroll c 16
conversion omvandling c 157
cookie kex nt 64
cool bag kylväska c 106
cool box kylbox c 106
copper koppar c 122
corduroy manchester c 114
corkscrew korkskruv c 106
corn (Am.) majs c 51; (foot) liktorn c 109
corner hörn nt 36; (street) gathörn nt 21, 77
corn plaster liktornsplåster nt 109
cost kostnad c 131
cost, to kosta 11, 24, 80, 133, 136
cot barnsäng c 24
cotton bomull c 114
cotton wool bomull c 109
cough hosta c 108, 141
cough, to hosta 142
cough drops halstabletter c/pl 109
counter lucka c 133
country land nt 92
countryside land nt 85
court house tingshus nt 81
cousin kusin c 93
crab krabba c 43, 46, 47
cramp kramp c 141
cranberry lingon nt 54
crayfish (freshwater) kräfta c 46
crayon färgkrita c 104
cream grädde c 38, 55, 59; (toiletry) kräm (crème) c 110; (pharmaceutical) salva c 109

crease resistant skrynkelfri 114
credit card kreditkort nt 20, 31, 61, 102, 130
cress krasse c 53
crispbread knäckebröd nt 38; hårt bröd nt 120
crisps chips nt/pl 64
crockery porslin nt/pl 106, 107
cross kors nt 121
cross-country skiing längdåkning c 91
crossing (by sea) överfart c 74
crossroads korsning c 77
crown (money) krona c 18, 101, 129
cruise kryssning c 74
crystal kristall c 122, 127
cucumber gurka c 51
cuff link manschettknapp c 121
cuisine kök nt 35
cup kopp c 36, 59, 107
curler papiljott c 111
currant vinbär nt 54
currency valuta c 129
currency exchange office växelkontor nt 18, 67, 129
current ström c 90
curtain gardin c 28
curve kurva c 79
customs tull c 16, 102
cut (wound) skärsår nt 139
cut, to (scissors) klippa 30
cut off, to avbryta 136
cut glass slipat glas nt 122
cuticle remover nagelbandsvatten nt 110
cutlery bestick nt/pl 106, 107, 121
cycle path cykelbana c 79
cycling cykel c 89
cystitis urinvägsinfektion c 142

D

dairy ostaffär c 98
dance, to dansa 88, 96
danger fara c 155, 156
dangerous farlig 79, 90
Danish pastry wienerbröd nt 63
dark mörk 25, 101, 112, 113
date (day) datum nt 25, 151; (appointment) träff c 95; (fruit) dadel c 54
daughter dotter c 93
day dag c 16, 20, 24, 32, 80, 150, 151

DICTIONARY

daylight dagsljus *nt* 124
day off ledig dag *c* 151
decade årtionde *nt* 149
decaffeinated koffeinfri 38, 59
December december *(c)* 150
decision beslut *c* 25, 102
deck *(ship)* däck *nt* 74
deck chair solstol *c* 91, 106
declare, to *(customs)* förtulla 17
deep djup 90, 142
deep fried friterad 46
deer hjort *c* 50
delicatessen delikatessaffär *c* 98
deliver, to leverera 102
delicious utsökt 61
delivery leverans *c* 102
Denmark Danmark *(nt)* 146
dentist tandläkare *c* 98, 145
denture tandprotes *c* 145
deodorant deodorant *c* 110
department avdelning *c* 83, 100
department store varuhus *nt* 98
departure avgång *c* 65
deposit *(car hire)*
  deponeringsavgift *c* 20; *(bank)*
  insättning *c* 130
dessert efterrätt *c* 37, 55
detour *(traffic)* trafikomläggning
  c 79
diabetic diabetiker *c* 37, 141
dialling code riktnummer *nt* 134
diamond diamant *c* 122
diaper blöja *c* 111
diarrhoea diarré *c* 140
dictionary ordbok *c* 104
diesel diesel 75
diet diet *c* 37
difficult svår 14
difficulty svårighet *c* 28; problem
  nt 102
digital digital 122
dill dill *c* 53
dining car restaurangvagn *c* 68, 71
dining room matsal *c* 27
dinner middag *c* 34, 94
direct direkt 65
direct, to visa vägen 13
direction riktning *c* 76
director *(theatre)* regissör *c* 86
directory *(phone)* telefonkatalog *c*
  134
disabled handikappad *c* 82
disc skiva *c* 127
discotheque diskotek *nt* 88, 96
discount rabatt *c* 131

disease sjukdom *c* 142
dish rätt *c* 37
dish of the day dagens rätt *c* 40
disinfectant desinfektionsmedel *nt*
  109
dislocated ur led 140
display case monter *c* 100
dissatisfied missnöjd 103
district *(town)* kvarter *nt* 81
disturb, to störa 155
dive dyka 90
diversion *(traffic)*
  trafikomläggning *c* 79
dizzy yr 140
do, to göra 163
doctor läkare *c* 79, 137, 156;
  doktor *c* 98, 137, 144
doctor's office läkarmottagning *c*
  137
dog hund *c* 155
doll docka *c* 128
dollar dollar *c* 18, 102, 130
door dörr *c* 155
double dubbel 74
double bed dubbelsäng *c* 23
double room dubbelrum *nt* 19, 23
down ner 15
downhill skiing utförsåkning *c* 91
downstairs där nere 15
downtown (stads)centrum *nt* 81
dozen dussin *c* 148
draught beer fatöl *nt* 56
drawing pad ritblock *nt* 104
drawing pin häftstift *nt* 104
dress klänning *c* 116
dressing gown morgonrock *c* 116
drink dryck *c* 56, 58, 59; drink *c*
  60, 95
drink, to dricka 35, 36, 37, 59
drinking water dricksvatten *nt* 32
drip, to droppa 28
drive, to köra 21, 76
driving licence körkort *nt* 20, 79
drop *(liquid)* droppe *c* 109
drugstore apotek *c* 98, 108
dry torr 30, 58, 111
dry cleaner's kemtvätt *c* 29, 98
dry shampoo torrshampo *nt* 111
Dublin bay prawn havskräfta *c* 45
duck anka *c* 50
dummy napp *c* 111
during under 15, 149, 151
duty *(customs)* tull *c* 16, 17
duty-free shop taxfree-shop *c* 19
dye, to färga 30

Ordlista

E

each varje 125, 143, 149
ear öra nt 138
earache ont i örat 141
ear drops örondroppar c/pl 109
early tidig 14, 31
earring örhänge nt 121
east öster 77
Easter påsk c 152
easy lätt, enkel 14
eat, to äta 36, 37, 144
eat out, to äta ute 33
eel ål c 41, 42, 46
egg ägg nt 38, 42, 45, 62, 64
eggplant äggplanta c 51
eight åtta 147
eighteen arton 147
eighth åttonde 148
eighty åttio 147
elastic elastisk 109
elastic bandage elastisk binda c 109
Elastoplast plåster nt 109
electric(al) elektrisk 119
electrical appliance elektrisk artikel c 119
electrical goods shop elaffär c 98
electricity elektricitet c 32
electronic elektronisk 125, 128
elevator hiss c 27, 100, 155
eleven elva 147
elk älg c 50
embassy ambassad c 156
emergency nödsituation c 156
emergency exit nödutgång c 27, 155
emery board sandpappersfil c 110
empty tom 14
enamel emalj c 122
end slut nt 150
endive endiv c 51
engaged (phone) upptaget 136
engagement ring förlovningsring c 122
engine (car) motor c 78
England England (nt) 146
English engelsk 104, 126
English engelska (c) 12, 82, 84; (person) engelsman c 93
engrave gravera 121
enjoyable trevlig 31
enlarge, to förstora 125
enough tillräcklig 15
enquiry förfrågan c 68
entrance ingång c 67, 99, 155; infart c 79

entrance fee inträde nt 82
envelope kuvert nt 27, 104
equipment utrustning c 91, 106
eraser radergummi nt 104
escalator rulltrappa c 100
estimate (cost) uppskattning c 131
Europe Europa (nt) 146
evening kväll c 87, 95, 96, 151, 153
evening dress (woman's) aftonklänning c 116
everything allt 31
examine, to undersöka 137
exchange, to byta 103
exchange rate växelkurs c 18, 130
excursion rundtur c 80
excuse, to förlåta, ursäkta 11
exercise book skrivbok c 104
exhaust pipe avgasrör nt 78
exhibition utställning c 81
exit utgång c 67, 99, 155; utfart c 79
expect, to vänta 130
expenses omkostnad c 131
expensive dyr 14, 19, 24, 101
exposure (photography) bild c 124
exposure counter exponeringsmätare c 125
express express 133
expression uttryck nt 10
expressway motorväg c 76
extension (phone) anknytning c 135
extension cord/lead förlängningssladd c 119
extra extra 27, 40
eye öga nt 139
eyebrow pencil ögonbrynspenna c 110
eye drops ögondroppar c/pl 109
eye liner eyeliner c 110
eye shadow ögonskugga c 110
eyesight syn f 123
eye specialist ögonläkare c 137

F

fabric (cloth) tyg nt 113
face ansikte nt 138
face pack ansiktsmask c 30
face powder puder nt 110
factory fabrik c 81
fair mässa c 81
fall (autumn) höst c 149

fall, to ramla 139
family familj c 93
fan belt fläktrem c 75
far långt (bort) 11, 14, 100
fare pris nt 69
farm bondgård c 85
fast snabb 124
fat (meat) fett nt 37
father far c 93
faucet kran c 28
February februari (c) 150
fee (doctor) arvode nt 144
feeding bottle nappflaska c 111
feel, to (physical state) känna
sig 140, 142
felt filt c 114
felt-tip pen filtpenna c 104
fennel fänkål c 51
ferry färja c 74
fever feber c 140
few få 14; (a) några 14
field fält nt 85
fifteen femton 147
fifth femte 148
fifty femtio 147
fig fikon nt 54
file (tool) fil c 110
fill in, to fylla i 26, 144
filling (tooth) plomb c 145
filling station bensinstation c 75
film film c 86, 124, 125
film winder frammatning c 125
filter filter nt 125
filter-tipped med filter 126
find, to hitta 11, 12, 100
fine (OK) bra 11, 25
finger finger nt 138
finish, to sluta 87
Finland Finland (nt) 146
fire eld c 156
first första 68, 69, 148
first-aid kit förbandslåda c 106
first class första klass c 69
first name förnamn nt 25
fish fisk c 45
fish, to fiska 90
fishing permit fiskekort nt 90
fishing tackle fiskeutrustning c
106
fishmonger's fiskaffär c 98
fit, to passa 115
five fem 147
fix, to laga 75, 145
fizzy (mineral water) med kolsyra
59

flash (photography) blixt c 125
flash attachment blixtaggregat nt
125
flashlight ficklampa c 106
flat platt 118
flat (apartment) våning c 19
flat tyre punktering c 75, 78
flea market loppmarknad c 81
flight flyg nt 65
floor våning c 23, 27
floor show show c 88
florist's blomsteraffär c 98
flounder flundra c 45
flour mjöl nt 37
flower blomma c 85
flu influensa c 142
fluid vätska c 75, 123
fog dimma c 94
folding chair fällstol c 106
folding table fällbord nt 107
folk art allmogekonst c 83
folk music folkmusik c 128
follow, to följa 77
food mat c 37, 60
food box matlåda c 106
food poisoning matförgiftning c
142
foot fot c 138
football fotboll c 89
foot cream fotkräm c 110
footpath stig c 85
for för 15; (time) i 143, 151
forbid, to förbjuda 155
forest skog c 85
forget, to glömma 60
fork gaffel c 36, 60, 107
form (document) blankett c 25, 26,
133
fortnight fjorton dagar c/pl 151
fortress borg c 81
forty fyrtio 147
forwarding address
eftersändningsadress c 31
foundation cream puderunderlag nt
110
fountain fontän c 81
fountain pen reservoarpenna c 105
four fyra 147
fourteen fjorton 147
fourth fjärde 148
fowl fågel c 50
frame (glasses) båge c 123
France Frankrike (nt) 146
free (vacant) ledig 14, 70, 96,
155

free (of charge) fri 155
French beans haricots verts c/pl 51
French fries pommes frites c/pl 52
fresh färsk 54, 60
Friday fredag c 150
fried stekt 46, 49
fried egg stekt ägg nt 38, 45
friend vän c 92, 93, 95
from från 15
frost frost c 94
fruit frukt c 54
fruit juice juice c 37, 38, 59
fruit salad fruktsallad c 54
frying pan stekpanna c 106
full full 14
full board helpension c 24
full insurance helförsäkring c 20
fur coat päls c 116
furniture möbler c/pl 83
furrier's körsnär c 98

G

gallery galleri nt 98
game spel nt 128; (food) vilt nt 50
gangway landgång c 74
garage (parking) garage nt 26; (repairs) verkstad c 78
garden(s) trädgård c 85
garlic vitlök c 52, 53
gas gas c 126, 156
gasoline bensin c 75, 78
gastritis magkatarr c 142
gauze gasbinda c 109
gem ädelsten c 121
general allmän 27, 100
general delivery poste restante 133
general practitioner allmänpraktiker c 137
genitals könsorgan nt 138
gentleman herre c 155
genuine äkta 118, 121
geology geologi c 83
Germany Tyskland (nt) 146
get, to få 108; (fetch) skaffa 21, 31, 137; (find) få tag på 11, 19, 21, 32
get off, to stiga av 72
get to, to komma till 19, 70, 76
get up, to stiga upp 144
gherkin ättiksgurka c 51, 64
gift present c 17

gin gin c 58
gin and tonic gin och tonic c 58
girdle höfthållare c 116
girl flicka c 112, 128
girlfriend flickvän c 93
give, to ge 13, 135
give way, to (traffic) lämna företräde 79
gland körtel c 138
glass glas nt 36, 57, 59, 60, 143
glasses glasögon c/pl 123
glasses case glasögonfodral nt 123
glassware glas nt 127
gloomy dyster 84
glove handske c 116
glue klister nt 105
go, to gå 96
go away! ge er i väg! 156
gold guld nt 121, 122
golden guldfärgad 113
gold plate gulddoublé c 122
golf golf c 89
golf course golfbana c 89
good bra 14, 101
good afternoon god middag 10
good-bye adjö 10
good evening god afton 10
Good Friday långfredag c 152
good morning god morgon 10
good night god natt 10
goods vara c 16
goose gås c 50
go out, to gå ut 96
gram gram nt 120
grammar book grammatik c 105
grape vindruva c 54
grapefruit grapefrukt c 54
grapefruit juice grapefruktjuice c 38, 59
gravy sky c 52
gray grå 113
graze skrubbsår nt 139
greasy fet 30, 111
Great Britain Storbritannien (nt) 146
green grön 113
green beans haricots verts c/pl 51
greengrocer's grönsaksaffär c 98
greeting hälsning c 151
grey grå 113
grilled grillad 46, 49
grocer's livsmedelsaffär c 98, 120
groundsheet tältunderlag nt 106
group grupp c 82
guesthouse pensionat nt 19, 22

guide guide c 80
guidebook guidebok c 82, 104, 105
gum *(teeth)* tandkött nt 145
gynaecologist gynekolog c 137

H

habit vana c 34
haddock kolja c 46
hair hår nt 30, 111
hairbrush hårborste c 111
haircut klippning c 30
hairdresser's frisersalong c 27, 30; frisör c 98
hair dryer hårtork c 119
hair dye hårfärgningsmedel nt 111
hair gel frisyrgelé nt 111
hairgrip hårklämma c 111
hair lotion hårvatten nt 111
hair pin hårnål c 111
hair slide hårspänne nt 111
hairspray (hår)spray c 30, 111
half halv 148
half halva c 148
half an hour halvtimme c 153
half board halvpension c 24
half price ticket halv biljett c 69
halibut hälleflundra c 46
hall porter portier c 26
hallo hej 10
ham skinka c 48, 62, 64
ham and eggs skinka och ägg 38
hamburger pannbiff c 48
hammer hammare c 106
hammock hängmatta c 106
hand hand c 138
handbag handväska c 116, 156
hand cream handkräm c 110
handicrafts konsthantverk nt 83; slöjd c 127
handkerchief näsduk c 116
handmade handgjord 113
hanger hängare c 27
hangover baksmälla c 108
happy glad 152
harbour hamn c 81
hard hård 123
hard-boiled hårdkokt 38
hardware store järnhandel c 98
hare hare c 50
hat hatt c 116
have, to ha 162
hayfever hösnuva c 108, 141
hazelnut hasselnöt c 54

he han 162
head huvud nt 138, 139
headache huvudvärk c 141
headphones hörlurar c/pl 119
head waiter hovmästare c 61
health food shop hälsokostaffär c 98
health insurance sjukförsäkring c 144
health insurance form sjukförsäkringsblankett c 144
heart hjärta nt 138
heart attack hjärtattack c 141
heat, to värma upp 90
heating värme c 23, 28
heavy tung 14, 101
heel klack c 118
helicopter helikopter c 74
hello *(phone)* hallå 135
help hjälp c 156
help! hjälp! 156
help, to hjälpa 13, 21, 71, 100, 134; *(oneself)* ta själv 120
her hennes l62; sin, sitt *(pl* sina) 161
herb ört c 53
here här 13
herring sill c 41, 42, 43, 46, 47
hi hej 10
high hög 85, 141
high season högsäsong c 149
hill kulle c 85
hire uthyrning c 20, 74
hire, to hyra 19, 20, 74, 90, 91, 119, 155
his hans 162; sin, sitt *(pl* sina) 161
history historia c 83
hitchhike, to lifta 74
hold on! *(phone)* var god dröj! 136
hole hål nt 29
holiday helgdag c 151, 152
holidays semester c 16, 151, 152; *(school)* skollov nt 151
home address bostadsadress c 31
home town hemort c 25
honey honung c 38
hope, to hoppas 96
horse häst c 127
horseback riding ridning c 89
horse racing hästkapplöpning c 89
horseradish pepparrot c 49, 52
hospital sjukhus nt 99, 144
hot varm 14, 25, 38, 94, 155
hotel hotell nt 19, 21, 22
hotel guide hotellguide c 19

hotel reservation hotellreservation c 19

hot water varmvatten nt 23, 28

hot-water bottle varmvattensflaska c 27

hour timme c 80, 143, 153

house hus nt 83, 85

how hur 11

how far hur långt 11, 76, 85

how long hur länge 11, 24

how many hur många 11

how much hur mycket 11, 24

hundred hundra 147

hungry hungrig 13, 35

hunt, to jaga 89

hunting jakt c 89

hurry (to be in a) ha bråttom 21

hurt, to göra ont 139, 140, 145; *(oneself)* slå sig 139

husband man c 93

hydrofoil svävare c 74

I

I jag 162

ice is c 94

ice-cream glass c 55, 62

ice cube is c 27

iced tea iste nt 59

icehockey ishockey c 91

Iceland Island *(nt)* 146

ice pack frysklamp c 106

ill sjuk 140, 156

illness sjukdom c 140

important viktig 13

imported importerad 113

impressive imponerande 84

in i 15

include, to ingå 24, 80

included inräknad 20, 40, 61; inkluderad 31

India Indien *(nt)* 146

indigestion dålig matsmältning c 141

indoor inomhus 90

inexpensive billig 35, 124

infected infekterad 140

infection infektion c 141

inflammation inflammation c 142

inflation inflation c 131

influenza influensa c 142

information information c 67; upplysning c 155

injection injektion c 144; spruta c 142

injure, to skada 139

injured skadad 79, 139

injury skada c 139

ink bläck nt 105

inn värdshus nt 33

inquiry förfrågan c 68

insect bite insektsbett nt 108, 139

insect repellent insektsspray c 109

insect spray insektsspray c 109

inside inne 15

instant coffee snabbkaffe nt 64

instead i stället 37

insurance försäkring c 20, 144

insurance company försäkrings-bolag nt 79

interest ränta c 131

interested, to be intresserad 83

interesting intressant 84

international internationell 133

international operator utlandstelefonist c 134

interpreter tolk c 131

intersection korsning c 77

introduce, to presentera 92

introduction *(social)* presentation 92

investment investering c 131

invitation inbjudan c 94

invite, to bjuda 94

invoice faktura c 131

iodine jod c 109

Ireland Irland *(nt)* 146

Irish irländare c 93

iron *(laundry)* strykjärn nt 119

iron, to stryka 29

ironmonger's järnhandel c 99

Israel Israel *(nt)* 146

its dess 162; sin, sitt *(pl* sina) 161

J

jacket kavaj c 116

jam sylt c 38, 63

jam, to fastna 28, 125

January januari *(c)* 150

Japan Japan *(nt)* 146

jar burk c 120

jaundice gulsot c 142

jaw käke c 138

jeans jeans c/pl 116

jersey jumper c, tröja c 116

jetty brygga c 74

jewel box smyckeskrin nt 121

jeweller's juvelerare c, guldsmedsaffär c 99, 121

jewellery smycke *nt* 127
joint led *c* 138
journey *(trip)* resa *c* 152
juice juice *c* 37, 38, 59
July juli *(c)* 150
June juni *(c)* 150
juniper berry enbär *nt* 53
just *(only)* bara 16, 37, 100

K

kale grönkål *c* 51
keep, to behålla 61
kerosene fotogen *c* 106
key nyckel *c* 27
kidney njure *c* 48, 138
kilo(gram) kilo(gram) *nt* 120
kilometre kilometer *c* 20
kind snäll 96
kind *(type)* slags *nt/c* 48, 140
knapsack ryggsäck *c* 106
knee knä *nt* 138
kneesocks knästrumpor *c/pl* 116
knife kniv *c* 36, 60, 107, 127
know, to veta 16, 24, 96; känna
    till 114

L

label etikett *c* 105
lace spets *c* 114
lady dam *c* 155
lake sjö *c* 81, 85, 90
lamb lamm *nt* 48
lamp lampa *c* 29, 106, 119
landmark landmärke *nt* 85
lantern lykta *c* 106
large stor 20, 101, 118, 130
last sista 14, 68; förra 149, 150,
    151
late sen 14; försenad 69
later senare 135
laugh, to skratta 95
launderette snabbtvätt *c* 99
laundry *(place)* tvättinrättning *c*
    99; *(clothes)* tvätt *c* 29
laundry service tvättservice *c* 23
laxative laxermedel *nt* 109
lead *(metal)* bly *nt* 75
leap year skottår *nt* 149
leather läder *nt* 114, 118; skinn
    nt 114
leave, to lämna 20, 26, 71, 156;
    (go) gå 95; åka 31; *(train)*
    (av)gå 68, 69, 74
leek purjolök *c* 51

left vänster 21, 62, 69, 77
left-luggage office
    effektförvaring *c* 67, 71
leg ben *nt* 138
lemon citron *c* 37, 38, 54, 59
lemonade läsk *c* 59
lens *(glasses)* glas *nt* 123; *(came-
    ra)* objektiv *nt* 125
lens cap linsskydd *nt* 125
less mindre 14
lesson lektion *c* 90
let, to *(hire out)* hyra 155
letter brev *nt* 28, 132
letter box brevlåda *c* 132
letter of credit remburs *c* 130
lettuce grönsallad *c* 44, 51
level crossing järnvägskorsning *c*
    79
library bibliotek *nt* 81, 99
licence *(driving)* körkort *nt* 20, 79
lie down, to lägga sig 142
life belt livbälte *nt* 74
life boat livbåt *c* 74
lift hiss *c* 27, 100, 155
ligament ligament *nt* 140
light lätt 14, 55, 58, 101, 128;
    (colour) ljus 101, 112, 113
light ljus *nt* 28, 124; *(cigarette)*
    eld *c* 95
lighter tändare *c* 126
lighter fluid bensin till tändare
    c 126
lighter gas gas till tändare *c* 126
light meter ljusmätare *c* 125
lightning blixt *c* 94
like, to tycka om 25, 61, 92, 112;
    ha lust 96; *(want)* vilja 13, 20,
    23; önska 103
line linje *c* 73
linen *(cloth)* linne *nt* 114
lip läpp *c* 138
lipbrush läppstiftpensel *c* 110
lipsalve cerat *nt* 110
lipstick läppstift *nt* 110
liqueur likör *c* 58
liquid vätska *c* 123
liquor store systembolag *nt* 99
listen, to lyssna 128
litre liter *c* 75, 120
little *(a)* lite 14
live, to leva 83; *(reside)* bo 83
liver lever *c* 48, 138
lobster hummer *c* 43, 46
local lokal 36
local train lokaltåg *nt* 66, 69

long lång 116; *(time)* lång tid 60, 62, 76, 116; länge 77, 92
long-sighted långsynt 123
look, to se 123; titta 100
look for, to leta efter 13
look out! se upp! 156
loose lös 145; *(clothes)* vid 116
lose, to tappa 123, 156; förlora 156
loss förlust *c* 131
lost, to be inte hitta 13; gå vilse 156
lost and found office hittegodsexpedition *c* 67, 156
lost property office hittegodsexpedition *c* 67, 156
lot *(a)* mycket 14
loud *(voice)* hög 135
love, to älska 92
lovely underbar 94
low låg 141
lower under- 69, 70
low season lågsäsong *c* 149
luck lycka *c* 152
luggage bagage *nt* 18, 26, 31, 71; *(registered)* resgods *nt/pl* 71
luggage locker förvaringsbox *c* 18, 67, 71
luggage trolley bagagekärra *c* 18, 71
lump *(bump)* knöl *c* 139
lunch lunch *c* 34, 80, 94
lung lunga *c* 138

M

macaroni makaroner *c/pl* 52
machine maskin *c* 114
mackerel makrill *c* 46
magazine veckotidning *c* 105
magnificent storslagen 84
maid städerska *c* 26
mail post *c* 28, 133
mail, to posta 28
mailbox brevlåda *c* 132
make, to göra 114, 131, 163
make up, to *(prepare)* göra i ordning 108
make-up bag sminkväska *c* 110
make-up remover pad make-up remover pad *c* 110
mallet träklubba *c* 106
man man *c* 156; herre *c* 115, 155
manager direktör *c* 26
manicure manikyr *c* 30

many många 11, 14
map karta *c* 76, 105
March mars *(c)* 150
marinated gravad 41, 43, 46; marinerad 46
market marknad *c* 99, torghandel *c* 99
marmalade apelsinmarmelad *c* 38
married gift 93
mashed potatoes potatismos *nt* 52, 62
mass *(church)* mässa *c* 84
match tändsticka *c* 106, 126; *(sport)* match *c* 89
match, to *(colour)* passa till 112
matinée matiné *c* 87
mattress madrass *c* 106
May maj *(c)* 150
may *(can)* kunna 12, 162
meadow äng *c* 85
meal måltid *c* 24, 143
mean, to betyda 11, 26
measles mässling *c* 142
measure, to ta mått 114
meat kött *nt* 48, 60
meatball köttbulle *c* 42, 48, 62
mechanic mekaniker *c* 78
mechanical pencil stiftpenna *c* 105, 121
medical certificate läkarintyg *nt* 144
medicine medicin *c* 83, 143
medium medium 49
meet, to träffa 92, 96; ses 96
melon melon *c* 54
memorial minnesmärke *nt* 81
mend, to laga 29, 75
menthol *(cigarettes)* mentol 126
menu meny *c* 37, 39; *(printed)* matsedel *c* 36, 39, 40
message meddelande *nt* 28, 136
methylated spirits rödsprit *c* 106
metre meter *c* 112
mezzanine *(theatre)* första raden 87
middle mitten 69, 87, 150; mellan 69
midnight midnatt *c* 153
midnight sun midnattssol *c* 94
mileage kilometerkostnad *c* 20
milk mjölk *c* 38, 59, 64
milkshake milkshake *c* 59
milliard milliard *c* 148
million million *c* 148

mineral water mineralvatten nt 59
minister (religion) protestantisk
präst c 84
minute minut c 21, 153
mirror spegel c 115, 123
miscellaneous diverse 127
Miss fröken c 10
miss, to fattas 18, 29, 60
mistake fel nt 31, 61, 102;
misstag nt 60
modified American plan halvpension
c 24
moisturizing cream
fuktighetsbevarande kräm c 110
moment ögonblick nt 12, 136
monastery kloster nt 81
Monday måndag c 150
money pengar c/pl 129, 130
money order postanvisning c 133
month månad c 16, 150
monument monument nt 81
moon måne c 94
moped moped c 74
more mer 14
morning morgon c 31, 151, 153
mortgage hypotek nt 131
mosque moské c 84
mosquito net myggnät nt 106
motel motell nt 22
mother mor c 93
motorbike motorcykel c 74
motorboat motorbåt c 91
motorway motorväg c 76
mountain berg nt 85
moustache mustasch c 31
mouth mun c 138, 142
mouthwash munvatten nt 109
move, to röra 139
movie film c 86
movie camera filmkamera c 124
movies bio c 86, 96
Mr. herr c 10
Mrs. fru c 10
much mycket 11, 14
mug mugg c 107
muscle muskel c 138
museum museum nt 81
mushroom svamp c 51
music musik c 83, 128
musical musical c 86
music box speldosa c 121
mussel mussla c 43
must (have to) måste 23, 31, 95
mustard senap c 64
my min, mitt (pl mina) 161

N

nail (human) nagel c 110
nail brush nagelborste c 110
nail clippers nageltång c 110
nail file nagelfil c 110
nail polish nagellack nt 110
nail polish remover nagellacks-
borttagningsmedel nt 110
nail scissors nagelsax c 110
name namn nt 23, 79, 133;
(surname) efternamn nt 25
napkin servett c 36, 105, 106
nappy blöja c 111
narrow trång 118
nationality nationalitet c 92
natural history naturhistoria c 83
near nära 14
nearby i närheten 77
nearest närmaste 73, 75, 78, 132
neat (drink) ren 58
neck nacke c 30, 138
necklace halsband nt 121
need, to behöva 29, 118, 137
needle nål c 27
negative negativ nt 124, 125
nerve nerv c 138
nervous system nervsystem nt
138
Netherlands Nederländerna (nt/pl),
Holland (nt) 146
never aldrig 15
new ny 14, 149
newspaper tidning c 104, 105
newsstand tidningskiosk c 19, 67,
99, 104
New Year nyår nt 152
New Zealand Nya Zeeland (nt) 146
next nästa 14, 65, 68, 73, 76,
149, 150, 151
next time nästa gång 95
next to bredvid 15, 77
nice (beautiful) vacker 94
night natt c 10, 24, 151; kväll c
88, 96
night club nattklubb c 88
night cream nattkräm c 110
nightdress nattlinne nt 116
nine nio 147
nineteen nitton 147
ninety nittio 147
ninth nionde 148
no nej 10
nonalcoholic alkoholfri 59
none ingen 15
nonsmoker icke rökare c 70, 155

DICTIONARY

noon klockan tolv (på dagen) 153
normal normal 30
north norr 77
North America Nordamerika (nt) 146
Norway Norge (nt) 146
nose näsa c 138
nosebleed näsblod nt 141
nose drops näsdroppar c/pl 109
not inte 15, 163
note (banknote) sedel c 130
notebook anteckningsbok c 105
note paper brevpapper c 105
nothing ingenting 15; inget 16, 17
notice (sign) anslag nt 155
notify, to underrätta 144
November november (c) 150
now nu 15
number nummer nt 25, 135, 136;
    räkneord nt 147
nurse sköterska c 144

O

observatory observatorium nt 81
occupation yrke nt 25
occupied upptagen 14, 155
o'clock klockan c 154
October oktober (c) 150
octopus bläckfisk c 45
office kontor nt 132
oil olja c 37, 75, 111
oily (greasy) fet 30, 111
old gammal 14, 149
old town gamla stan c 81
omelet omelett c 45
on på 15
once en gång 148
one ett 147
one-way (ticket) enkel (biljett c)
    65, 69
on foot till fots 76
onion lök c 51
only bara 15, 24, 80
on time i tid 68
open öppen 14, 82, 155
open, to öppna 11, 17, 82, 108,
    130, 132, 142
opening hours öppettider c/pl 155
opera opera c 88
opera house opera c 81, 88
operation operation c 144
operetta operett c 88
opposite mitt emot 77
optician optiker c 99, 123
or eller 15

orange orange 113
orange apelsin c 54
orange juice apelsinjuice c 38, 59
orchestra orkester c 88; (seats)
    parkett c 87
order (goods, meal) beställning c
    40, 102
order, to (goods, meal) beställa
    36, 60, 102, 103
ornithology ornitologi c 83
other andra 58, 74
our vår, vårt (pl våra) 161
out of order trasig 136; ur
    funktion 155
out of stock slut på lagret 103
outlet (electric) uttag nt 27
outside ute 15, 36
oval oval 101
overalls overall c 116
overdone för mycket stekt 60
overheat, to (engine) gå varm 78
overnight (stay) över natt 24
overtake, to köra om 79
owe, to vara skyldig 144
oyster ostron nt 43

P

pacifier napp c 111
packet paket nt 120, 126
page (hotel) pickolo c 26
pail hink c 106, 128
pain smärta c 140, 143
paint, to måla 83
paintbox färglåda c 105
painter konstnär c 83
painting måleri nt 83
pair par nt 116, 118, 148
pajamas pyjamas c 117
palace slott nt 81
palpitation hjärtklappning c 141
pancake pannkaka c 45; (small)
    plätt c 55
panties trosor c/pl 116
pants (trousers) (lång)byxor c/pl 116
panty girdle byxgördel c 116
panty hose strumpbyxor c/pl 117
paper papper c 105
paperback pocketbok c 105
paperclip gem nt 105
paper napkin pappersservett c 105,
    106
paraffin (fuel) fotogen c 106
parcel paket nt 132

pardon förlåt 11
parents föräldrar c/pl 93
park park c 81
park, to parkera 26, 77
parka anorak c 117
parking parkering c 77, 79
parking meter parkeringsautomat c 77
parliament riksdag c 81
parliament building riksdagshus nt 81
parsley persilja c 53
part del c 138
party (social gathering) fest c 95
pass, to (overtake) köra om 79
passport pass nt 16, 17, 25, 26, 156
passport photo passfoto nt 124
pass through, to vara på genomresa 16
pastry bakverk nt 63
pastry shop konditori nt 99
path stig c 85
patient patient c 144
pattern mönster nt 112
pay, to betala 31, 61, 100, 102
payment betalning c 102, 131
pea ärta c 51
peach persika c 54
peak topp c 85
pear päron nt 54
pearl pärla c 122
peg (tent) pinne c 107
pen penna c 105
pencil blyertspenna c 105
pencil sharpener pennvässare c 105
pendant hängsmycke nt 121
penicilline penicillin nt 143
penknife pennkniv c 106
pensioner pensionär c 82
people människor c/pl 92
pepper peppar c 37, 38, 53
per cent procent c 148
percentage procentsats c 131
perch abborre c 45, 47
per day per dag 20, 32, 89
perfume parfym c 110
perfume shop parfymeri nt 99
perhaps kanske 15
per hour per timme 77, 89
period (monthly) mens(truation) c 141
period pains mens(truations)-smärtor c/pl 141
permanent wave permanent c 30
per night per natt 24

per person per person 32
person person c 32
personal personlig 17
personal call personligt samtal nt 134
person-to-person call personligt samtal nt 134
per week per vecka 20, 24
petrol bensin c 75, 78
pewter tenn nt 122
pheasant fasan c 50
photo foto nt 124; kort nt 125
photocopy fotokopia c 131
photograph, to fotografera 82
photographer fotograf c 99
photography fotografering c 124
phrase uttryck nt 12
pick up, to (person) hämta 80, 96
pickled gherkin ättiksgurka c 51, 64
picnic picknick c 64
picture (painting) tavla c 83; (photo) bild nt 105
picture-book bilderbok c 105
piece bit c 63, 120
pier pir c 74
pill tablett c 109, 143; (contraceptive) p-piller nt 141
pillow kudde c 27
pin nål c 110, 111, 122
pineapple ananas c 54
pink rosa 113
pipe pipa c 126
pipe cleaner piprensare c 126
pipe tool pipverktyg nt 126
place ort c 25; plats c 76
place of birth födelseort c 25
plaice rödspätta c 46
plane flyg nt 65
planetarium planetarium nt 81
plaster, to put in gipsa 140
plastic plast c 107
plastic bag plastpåse c 107
plate tallrik c 36, 60, 107
platform (station) perrong c 67, 68, 69, 70
platinum platina c 122
play (theatre) pjäs c 86
play, to spela 86, 88, 89, 93
playground lekplats c 32
playing card spelkort nt 105
please var snäll och ... 10; tack 10
pliers tång c 107
plimsoll tennissko c 118
plug (electric) stickkontakt c 29, 119
plum plommon nt 54
pneumonia lunginflammation c 142

poached pocherad 46; *(egg)* förlorat 45
pocket ficka *c* 117
pocket calculator fickräknare *c* 105
pocket dictionary fickordbok *c* 104
pocket watch fickur *nt* 121
point, to peka 12
poison gift *nt* 109, 156
poisoning förgiftning *c* 142
Poland Polen *(nt)* 146
pole *(ski)* stav *c* 91; *(tent)* stång *c* 107
police polis *c* 78, 156
police station polisstation *c* 99, 156
pond damm *c* 85
pork fläskkött *nt* 48
port hamn *c* 74; *(wine)* portvin *nt* 58
portable bärbar 119
porter bärare *c* 18, 26, 71
portion portion *c* 37, 60
possible möjlig 137
post *(mail)* post *c* 133; brev *nt* 28
post, to posta 28
postage porto *nt* 132
postage stamp frimärke *nt* 28, 126, 132
postcard vykort *c* 105, 126, 132
poste restante poste restante 133
post office postkontor *nt* 99, 132; post *c* 132
pot kanna *c* 59
potato potatis *c* 52
pottery lergods *nt* 83
poultry fågel *c* 50
pound *(money)* pund *nt* 18, 102, 130; *(weight)* halvt kilo *nt* 120
powder puder *nt* 110
powder compact puderdosa *c* 122
prawn räka *c* 43, 46
prefer, to föredra 101
pregnant gravid 141
premium *(gasoline)* högoktanig 75
prescribe, to skriva ut 143
prescription recept *nt* 108, 143; ordination *c* 143
present present *c* 17, 121
press, to *(iron)* pressa 29
press stud tryckknapp *c* 117
pressure tryck *nt* 75, 141
pretty söt 84
price pris *nt* 24
priest katolsk präst *c* 84
print *(photo)* kopia *c* 125
private privat 79, 80, 155

processing *(photo)* framkallning *c* 124, 125
profession yrke *nt* 25
profit vinst *c* 131
programme program *nt* 87
prohibit, to förbjuda 79
pronunciation uttal *nt* 6
propelling pencil stiftpenna *c* 105, 122
propose, to rekommendera 40
Protestant protestantisk 84
provide, to skaffa 131
prune katrinplommon *nt* 54, 55
public holiday allmän helgdag *c* 152
pull, to dra 155
pullover jumper *c*, tröja *c* 117
puncture punktering *c* 75
purchase köp *nt* 131
pure ren 114
push, to *(button)* trycka 155
put, to ställa 24
pyjamas pyjamas *c* 117

Q

quality kvalitet *c* 103, 113
quantity kvantitet *c* 14
quarter fjärdedel *c* 148; *(part of town)* kvarter *nt* 81
quarter of an hour kvart *c* 153
quartz quartz 122
question fråga *c* 11
quick snabb 14
quickly fort 79, 137, 156
quiet tyst 23, 25

R

rabbi rabbin *c* 84
race tävling *c* 89
race course/track hästkapp-löpningsbana *c* 90
racket *(sport)* racket *c* 90
radiator *(car)* kylare *c* 78
radio radio *c* 23, 28, 119
radish rädisa *c* 51
railway järnväg *c* 154
railroad crossing järnvägskorsning *c* 79
railway station järnvägsstation *c* 19, 21, 67
rain regn *nt* 94
rain, to regna 94
raincoat *(man's)* regnrock *c* 117; *(woman's)* regnkappa *c* 117

raisin russin *nt* 54
rangefinder ljusmätare *c* 125
rare *(meat)* blodig 49, 60
rash utslag *nt* 139
raspberry hallon *nt* 54
rate *(price)* pris *nt* 20;
  (exchange) kurs *c* 18, 130
razor rakhyvel *c* 110
razor blade rakblad *nt* 110
reading-lamp läslampa *c* 27
ready klar 29, 31, 118, 123, 125,
  145
real *(genuine)* äkta 118, 121
rear bak 75
receipt kvitto *nt* 103, 144
reception reception *c* 23
receptionist receptionist *c* 26
recommend, to rekommendera 35,
  36, 88, 137, 145; *(suggest)*
  föreslå 35, 44, 80
record *(disc)* skiva *c* 127, 128
record player skivspelare *c* 119
rectangular rektangulär 101
red röd 58, 113
reduction rabatt *c* 24, 82
refill *(pen)* refill *c* 105
refund, to get a få pengarna
  tillbaka 103
regards hälsningar *c/pl* 152
register, to *(luggage)* pollettera
  71
registered mail rekommenderat 133
registration incheckning *c* 25
registration form inskrivningsblankett *c* 25
regular *(petrol)* lågoktanig 75
reindeer ren *c* 42, 50
religion religion *c* 83
religious service gudstjänst *c* 84
rent, to hyra 19, 20, 74, 90, 91,
  119, 155
rental uthyrning *c* 20, 74
repair reparation *c* 125
repair, to laga 29, 118, 119, 121,
  123, 125, 145
repeat, to upprepa 12
report, to *(a theft)* anmäla 156
reservation reservation *c* 19, 65;
  beställning *c* 69
reservations office biljettkontor
  nt 19, 67
reserve, to beställa 19, 23, 36,
  87; reservera 69, 155
restaurant restaurang *c* 19, 32,
  33, 35, 67

return *(ticket)* tur och retur 65,
  69
return, to *(come back)* vara
  tillbaka 21, 80; *(give back)*
  lämna tillbaka 103
reverse-charge call Ba-samtal
  nt 135
revue revy *c* 86
rheumatism reumatism *c* 141
rhubarb rabarber *c* 54
rib revben *nt* 138
ribbon band *nt* 105
rice ris *nt* 52
right höger 21, 62, 69, 77; *(correct)* rätt 14, 70
ring *(on finger)* ring *c* 122
ring, to ringa 134, 155
river flod *c* 85, 90
road väg *c* 76, 77, 85
road assistance hjälp på vägen *c*
  78
road map vägkarta *c* 105
road sign vägmärke *nt* 79
roasted stekt 49
roast beef rostbiff *c* 48
roll *(bread)* småfranska *nt* 38;
  bröd *nt* 62
roller skates rullskridskor *c/pl*
  128
roll film filmrulle *c* 124
romantic romantisk 84
room rum *nt* 19, 23, 24, 25;
  (space) plats *c* 32
room number rumsnummer *nt* 26
room service rumsbetjäning *c* 23
rope rep *nt* 107
rosé rosé 58
rouge rouge *c* 110
round rund 101
round *(golf)* runda *c* 89
round-neck rundringad 117
round trip *(ticket)* tur och retur
  65, 69
route väg *c* 85
rowing boat roddbåt *c* 74, 91
royal kunglig 82
rubber *(material)* gummi *nt* 118;
  (eraser) radergummi *nt* 105
rubber band gummisnodd *c* 105
rucksack ryggsäck *c* 107
ruin ruin *c* 81
ruler *(for measuring)* linjal *c* 105
rum rom *c* 58
running water rinnande vatten *nt*
  23

S

safe *(not dangerous)* riskfri 90
safe kassaskåp *nt* 26
safety pin säkerhetsnål *c* 110
sailing boat segelbåt *c* 74, 91
salad sallad *c* 44, 51
sale försäljning *c* 131; *(bargains)* rea(lisation) *c* 100, 155
sales tax moms *c* 24, 102
salmon lax *c* 42, 43, 46, 47
salmon trout laxöring *c* 46
salt salt *nt* 37, 38, 53,
salty salt 60
sand sand *c* 90
sandal sandal *c* 118
sandwich sandwich *c* 43; smörgås *c* 62
sanitary towel/napkin dambinda *c* 109
sardine sardin *c* 46
satin satin *c* 114
Saturday lördag *c* 150
sauce sås *c* 52
saucepan kastrull *c* 107
saucer tefat *nt* 107
sauna bastu *c* 23, 32
sausage korv *c* 48, 64
scarf scarf *c* 117
school skola *c* 79
school holidays skollov *nt* 151
scissors sax *c* 107, 110
scooter skoter *c* 74
Scotland Skottland *(nt)* 146
scrambled egg äggröra *c* 38, 45
screwdriver skruvmejsel *c* 107
sculptor skulptör *c* 83
sculpture skulptur *c* 83
sea hav *nt* 85, 90
seafood skaldjur *nt/pl* 45
season årstid *c* 149
seasoning krydda *c* 37
seat plats *c* 69, 70, 87
seat belt bilbälte *nt* 75
second andra 148
second sekund *c* 153
second class andra klass *c* 69
second hand sekundvisare *c* 122
second-hand *(book)* antikvarisk 104
second-hand shop andrahandsaffär *c* 99
secretary sekreterare *c* 27, 131
see, to se 12, 89; *(examine)* undersöka 137
sell, to sälja 100

send, to skicka 78, 102, 103, 132, 133
send up, to skicka upp 26
sentence mening *c* 12
September september *(c)* 150
serve, to servera 41
service (charge) betjäningsavgift *c* 24; serveringsavgift *c* 61; *(religion)* gudstjänst *c* 84
serviette servett *c* 36
set menu meny *c* 36, 40
setting lotion läggningsvätska *c* 30, 111
seven sju 147
seventeen sjutton 147
seventh sjunde 148
seventy sjuttio 147
sew, to sy 29
shade *(colour)* nyans *c* 112
shallow långrunt 90
shampoo shampo *nt* 30, 111
shampoo and set tvättning och läggning *c* 30
shape form *c* 103
share *(finance)* aktie *c* 131
shave rakning *c* 31
shaver rakapparat *c* 27, 119
shaving brush rakborste *c* 111
shaving cream rakkräm *c* 111
she hon 162
sherry sherry *c* 58
ship fartyg *nt* 74
shirt skjorta *c* 117
shoe sko *c* 118
shoelace skosnöre *nt* 118
shoemaker's skomakare *c* 99
shoe polish skokräm *c* 118
shoe shop skoaffär *c* 99
shop affär *c* 98
shopping shopping *c* 97
shopping area affärscentrum *nt* 81, 100
shopping centre shoppingcenter *nt* 99
shop window (skylt)fönster *nt* 100, 112
short kort 30, 116
shorts shorts *c/pl* 117
short-sighted närsynt 123
shoulder axel *c* 138
shovel spade *c* 128
show show *c* 88; *(theatre)* föreställning *c* 87
show, to visa 12, 13, 76, 100, 101, 119, 124

shower dusch *c* 23, 32
shrimp räka *c* 43, 46, 62
shrink, to krympa 114
shut stängd 14
shutter *(camera)* slutare *c* 125
sick *(ill)* sjuk 140, 156
sickness *(illness)* sjukdom *c* 140
side sida *c* 30
sideboards/burns polisonger *c/pl*
sightseeing sightseeing *c* 80
sightseeing tour sightseeingtur *c* 80
sign *(notice)* skylt *c* 79, 155
sign, to skriva under 26, 130
signature underskrift *c* 25
signet ring signetring *c* 122
silk siden *nt*, silke *nt* 114
silver *(colour)* silverfärgad 113
silver silver *nt* 121, 122
silver plate nysilver *nt* 122
silversmith silversmed *c* 99
simple enkel 124
since sedan 15, 150
sing, to sjunga 88
single *(not married)* ogift 93;
  (ticket) enkel 65, 69
single room enkelrum *nt* 19, 23
sister syster *c* 93
sit down, to sätta sig 95
six sex 147
sixteen sexton 147
sixth sjätte 148
sixty sextio 147
size format *nt* 124; *(clothes)*
  storlek *c* 114, 115, 118
skate skridsko *c* 91
skating rink skridskobana *c* 91
ski skida *c* 91
ski, to åka skidor 91
ski boot pjäxa *c* 91
skiing skidåkning *c* 89
ski lift skidlift *c* 91
skin hud *c* 138
skirt kjol *c* 117
ski run (skid)backe *c* 91
sky himmel *c* 94
sleep, to sova 144
sleeping bag sovsäck *c* 107
sleeping car sovvagn *c* 68, 69, 70
sleeping pill sömntablett *c* 143
sleeve ärm *c* 116
slice skiva *c* 120
slide *(photo)* diapositiv *nt* 124
slip underklänning *c* 117
slipper toffel *c* 118
slow långsam 14

slow down, to köra sakta 79
slowly långsamt 12, 21, 135
small liten 14, 20, 25, 101, 118
smoke, to röka 95
smoked rökt 42, 43, 46, 49
smoker rökare *c* 70, 155
snack mellanmål *nt* 62
snack bar snackbar *c* 67
snail snigel *c* 43
snap fastener tryckknapp *c* 117
sneakers tennisskor *c/pl* 118
snorkel snorkel *c* 128
snow snö *c* 94
snow, to snöa 94
snuff snus *nt* 126
soap tvål *c* 27, 111
soccer fotboll *c* 89
sock socka *c* 117
socket *(outlet)* uttag *nt* 27
soda water sodavatten *nt* 58
soft mjuk 123
soft-boiled *(egg)* löskokt 38
soft drink juice *c*, läsk *c* 59
sold out *(theatre)* utsålt 87, 155
sole sula *c* 118; *(fish)* sjötunga *c* 46
soloist solist *c* 88
some några 15
someone någon 31, 95
something något 29, 36, 108, 112,
  125, 139; någonting 55, 113
somewhere någonstans 87
son son *c* 93
song sång *c* 128
soon snart 15, 137
sore *(painful)* öm 145
sore throat ont i halsen 141
sorry *(I'm)* förlåt 11, 16; jag är
  ledsen 103
sort *(kind)* slag *nt* 86; sort *c* 120
soup soppa *c* 44
sour cream gräddfil *c* 52
south söder 77
South Africa Sydafrika *(nt)* 146
South America Sydamerika *(nt)*
  146
souvenir souvenir *c* 127
souvenir shop souveniraffär *c* 99
Soviet Union Sovjetunionen *(nt)* 146
spade spade *c* 128
Spain Spanien *(nt)* 146
sparerib revbensspjäll *nt* 42, 48
spare tyre reservdäck *nt* 75
spark(ing) plug tändstift *nt* 75
sparkling *(wine)* mousserande 58
speak, to tala 12, 135

speaker (loudspeaker) högtalare c 119
special special- 20, 37
special delivery express 133
specialist specialist c 142
speciality specialitet c 36
specimen (medical) prov nt 142
spell, to bokstavera 12
spend, to lägga ut 101
spice krydda c 53
spinach spenat c 51
spine ryggrad c 138
sponge tvättsvamp c 111
sponge bag necessär c 111
spoon sked c 36, 60, 107
sport sport c 89
sporting goods shop sportaffär c 99
sprain, to vricka 140
sprat skarpsill c 46
spring (season) vår c 149; (water) källa c 85
square kvadratisk 101
square torg nt 82
stadium stadion nt 82
staff personal c 26
stain fläck c 29
stainless steel rostfritt stål nt 107, 122
stalls (theatre) parkett c 87
stamp (postage) frimärke nt 28, 126, 132, 133
stapler häftapparat c 105
staple häftklammer c 105
star stjärna c 94
start, to börja 87, 88; starta 80; (car) starta 78
starter (appetizer) förrätt c 43
station (railway) (järnvägs)station c 19, 21, 67, 70; (underground, subway) tunnelbanestation c 73
stationer's pappershandel c 99, 104
statue staty c 82
stay vistelse c 31
stay, to stanna 16, 24, 26; (reside) bo 93
steak tartare råbiff c 48
steal, to stjäla 156
steamed ångkokt 46
steamer ångbåt c 74
stew pot gryta c 107
stewed stuvad 49
stiff neck stel nacke c 141
still (mineral water) utan kolsyra 59
sting stick nt 139

sting, to bita 139
stitch, to (clothes) sy ihop 29, 118
stock (in shop) lager nt 103
stock exchange (fond)börs c 82
stocking strumpa c 117
stomach mage c 138
stomach ache ont i magen 141
stools avföring c 142
stop (bus) (buss)hållplats c 72
stop, to stanna 21, 68, 70, 72
stop thief! stoppa tjuven! 156
store (shop) affär c 98
straight (drink) ren 58
straight ahead rakt fram 21, 77
strange underlig 84
strawberry jordgubbe c 54, 55
street gata c 25
streetcar spårvagn c 72
street map karta c 19, 105
string snöre nt 105
strong stark 126, 143
student studerande c 82
study, to studera 93
stuffed fylld 51
sturdy kraftig 101
subway (railway) tunnelbana c 73
suede mocka c 114, 118
sugar socker nt 37, 64
suit (man's) kostym c 117; (woman's) dräkt c 117
suitcase väska c 18
summer sommar c 149
sun sol c 94
sunburn solsveda c 108
Sunday söndag c 150
sunglasses solglasögon c/pl 123
sunshade (beach) parasoll nt 91
sunstroke solsting nt 141
sun-tan cream solkräm c 110
sun-tan oil sololja c 111
super (petrol) högoktanig 75
superb utomordentlig 84
supermarket snabbköp nt 99
suppository stolpiller nt 109
surcharge extra kostnad c 40
surgery (consulting room) läkarmottagning c 137
surname efternamn nt 25
suspenders (Am.) hängslen nt/pl 117
swallow, to svälja 143
sweater tröja c 117
sweatshirt sweatshirt c 117
Sweden Sverige (nt) 146

DICTIONARY

Swedish svensk 18, 114
Swedish svenska c 11, 12, 98
sweet söt 54, 58, 60
sweet (candy) godis c 126
sweet corn majs c 51
sweetener sötningsmedel nt 37
sweet pepper paprika c 51
sweet shop godisaffär c 99
swell, to svullna 139
swelling svullnad c 139
swim, to simma, bada 90
swimming simning c 89; badning c 91
swimming pool simbassäng c 23, 32, 90
swimming trunks badbyxor c/pl 117
swimsuit baddräkt c 117
switch (light) strömbrytare c 29
switchboard operator telefonist c 26
swollen svullen 139
synagogue synagoga c 84
synthetic syntetisk 114
system system nt 138

T

table bord nt 36, 107; (list) tabell c 157
table tennis bordtennis c 89
tablet tablett c 109
tailor's skräddare c 99
take, to ta 18, 25, 60, 73, 76, 102
take away, to (carry) ta med 62, 102
talcum powder talkpuder nt 111
tampon tampong c 109
tap (water) kran c 28
tape recorder bandspelare c 119
tarragon dragon c 53
taste, to smaka 60
taxi taxi c 18, 19, 21, 31, 67
taxi stand taxistation c 21
tea te nt 38, 59, 64
team lag nt 89
tear, to (ligament) slita av 140
teaspoon tesked c 107, 143
telegram telegram nt 133
telegraph office telegraf c 99, 133; telebutik c 134
telephone telefon c 27, 28, 78, 134
telephone, to ringa 134, 136
telephone booth telefonkiosk c 134

telephone call (telefon)samtal nt 136; telefon c 136
telephone directory telefonkatalog c 134
telephone number (telefon)nummer nt 134, 135, 136
telephoto lens teleobjektiv nt 125
television (set) TV c 23, 28, 119
telex telex nt 133
telex, to skicka ett telex 130
tell, to säga 13, 72, 76, 153; tala om 76, 136
temperature temperatur c 142; (fever) feber c 140
temporary provisorisk 145
ten tio 147
tendon sena c 138
tennis tennis c 89
tennis court tennisbana c 89
tennis racket tennisracket nt 90
tent tält nt 32, 107
tenth tionde 148
tent peg tältpinne c 107
tent pole tältstång c 107
terrible hemsk 84
tetanus stelkramp c 140
than än 14
thank you tack 10, 95, 96
that den där 160; det där 11, 100, 160
the -en, -ett 159
theatre teater c 82, 86
theft stöld c 156
their deras 161
then då, sedan 15
there där 13
thermometer termometer c 109, 144
these de här 62, 160
they de, dem 162
thief tjuv c 156
thigh lår nt 138
thin tunn 113
think, to (believe) tro 31, 94
third tredje 148
third tredjedel c 148
thirsty törstig 13, 35
thirteen tretton 147
thirty trettio 147
this den här 160; det här 11, 100, 160
those de där 62, 120, 160
thousand tusen 148
thread tråd c 27
three tre 147
throat hals c 138, 141
throat lozenge halstablett c 109

Ordlista

through genom 15
through train direktgående tåg nt 68, 69
thumb tumme c 138
thumbtack häftstift nt 105
thunder åska c 94
thunderstorm åskväder nt 94
Thursday torsdag c 150
ticket biljett c 65, 69, 72, 87, 89
ticket office biljettluckan c 67
tie slips c 117
tie clip slipshållare c 122
tie pin kravattnål c 122
tight (clothes) trång 116
tights strumpbyxor c/pl 117
time tid c 80; (occasion) gång c 95, 148
timetable tidtabell c 68
tin (can) burk c 120
tinfoil aluminiumfolie c 107
tin opener konservöppnare c 107
tint toningsmedel nt 111
tint, to tona 30
tinted färgad 123
tire däck nt 75
tired trött 13
tissue (handkerchief) pappersnäsduk c 111
tissue paper silkespapper nt 105
to till 15
toast rostat bröd nt 38
tobacco tobak c 126
tobacconist's tobaksaffär c 99, 126
today idag 29, 150, 151
toe tå c 138
toilet paper toalettpapper nt 111
toiletry toilettartikel c 110
toilets toalett c 27, 32, 37, 67
toilet water eau de toilette c 111
tomato tomat c 51
tomato juice tomatjuice c 59
tomb grav c 82
tomorrow i morgon 29, 96, 151
tongue tunga c 48, 138
tonic water tonic c 59
tonight i kväll 29, 86, 87, 96
tonsils mandlar c/pl 138
too för 15; (also) också 15
tooth tand c 145
toothache tandvärk c 145
toothbrush tandborste c 111, 119
toothpaste tandkräm c 111
torch (flashlight) ficklampa c 107

torn (ligament) avsliten 140
touch, to (vid)röra 155
tough (meat) seg 60
tour tur c 80
tourist office turistbyrå c 22, 80
towards mot 15
towel handduk c 111
tower torn nt 82
town stad c 19, 88
town hall rådhus nt 82
tow truck bärgningsbil c 78
toy leksak c 128
toy shop leksaksaffär c 99
track (station) spår nt 67, 68, 69
tracksuit träningsoverall c 117
traffic trafik c 76
traffic light trafikljus nt 77
trailer husvagn c 32
train tåg nt 66, 67, 68, 69, 70
tram spårvagn c 72
tranquillizer något nervlugnande 143
transfer (bank) överföring c 131
transformer transformator c 119
translate, to översätta 12
transport transport c 74
travel, to resa 93
travel agency resebyrå c 99
travel guide reseguide c 105
traveller's cheque resecheck c 18, 61, 102, 130
travelling bag bag c 18
travel sickness åksjuka c 108
treatment behandling c 143
tree träd nt 85
tremendous förfärlig 84
trim, to (beard) putsa 31
trip resa c 93, 152; tur c 73
trolley kärra c 18, 71
trousers (lång)byxor nt/pl 117
trout forell c 45
try, to försöka 135; (try on) prova 115; (sample) smaka 63, 64
T-shirt T-shirt c 117
tube tub c 120
Tuesday tisdag c 150
tumbler dricksglas nt 107
tuna/tunny tonfisk c 44, 46
turbot piggvar c 46
turkey kalkon c 50
turn, to (change direction) svänga 21, 77
turquoise turkos 113
turquoise turkos c 122
turtleneck polokrage c 117

tweezers pincett *c* 111
twelve tolv 147
twenty tjugo 147
twice två gånger 148
twin beds två sängar *c/pl* 23
two två 147
typewriter skrivmaskin *c* 27
typewriter ribbon skrivmaskinsband *nt* 105
typically typisk 127
typing paper skrivmaskinspapper *nt* 105
tyre däck *nt* 75, 76

U

ugly ful 14, 84
umbrella paraply *nt* 117; *(beach)* parasoll *nt* 91
uncle farbror *c*, morbror *c* 93
unconscious medvetslös 139
under under 15
underdone *(meat)* blodig 49, 60
underground *(railway)* tunnelbana *c* 73
underpants kalsonger *c/pl* 117
undershirt undertröja *c* 117
understand, to förstå 12, 16
undress, to klä av sig 142
United States USA *(nt)* 146
university universitet *nt* 82
unleaded blyfri 75
until till 15, 150
up upp 15
upper över- 69
upset stomach orolig mage *c* 108
upstairs där uppe 15; uppför trappan 69
urgent brådskande 13
urine urin *c* 142
use bruk *nt* 17, 109
useful användbar 15
usual vanlig 143

V

vacancy ledigt rum *nt* 23
vacant ledig 14
vacation semester *c* 151
vaccinate, to vaccinera 140
vacuum flask termos *c* 107
vaginal infection underlivsinfektion *c* 141
valley dal *c* 85
value värde *nt* 131

value-added tax moms *c* 24, 102, 154
vanilla vanilj *c* 55
vase vas *c* 127
VAT *(sales tax)* moms *c* 24, 102, 154
veal kalv *c* 48, 49
vegetable grönsak *c* 40, 51
vegetable store grönsaksaffär *c* 99
vegetarian vegetarisk 37
vein ven *c*, åder *c* 138
velvet sammet *c* 114
velveteen bomullssammet *c* 114
venereal disease könssjukdom *c* 142
venetian blind persienn *c* 29
venison rådjur *nt* 50
vermouth vermouth *c* 58
very mycket 15
vest undertröja *c* 117; *(Am.)* väst *c* 117
veterinarian veterinär *c* 99
video cassette videokassett *c* 119, 127
video recorder videobandspelare *c* 119
view utsikt *c* 23, 25
village samhälle *nt* 76; by *c* 85
vinegar vinäger *c* 37
visit, to *(a person)* hälsa på 95; *(a place)* titta på 84
visit besök *nt* 92
visiting hours besökstid *c* 144
vitamin pill vitamintablett *c* 109
V-neck V-ringad 117
vodka vodka *c* 58
voltage spänning *c* 27
vomit, to kräkas 140

W

waistcoat väst *c* 117
wait, to vänta 21, 95, 108, 155
waiter kypare *c*, servitör *c* 26
waiting room väntsal *c* 67
waitress servitris *c* 26
wake, to väcka 27, 71
Wales Wales *(nt)* 146
walk, to gå 74, 85
wall mur *c* 85
wallet plånbok *c* 156
walnut valnöt *c* 54
want, to vilja, *(wish)* önska 13
warm varm 94
wash to tvätta 29, 114
washbasin handfat *nt* 28

washing powder tvättmedel nt 107
washing-up liquid diskmedel nt 107
watch klocka c 121, 122
watchmaker's urmakare c 99, 121
watchstrap klockarmband nt 122
water vatten nt 23, 28, 32, 38, 75, 90
waterfall vattenfall nt 85
water flask fältflaska c 107
watermelon vattenmelon c 54
waterproof vattentät 122
water ski vattenskida c 91
way väg c 76, 77
we vi 162
weather väder nt 94
weather forecast väderleksutsikt c 94
wedding ring vigselring c 122
Wednesday onsdag c 150
week vecka c 16, 20, 24, 80, 151
weekend weekend c 151
well bra 10, 140
well källa c 85
well-done (meat) genomstekt 49
west väster 77
wet paint nymålat 155
what vad 11
wheel hjul nt 78
when när 11
where var 11
which vilken 11
whipped cream vispgrädde c 55
whisky whisky c 17, 58
white vit 58, 113
Whit Sunday Pingstdagen c 152
who vem 11
why varför 11
wick veke c 126
wide bred 118
wide-angle lens vidvinkelobjektiv nt 125
wife fru c 93
wig peruk c 111
wild duck vildand c 50
wind vind c 94
window fönster nt 28, 36; (shop) skyltfönster nt 100, 112
window seat plats vid fönstret c 65; fönsterplats c 69
windscreen/shield vindruta c 76
wine vin nt 57, 60
wine list vinlista c 57
wine merchant's systembolag nt 99
winter vinter c 149
winter sports vintersport c 91

wiper vindrutetorkare c 75
wish gratulation c 151; välgångsönskning c 152
with med 15
withdraw, to (bank) ta ut 131
without utan 15
woman kvinna c 156; dam c 115
wonderful underbar 96
wood (material) trä nt 127; (forest) skog c 85
wood alcohol rödsprit c 107
wool ull c, ylle nt 114
word ord nt 12, 15, 133
work arbete nt 79
work, to arbeta 79; (function) fungera 28, 119
working day arbetsdag c 151
worse sämre 14
wound sår nt 139
wrap, to slå in 103
wrapping paper omslagspapper nt 105
wrinkle resistant skrynkelfri 114
wristwatch armbandsur nt 122
write, to skriva 12, 101
writing pad skrivblock nt 105
writing paper brevpapper nt 27, 105
wrong fel 14, 135

X

X-ray (photo) röntgenbild c 140

Y

year år nt 149
yellow gul 113
yes ja 10
yesterday igår 151
yet än 15, 16
yield, to (traffic) lämna företräde 79
yoghurt yoghurt c 38, 64
you du, ni 10, 162
young ung 14, 149
your din, ditt (pl dina) 161; er, ert (pl era) 161
youth hostel vandrarhem nt 22, 32

Z

zero noll 147
zip(per) blixtlås nt 117
zoo djurpark c 82
zoology zoologi c 83

Svenskt register